SOME BRITISH ROMANTICS

A Collection of Essays

SOME BRITISH

ROMANTICS

A Collection of Essays

by

Northrop Frye, Vivian Mercier, Geoffrey Tillotson,
Stephen F. Fogle, Douglas Grant, Kathleen Coburn,
Ian Jack, John Henry Raleigh, Karl Kroeber,
and William S. Ward

Edited by

James V. Logan, John E. Jordan, and Northrop Frye

Ohio State University Press

PREFACE

This collection of essays is the fourth book of a series on British Romanticism sponsored by the Committee on Research Projects of that group of the Modern Language Association concerned with early nineteenth-century British writers. The series consists of two reviews of research (*The English Romantic Poets,* T. M. Raysor, ed., and *The English Romantic Poets and Essayists,* Carolyn W. and Lawrence H. Houtchens, eds.); and two books of criticism (*The Major English Romantic Poets,* Clarence D. Thorpe, Carlos Baker, and Bennett Weaver, eds., and the present volume). The Raysor and Thorpe books are concerned with the same writers, and the present book contains essays on writers included in the Houtchens volume, although we have shortened the list and added chapters on John Clare, on Romantic narrative poetry, and on periodicals.

The ten contributors represent a wide selection of British, Canadian, and American scholars. The editors have avoided a strictly planned program, and have given the contributors complete freedom in writing what and how they please on their respective subjects. Our hope was simply to achieve fresh and stimulating comments and interpretations.

J.V.L.   J.E.J.   N.F.

CONTENTS

THE KEYS TO THE GATES

Northrop Frye

The criticism of Blake, especially of Blake's prophecies, has developed in direct proportion to the theory of criticism itself. The complaints that Blake was "mad" are no longer of any importance, not because anybody has proved him sane, but because critical theory has realized that madness, like obscenity, is a word with no critical meaning. There are critical standards of coherence and incoherence, but if a poem is coherent in itself the sanity of its author is a matter of interest only to the more naïve type of biographer. Those who have assumed that the prophecies are incoherent because they have found them difficult often use the phrase "private symbolism." This is also now a matter of no importance, because in critical theory there is no such thing as private symbolism. There may be allegorical allusions to a poet's private life that can only be interpreted by biographical research, but no set of such allusions can ever form a poetic structure. They can only be isolated signposts, like the allusions to the prototypes of the beautiful youth, dark lady, and rival poet which historians and other speculative critics are persuaded that they see in the Shakespeare sonnets.

When I first embarked on an intensive study of Blake's prophecies, I assumed that my task was to follow the trail blazed by Foster Damon's great book, and take further steps to demonstrate the coherence of those poems. My primary interests, like Damon's, were literary, not occult or philosophical or religious. Many other writers had asserted that while the prophecies were doubtless coherent enough intellectually, they would turn out to depend for their coherence on some extra-poetic system of ideas. A student interested in Blake's prophecies as poems would have to begin by rejecting this hypothesis, which contradicts all Blake's views about the primacy of art and the cultural disaster of substituting abstractions for art. But as I went on, I was puzzled and annoyed by a schematic quality in these prophecies that refused to dissolve into what I then regarded as properly literary forms. There were even diagrams in Blake's own designs which suggested that he himself attached a good deal of value to schematism, and such statements as "I must create a system." Perhaps, then, these critics I had begun by rejecting were right after all: perhaps Blake was not opposed to abstraction but only to other people's abstractions, and was really interested merely in expounding some conceptual system or other in an oblique and allegorical way. In any event, the schematic, diagrammatic quality of Blake's thought was there, and would not go away or turn into anything else. Yeats had recognized it; Damon had recognized it; I had to recognize it. Like Shelley, Blake expressed an abhorrence of didactic poetry but continued to write it.

This problem began to solve itself as soon as I realized that poetic thought is inherently and necessarily schematic. Blake soon led me, in my search for poetic analogues, to Dante and Milton, and it was clear that the schematic cosmologies of Dante and Milton, however they got into Dante and Milton, were, once they got there, poetic constructs, examples of the way poets think,

4

and not foreign bodies of knowledge. If the prophecies are normal poems, or at least a normal expression of poetic genius, and if Blake nevertheless meant to teach some system by them, that system could only be something connected with the principles of poetic thought. Blake's "message," then, is not simply *his* message, nor is it an extra-literary message. What he is trying to say is what he thinks poetry is trying to say: the imaginative content implied by the existence of an imaginative form of language. I finished my book in the full conviction that learning to read Blake was a step, and for me a necessary step, in learning to read poetry, and to write criticism. For if poetic thought is inherently schematic, criticism must be so too. I began to notice that as soon as a critic confined himself to talking seriously about literature, his criticism tightened up and took on a systematic, even a schematic, form.

The nature of poetic "truth" was discussed by Aristotle in connection with action. As compared with the historian, the poet makes no specific or particular statements: he gives the typical, recurring, or universal event, and is not to be judged by the standards of truth that we apply to specific statements. Poetry, then, does not state historical truth, but contains it: it sets forth what we may call the *myth* of history, the kind of thing that happens. History itself is designed to record events, or, as we may say, to provide a primary verbal imitation of events. But it also, unconsciously perhaps, illustrates and provides examples for the poetic vision. Hence we feel that *Lear* or *Macbeth* or *Oedipus Rex,* although they deal almost entirely with legend rather than actual history, contain infinite reserves of historical wisdom and insight. Thus poetry is "something more philosophical" than history.

This last observation of Aristotle's has been of little use to critics except as a means of annoying historians, and it is difficult to see in what sense Anacreon is more philosophical than Thucydides. The statement is best interpreted, as it was by Renaissance critics, schematically, following a diagram in which poetry is intermediate between history and philosophy, pure example and pure precept. It follows that poetry must have a relation to thought paralleling its relation to action. The poet does not think in the sense of producing concepts, ideas or propositions, which are specific predications to be judged by their truth or falsehood. As he produces the mythical structures of history, so he produces the mythical structures of thought, the conceptual frameworks that enter into and inform the philosophies contemporary with him. And just as we feel that the great tragedy, if not historical, yet contains an infinity of the kind of meaning that actual history illustrates, so we feel that great "philosophical" poetry, if not actually philosophical, contains an infinity of the kind of meaning that discursive writing illustrates. This sense of the infinite treasures of thought latent in poetry is eloquently expressed by several Elizabethan critics, and there is perhaps no modern poet who suggests the same kind of intellectual richness so immediately as Blake does.

Blake, in fact, gives us so good an introduction to the nature and structure of poetic thought that, if one

6

has any interest in the subject at all, one can hardly avoid exploiting him. There are at least three reasons why he is uniquely useful for this purpose. One is that his prophecies are works of philosophical poetry which give us practically nothing at all unless we are willing to grapple with the kind of poetic thought that they express. Another is that Blake also wrote such haunting and lucid lyrics, of which we can at first say little except that they seem to belong in the center of our literary experience. We may not know why they are in the center, and some readers would rather not know; but for the saving remnant who do want to know, there are the prophecies to help us understand. The third reason is Blake's quality as an illustrator of other poets. If a person of considerable literary experience is reading a poem he is familiar with, it is easy for him to fall—in fact it is very difficult for him not to fall—into a passive habit of not really reading the poem, but merely of spotting the critical clichés he is accustomed to associate with it. Thus, if he is reading Gray's "Ode on the Death of a Favorite Cat," and sees the goldfish described as "angel forms," "genii of the stream," and with "scaly armour," his stock response will start murmuring: "Gray means fish, of course, but he is saying so in terms of eighteenth-century personification, Augustan artificiality, his own peculiar demure humour," and the like. Such a reading entirely obliterates Gray's actual processes of poetic thought and substitutes something in its place that, whatever it is, is certainly not poetry or philosophy, any more than it is history. But if he is reading the poem in the context of

7

Blake's illustrations, Blake will compel him to see the angel forms, the genii of the stream, and the warriors in scaly armour, as well as the fish, in such a way as to make the unvisualized clichés of professional reading impossible, and to bring the metaphorical structure of the poem clearly into view.

I am suggesting that no one can read Blake seriously and sympathetically without feeling that the keys to poetic thought are in him, and what follows attempts to explain how a documentation of such a feeling would proceed. I make no claim that I am saying anything here that I have not said before, though I may be saying it in less compass.

EASTERN GATE: TWOFOLD VISION

The structure of metaphors and imagery that informed poetry, through the Middle Ages and the Renaissance, arranged reality on four levels. On top was heaven, the place of the presence of God: below it was the proper level of human nature, represented by the stories of the Garden of Eden and the Golden Age; below that was the physical world, theologically fallen, which man is in but not of: and at the bottom was the world of sin, death and corruption. This was a deeply conservative view of reality in which man, in fallen nature, was confronted with a moral dialectic that either lowered him into sin or raised him to his proper level. The raising media included education, virtue, and obedience to law. In the Middle Ages, this construct was closely linked with similar constructs in theology and science. These links weakened after the sixteenth century and eventually disappeared, leaving the construct to survive only in poetry, and, even there, increasingly by inertia. It is still present in Pope's *Essay on Man,* but accompanied with a growing emphasis on the limitation of poetic objectives. This limitation means, among other things, that mythopoeic literature, which demands a clear and explicit framework of imagery, is in the age of Pope and Swift largely confined to parody.

As the eighteenth century proceeded, the imaginative climate began to change, and we can see poets trying to move toward a less conservative structure of imagery. This became a crucial problem when the French Revolution confronted the Romantic poets. No major poet in the past had been really challenged by a revolutionary situation except Milton, and even Milton had reverted to the traditional structure for *Paradise Lost.* Blake was not only older than Wordsworth and Coleridge, but more consistently revolutionary in his attitude: again, unlike most English writers of the period, he saw the American Revolution as an event of the same kind as its French successor. He was, therefore, the first English poet to work out the revolutionary structure of imagery that continues through Romantic poetry and thought to our own time.

At the center of Blake's thought are the two conceptions of innocence and experience, "the two contrary states of the human soul." Innocence is characteristic of the child, experience of the adult. In innocence, there are two factors. One is an assumption that the world was made for the benefit of human beings, has a human shape and a human meaning, and is a world in which providence, protection, communication with other beings, including animals, and, in general, "mercy, pity, peace and love," have a genuine function. The other is ignorance of the fact that the world is not like this. As the child grows up, his conscious mind accepts "experience," or reality without any human shape or meaning, and his childhood innocent vision, having nowhere else to go, is driven underground into what we should call the subconscious, where it takes an essentially sexual form. The original innocent vision becomes a melancholy dream of how man once possessed a happy garden, but lost it forever, though he may regain it after he dies. The following diagram illustrates the process as well as the interconnection of *Songs of Innocence and Experience, The Marriage of Heaven and Hell,* and the early political prophecies *The French Revolution* and *America* in Blake's thought:

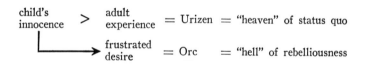

In place of the old construct, therefore, in which man regains his happy garden home by doing his duty and obeying the law, we have an uneasy revolutionary conception of conscious values and standards of reality sitting on top of a volcano of thwarted and mainly sexual energy. This construct has two aspects, individual or psychological, and social or political. Politically, it represents an ascendant class threatened by the growing body of those excluded from social benefits, until the latter are strong enough to overturn society. Psychologically, it represents a conscious ego threatened by a sexually-rooted desire. Thus the mythical structure that informs both the psychology of Freud and the political doctrines of Marx is present in *The Marriage of Heaven and Hell,* which gives us both aspects of the Romantic movement: the reaction to political revolution and the manifesto of feeling and desire as opposed to the domination of reason.

In the associations that Blake makes with Urizen and Orc, Urizen is an old man and Orc a youth: Urizen has the counterrevolutionary color white and Orc is a revolutionary red. Urizen is therefore associated with sterile winter, bleaching bones, and clouds; Orc with summer, blood, and the sun. The colors white and red suggest the bread and wine of a final harvest and vintage, prophesied in the fourteenth chapter of Revelation. Orc is "underneath" Urizen, and underneath the white cliffs of Albion on the map are the "vineyards of red France" in the throes of revolution. In a map of Palestine, the kingdom of Israel, whose other name, Jacob, means usurper, sits on top of Edom, the kingdom of the red and hairy Esau, the rightful heir. Isaiah's vision of a Messiah appearing in Edom with his body soaked in blood from "treading the winepress" of war, haunts nearly all Blake's prophecies. There are many other associations; perhaps we may derive the most important from the following passage in *America:*

The terror answerd: I am Orc, wreath'd round the accursed
    tree:
The times are ended: shadows pass the morning gins to
    break;
The fiery joy, that Urizen perverted to ten commands,
What night he led the starry hosts thro' the wide wilder-
    ness:
That stony law I stamp to dust: and scatter religion abroad
To the four winds as a torn book, & none shall gather the
    leaves:
But they shall rot on desart sands, & consume in bottomless
    deeps:
To make the desarts blossom, & the deeps shrink to their
    fountains,
And to renew the fiery joy, and burst the stony roof.
That pale religious letchery, seeking Virginity,
May find it in a harlot, and in coarse-clad honesty
The undefil'd tho' ravish'd in her cradle night and morn:
For every thing that lives is holy, life delights in life:
Because the soul of sweet delight can never be defil'd.
Fires inwrap the earthly globe, yet man is not consumd:
Amidst the lustful fires he walks: his feet become like
    brass,
His knees and thighs like silver, & his breast and head like
    gold.*

At various times in history, there has been a political
revolution symbolized by the birth or rebirth of Orc,
the "terrible boy": each one, however, has eventually

* Blake's punctuation is retained.

subsided into the same Urizenic form as its predecessor. Orc is the human protest of energy and desire, the impulse to freedom and to sexual love. Urizen is the "reality principle," the belief that knowledge of what is real comes from outside the human body. If we believe that reality is what we bring into existence through an act of creation, then we are free to build up our own civilization and abolish the anomalies and injustices that hamper its growth; but if we believe that reality is primarily what is "out there," then we are condemned, in Marx's phrase, to study the world and never to change it. And the world that we study in this way we are compelled to see in the distorted perspective of the human body with its five cramped senses, not our powers of perception as they are developed and expanded by the arts. Man in his present state is so constructed that all he can see outside him is the world under the law. He may believe that gods or angels or devils or fairies or ghosts are also "out there," but he cannot see these things: he can see only the human and the subhuman, moving in established and predictable patterns. The basis of this vision of reality is the world of the heavenly bodies, circling around automatically and out of reach.

One early Orc rebellion was the Exodus from Egypt, where Orc is represented by a pillar of fire (the "fiery joy") and Urizen by a pillar of cloud, or what *Finnegans Wake* calls "Delude of Isreal." Orc was a human society of twelve (actually thirteen) tribes; Urizen, a legal mechanism symbolized by the twelvefold Zodiac with its captive sun, which is why Urizen is said to have "led the

starry hosts" through the wilderness. The eventual victory
of Urizen was marked by the establishing of Aaron's
priesthood (the twelve stones in his breastplate symbolized the Zodiac as well as the tribes, according to
Josephus), and by the negative moral law of the Deca-
logue, the moral law being the human imitation of the
automatism of natural law. The final triumph of Urizen
was symbolized by the hanging of the brazen serpent
(Orc) on the pole, a form of the "accursed tree," and
recalling the earlier association of tree and serpent with
the exile of Adam into a wilderness, as well as anticipating
the Crucifixion.

Jesus was another Orc figure, gathering twelve followers
and starting a new civilization. Christian civilization, like
its predecessors, assumed the Urizenic form that it presented so clearly in Blake's own time. This historical perversion of Christianity is studied in *Europe,* where
Enitharmon, the Queen of Heaven, summons up twelve
starry children, along with Orc as the captive sun, to re-
impose the cult of external reality, or what Blake calls
natural religion, on Christendom. With the Resurrection,
traditionally symbolized by a red cross on a white ground,
Jesus made a definitive step into reality: the revolutionary
apocalypse Blake hopes for in his day is a second coming
or mass resurrection, which is why resurrection imagery
is prominently displayed in *America.* Now, at the end of
European civilization, comes another rebellion of Orc in
America, bearing on its various banners a tree, a serpent,
and thirteen red and white stripes. The spread of this

rebellion to Europe itself is a sign that bigger things are on the way.

The Israelites ended their revolt in the desert of the moral law: now it is time to reverse the movement, to enter the Promised Land, the original Eden, which is to Israel what Atlantis is to Britain and America. The Promised Land is not a different place from the desert, but the desert itself transformed (Blake's imagery comes partly from Isaiah 35, a chapter he alludes to in *The Marriage of Heaven and Hell*). The "deeps shrink to their fountains" because in the apocalypse there is no more sea: dead water is transformed to living water (as in Ezekiel's vision, Ezek. 47:8. The spiritual body of risen man is sexually free, an aspect symbolized by the "lustful fires" in which he walks. Man under the law is sexually in a prison of heat without light, a volcano: in the resurrection he is unhurt by flames, like the three Hebrews in Nebuchadnezzar's furnace who were seen walking with the son of God. According to *The Marriage of Heaven and Hell*, Jesus became Jehovah after his death, and Jehovah, not Satan, is the one who dwells in flaming fire. The risen man, then, is the genuine form of the metallic statue of Nebuchadnezzar's dream, without the feet of clay that made that statue an image of tyranny and the cycle of history.

The Resurrection rolled the stone away covering the tomb ("burst the stony roof"). The stone that covers the tomb of man under the law is the vast arch of the sky, which we see as a concave "vault of paved heaven" (a phrase in the early "Mad Song") because we are looking at it from under the "stony roof" of the skull. The risen body would be more like the shape of one of Blake's Last Judgment paintings, with an "opened centre" or radiance of light on top, in the place which is the true location of heaven. Finally, the entire Bible or revelation of the divine in and to man can be read either as the charter of human freedom or as a code of restrictive and negative moral commands. Orc proposes to use Urizen's version of the holy book as fertilizer to help make the desert blossom: what he would do, in other words, is to internalize the law, transform it from arbitrary commands to the inner discipline of the free spirit.

NORTHERN GATE: SINGLE VISION

The optimistic revolutionary construct set up in Blake's early prophecies is found again in Shelley, whose Prometheus and Jupiter correspond to Orc and Urizen. But in later Romanticism, it quickly turns pessimistic and once more conservative, notably in Schopenhauer, where the world as idea, the world of genuine humanity, sits on top of a dark, threatening, and immensely powerful world as will. A similar construct is in Darwin and Huxley, where the ethical creation of human society maintains itself precariously against the evolutionary force below it. In Freud, civilization is essentially an anxiety structure, where the "reality principle," Blake's Urizen, must maintain its ascendancy somehow over the nihilistic upthrusts of desire. It may permit a certain amount of expression to the "pleasure principle," but not to the extent of being taken over by it. And in Blake, if every revolt of Orc in history has been "perverted to ten commands," the inference seems to be that history exhibits only a gloomy series of cycles, beginning in hope and inevitably ending in renewed tyranny. In Blake's later prophecies, we do find this Spenglerian view of history, with a good many of Spengler's symbols attached to it.

The cyclical movement of history is summarized by Blake in four stages. The first stage is the revolutionary birth of Orc; the second, the transfer of power from Orc to Urizen at the height of Orc's powers, accompanied by the binding or imprisoning of Orc; the third, the consolidating of "natural religion" or the sense of reality as out there, symbolized by Urizen exploring his dens; the fourth, a collapse and chaos symbolized by the crucifixion of Orc, the hanging of the serpent on the dead tree. This fourth stage is the one that Blake sees his own age entering, after the triumph of natural religion or "Deism" in the decades following Newton and Locke. It is an age characterized by mass wars (Isaiah's treading of the winepress), by technology and complex machinery, by tyranny and "empire" (imperialism being the demonic enemy of culture), and by unimaginative art, especially in architecture. The central symbol of this final phase is the labyrinthine desert in which the Mosaic exodus ended. Jesus spent forty days in the desert, according to Mark, "with the wild beasts": the passage from empire to ruin, from the phase of the tyrant to the phase of the wild beast, is symbolized in the story of Nebuchadnezzar, whose metamorphosis is illustrated at the end of *The Marriage of Heaven and Hell.* The figure of Ijim in *Tiriel* has a parallel significance.

As Blake's symbolism becomes more concentrated, he tends to generalize the whole cycle in the conception of "Druidism." The Druids, according to Blake's authorities, worshipped the tree and the serpent, the Druid temple of Avebury, illustrated on the last plate of *Jerusalem,* being serpent-shaped; and they went in for orgies of human sacrifice which illustrate, even more clearly than warfare, the fact that the suppression or perversion of the sexual impulse ends in a death wish (I am not reading modern conceptions into Blake here, but following Blake's own symbolism). This "Druid" imagery is illustrated in the following passage from *Europe,* describing the reaction of the tyrannical "King" or guardian angel of the reactionary Albion and his councillors to the American revolution and kindred portents of apocalyptic disaffection:

> In thoughts perturb'd they rose from the bright
>   ruins silent following
> The fiery King, who sought his ancient temple
>   serpent-form'd
> That stretches out its shady length along the
>   Island white.
> Round him roll'd his clouds of war; silent the
>   Angel went,
> Along the infinite shores of Thames to golden
>   Verulam.

There stand the venerable porches that high-
  towering rear
Their oak-surrounded pillars, form'd of massy
  stones, uncut
With tool: stones precious: such eternal in
  the heavens,
Of colours twelve, few known on earth, give
  light in the opake,
Plac'd in the order of the stars, when the five
  senses whelm'd
In deluge o'er the earth-born man: then turn'd
  the fluxile eyes
Into two stationary orbs, concentrating all
  things.
The ever-varying spiral ascents to the heavens
  of heavens
Were bended downward, and the nostrils golden
  gates shut,
Turn'd outward barr'd and petrify'd against the
  infinite ...

Now arriv'd the ancient Guardian at the southern
  porch.
That planted thick with trees of blackest leaf,
  & in a vale
Obscure, inclos'd the Stone of Night; oblique
  it stood, o'erhung
With purple flowers and berries red: image of
  that sweet south
Once open to the heavens and elevated on the
  human neck,
Now overgrown with hair and cover'd with a
  stony roof:

> Downward 'tis sunk beneath th' attractive north,
>   that round the feet
> A raging whirlpool draws the dizzy enquirer to
>   his grave.

It is an intricate passage, but it all makes sense. The serpent temple of Avebury is identified with the white-cliffed Albion in its final Druid phase. It is centered at Verulam, which, as the site of a Roman camp, a "Gothic" cathedral, and the baronial title of Bacon, takes in the whole cycle of British civilization. As we approach the temple, it appears to be a Stonehenge-like circle of twelve precious stones, "plac'd in the order of the stars," or symbolizing the Zodiac. The imagery recalls the similar decadence of Israel in the desert: the twelve Zodiacal gems of Aaron's breastplate have been mentioned, and the Israelites also built megalithic monuments on which they were forbidden to use iron (Jos. 8:31), hence "uncut with tool," iron being in Blake the symbol of Los the blacksmith, the builder of the true city of gems (Isa. 54:16).

The central form of Druid architecture is the trilithic cromlech or dolmen, the arch of three stones. According to Blake, the two uprights of this arch symbolize the two aspects of creative power, strength and beauty, or sublimity and pathos, as he calls them in the *Descriptive Catalogue*, the horizontal stone being the dominant Urizenic reason. Human society presents this arch in the form of an "Elect" class tyrannizing over the "Reprobate," the unfashionable artists and prophets who embody human sublimity, and the "Redeemed," the gentler souls who are in the company of the beautiful and pathetic. This trilithic structure reappears in such later militaristic monuments as the Arch of Titus: in its "Druid" form, it is illustrated with great power in *Milton*, Plate 6, and *Jerusalem*, Plate 70. In the former, the balancing rock in front may represent the "Stone of Night" in the above passage. To pass under this arch is to be subjugated, in a fairly literal sense, to what is, according to the *Descriptive Catalogue*, both the human reason and the "incapability of intellect," as intellect in Blake is always associated with the creative and imaginative. Another form of tyrannical architecture characteristic of a degenerate civilization is the pyramid, representing the volcano or imprisoning mountain under which Orc lies. Blake connects the pyramids with the servitude of the Israelites among the brickkilns and the epithet "furnace of iron" (I Kings 8:51) applied to Egypt in the Bible. The association of pyramids and fire is as old as Plato's pun on the word πύρ.

The temple of Verulam is a monument to the fall of man, in Blake the same event as the deluge and the creation of the world in its present "out there" form. This form is that of the law, the basis of which is revolution in its mechanical sense of revolving wheels, the symbol of which is the *ouroboros*, the serpent with its tail in its mouth (indicated in a passage omitted above). We see the world from individual "opake" centers, instead of being identified with a universal Man who is also God, who created what we see as alien to us, and who would consequently see his world from the circumference instead of the center, the perspective reinstated in man by the arts. Such a God-Man would be "full of eyes," like the creatures of Ezekiel's vision, and by an unexpected but quite logical extension of the symbolism, Blake makes him full of noses too. Burning meat to gods on altars, after all, does assume that gods have circumferential noses.

The "Stone of Night," the opposite of the "lively stones" (I Peter 2:5) of the genuine temple, is an image of the human head, the phrase "stony roof" being repeated from the passage in *America* quoted above. It is in the south because the south is the zenith, the place of the sun in full strength in Blake's symbolism. Now it is covered with purple flowers and red berries, probably of the nightshade: the colors are those of the dying god, which is what Orc (usually Luvah in this context) comes to be in Blake's later poems. The Stone of Night has fallen like a meteor through the bottom or nadir of existence, represented by the north, and now has the same relation to its original that a gravestone has to a living body. We may compare the "grave-plot" that Thel reached when she passed under the "northern bar," and the black coffin which is the body of the chimney sweep (and the enslaved Negro, who also belongs in the "southern clime"). Blake's imagery of the north combines the magnetic needle and the legend of the northern maelstrom, the latter supplying a demonic parody of the ascending spiral image on the altar.

From the perspective of single vision, then, our original diagram of buried innocence trying to push its way into experience has to be completed by the death in which all life, individual or historical, ends. Death in Blake's symbolism is Satan, the "limit of Opacity," reduction to inorganic matter, who operates in the living man as a death wish or "accuser" of sin. His source in the outer world is the sky, Satan being the starry dragon of Revelation 12:4. Blake identifies this dragon with the Covering Cherub of Ezekiel 28, and the Covering Cherub again with the angel trying to keep us out of the Garden of Eden. Thus the sky is, first, the outward illusion of reality that keeps us out of our proper home; second, the macrocosmic Stone of Night, the rock on top of man's tomb designed to prevent his resurrection; and third, the circumference of what Blake calls the "Mundane Shell," the world as it appears to the embryonic and unborn imagination. Thus:

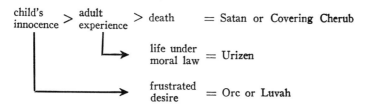

Ordinary human life, symbolized in Blake first by "Adam" and later by "Reuben," oscillates between the two submerged states.

The conception of Druidism in Blake, then, is a conception of human energy and desire continuously martyred by the tyranny of human reason, or superstition. The phrase "dying god" that we have used for Luvah suggests Frazer, and Blake's Druid symbolism has some remarkable anticipations of Frazer's *Golden Bough* complex, including the mistletoe and the oak. The anticipations even extend to Frazer's own unconscious symbolism: the colors of the three states above are, reading up, red, white, and black; and Frazer's book ends with the remark that the web of human thought has been woven of these three colors, though the status of the white or scientific one in Blake is very different. The following passage from *Jerusalem* 66 illustrates Blake's handling of sacrificial symbolism:

> The Daughters of Albion clothed in garments
>   of needle work
> Strip them off from their shoulders and bosoms,
>   they lay aside
> Their garments, they sit naked upon the
>   Stone of trial.
> The knife of flint passes over the howling
>   Victim: his blood
> Gushes & stains the fair side of the fair
>   Daughters of Albion.
> They put aside his curls: they divide his
>   seven locks upon
> His forehead: they bind his forehead with
>   thorns of iron,
> They put into hand a reed, they mock,
>   Saying: Behold
> The King of Canaan, whose are seven hundred
>   chariots of iron!
> They take off his vesture whole with their
>   Knives of flint:

But they cut asunder his inner garments:
  searching with
Their cruel fingers for his heart, & there
  they enter in pomp,
In many tears: & there they erect a temple
  & an altar:
They pour cold water on his brain in front,
  to cause
Lids to grow over his eyes in veils of tears:
  and caverns
To freeze over his nostrils, while they feed
  his tongue from cups
And dishes of painted clay.

The imagery combines the mockery and passion of Jesus with features from Aztec sacrifices, as Blake realizes that the two widely separated rituals mean essentially the same thing. In the Mexican rites, the "vesture whole" is the skin, not the garment, and the heart is extracted from the body, not merely pierced by a spear as in the Passion. As the passage goes on, the victim expands from an individual body into a country: that is, he is beginning to embody not merely the dying god, but the original universal Man, Albion, whose present dead body is England. The veils and caverns are religious images derived from analogies between the human body and the landscape. Serpent worship is for Blake a perennial feature of this kind of superstition, and the victim is fed from dishes of clay partly because, as Blake says in *The Everlasting Gospel*, "dust & Clay is the Serpent's meat."

An early Biblical dying-god figure is that of Sisera, the King of Canaan, whose murder at the hands of Jael suggests the nailing down of Jesus and Prometheus; and the reference to "needle work" in the first line also comes from Deborah's war song. The role given to the Daughters of Albion shows how clearly Blake associates the ritual of sacrifice, many features of which are repeated in judicial executions, with a perversion of the erotic instinct; and in fact Blake is clearer than Frazer about the role of the "white goddess" in the dying god cult, the Cybele who decrees the death of Attis.

Southern Gate: Threefold Vision

The conception of a cycle common to individual and to historical life is the basis of the symbolism of several modern poets, including Yeats, Joyce in *Finnegans Wake*, and Graves in *The White Goddess*. In its modern forms, it usually revolves around a female figure. *The Marriage of Heaven and Hell* prophesies that eventually the bound Orc will be set free and will destroy the present world in a "consummation," which means both burning up and the climax of a marriage. When the marriage is accomplished "by an improvement of sensual enjoyment," the world of form and reason will be possessed by energy and desire, and will be their "outward bound or circumference" instead of a separate and therefore tyrannizing principle. One would think then that a female figure would be more appropriate for the symbolism of the world of form than the aged and male Urizen.

In traditional Christian symbolism, God the Creator is symbolically male, and all human souls, whether of men or of women, are creatures, and therefore symbolically female. In Blake, the real man is creating man; hence all human beings, men or women, are symbolically male. The symbolic female in Blake is what we call nature, and has four relations to humanity, depending on the quality of the vision. In the world of death, or Satan, which Blake calls Ulro, the human body is completely absorbed in the body of nature—a "dark Hermaphrodite," as Blake says in *The Gates of Paradise*. In the ordinary world of experience, which Blake calls Generation, the relation of humanity to nature is that of subject to object. In the usually frustrated and suppressed world of sexual desire, which Blake calls Beulah, the relation is that of lover to beloved, and in the purely imaginative or creative state, called Eden, the relation is that of creator to creature. In the first two worlds, nature is a remote and tantalizing "female will"; in the last two she is an "emanation." Human women are associated with this female nature only when in their behavior they dramatize its characteristics. The relations between man and nature in the individual and historical cycle are different, and are summarized in *The Mental Traveller*, a poem as closely related to the cyclical symbolism of twentieth-century poetry as Keats's *La Belle Dame Sans Merci* is to pre-Raphaelite poetry.

The Mental Traveller traces the life of a "Boy" from infancy through manhood to death and rebirth. This Boy represents humanity, and consequently the cycle he goes

through can be read either individually and psychologically, or socially and historically. The latter reading
is easier, and closer to the center of gravity of what Blake
is talking about. The poem traces a cycle, but the cycle
differs from that of the single vision in that the emphasis
is thrown on rebirth and return instead of on death. A
female principle, nature, cycles in contrary motion against
the Boy, growing young as he grows old and vice versa,
and producing four phases that we may call son and
mother, husband and wife, father and daughter, ghost
(Blake's "spectre") and ghostly bride (Blake's "emanation"). Having set them down, we next observe that not
one of these relations is genuine: the mother is not really
a mother, nor the daughter really a daughter, and similarly with the other states. The "Woman Old," the nurse
who takes charge of the Boy, is Mother Nature, whom
Blake calls Tirzah, and who ensures that everyone enters
this world in the mutilated and imprisoned form of the
physical body. The sacrifice of the dying god repeats this
symbolism, which is why the birth of the Boy also contains the symbols of the Passion (we should compare this
part of *The Mental Traveller* with the end of *Jerusalem*
67).

As the Boy grows up, he subdues a part of nature to
his will, which thereupon becomes his mistress: a stage
represented elsewhere in the Preludium to *America*. As
the cycle completes what Yeats would call its first gyre,
we reach the opposite pole of a "Female Babe" whom,
like the newborn Boy, no one dares touch. This female
represents the "emanation" or accumulated form of what

the Boy has created in his life. If she were a real daughter and not a changeling, she would be the Boy's own permanent creation, as Jerusalem is the daughter of Albion, "a City, yet a Woman"; and with the appearance of such a permanent creation, the cycle of nature would come to an end. But in this world all creative achievements are inherited by someone else and are lost to their creator. This failure to take possession of one's own deepest experience is the theme of *The Crystal Cabinet* (by comparing the imagery of this latter poem with *Jerusalem* 70 we discover that the Female Babe's name, in this context, is Rahab). The Boy, now an old man at the point of death, acquires, like the aged king David, another "maiden" to keep his body warm on his deathbed. He is now in the desert or wilderness, which symbolizes the end of a cycle, and his maiden is Lilith, the bride of the desert, whom Blake elsewhere calls the Shadowy Female. The Boy as an old man is in an "alastor" relation to her: he ought to be still making the kind of creative effort that produced the Female Babe, but instead he keeps seeking his "emanation" or created form outside himself, until eventually the desert is partially renewed by his efforts, he comes again into the place of seed, and the cycle starts once more.

A greatly abbreviated account of the same cycle, in a more purely historical context, is in the "Argument" of *The Marriage of Heaven and Hell*. Here we start with Rintrah, the prophet in the desert, the Moses or Elijah or John the Baptist, who announces a new era of history; then we follow the historical cycle as it makes the desert blossom and produces the honey of the Promised Land. We notice how, as in the time of Moses, water springs up in the desert and how Orc's "red clay" puts life on the white bones of Urizen. Eventually the new society becomes decadent and tyrannical, forcing the prophet out into the desert once more to begin another cycle.

The poem called *The Gates of Paradise*, based on a series of illustrations reproduced in the standard edition of Blake, describes the same cycle in slightly different and more individualized terms. Here conception in the womb, the mutilation of birth which produces the "mother's grief," is symbolized by the caterpillar and by the mandrake. The mandrake is traditionally an aphrodisiac, a plant with male and female forms, an opiate, the seed of hanged men, a "man-dragon" that shrieks when uprooted (i.e., born), and recalls the frustrated sunflower of the *Songs of Experience*. The association of the mandrake with the mother in Genesis 30:14 is the main reason why Blake uses "Reuben" instead of "Adam" as the symbol of ordinary man in *Jerusalem*. The embryo then takes on the substance of the four elements and the four humors that traditionally correspond to them, of which "Earth's Melancholy" is the dominant one. Then the infant is born and grows into an aggressive adolescent, like the Boy in *The Mental Traveller* binding nature down for his delight. This attitude divides nature into a part that is possessed and a part that eludes, and the separation indicates that the boy in this poem also is bound to the cyclical movement. The youth then collides with Urizen, the spear in the revolutionary left hand being opposed to the sword of established order in the right. The caption of this emblem, "My Son! My Son!", refers to Absalom's revolt against David. Orc is not the son of Urizen, but Absalom, hung on a tree (traditionally by his golden hair, like the mistletoe: cf. *The Book of Ahania*, II, 9) is another dying god or Druid victim.

The other plates are not difficult to interpret: they represent the frustration of desire, the reaction into despair, and the growing of the youthful and rebellious Orc into a wing-clipping Urizen again. Finally the hero, like the early Tiriel and like the Boy of *The Mental Traveller* in his old age, becomes a wandering pilgrim making his way, like the old man in the Pardoner's Tale, toward his own death. He enters "Death's Door," the lower half of a design from Blair's *Grave* omitting the resurrection theme in the upper half, and is once more identified with Mother Nature, with a caption quoted from Job 17:14. The Prologue asks us why we worship this dreary womb-to-tomb treadmill as God—that is, why we think of God as a sky-god of automatic order, when this sky-god is really Satan, the corpse of God. The Epilogue returns to the same attack, and concludes by calling Satan "The lost traveller's Dream under the Hill." Apart from the general theme of the dreaming traveller which is common to this poem and to *The Mental Traveller* (where the "mental" travelling is done by the poet and reader, not the hero), there is a more specific allusion to the passage in *The Pilgrim's Progress* where Christian, after falling asleep under Hill Difficulty and losing his roll, is forced to retrace his steps like the Israelites in the desert, to whom Bunyan explictly refers.

The passage from death to rebirth is represented in Blake's symbolism by Tharmas, the power of renewing life. The ability of the individual to renew his life is resurrection, and the resurrection is a break with the cycle, but in ordinary life such a renewal takes place only in the group or species, and within the cycle. Tharmas is symbolized by the sea, the end and the beginning of life. As the original fall of man was also the deluge, we are in this world symbolically under water, our true home being Atlantis, or the Red Sea, which the Israelites found to be dry land. Tharmas and Orc are the strength and beauty, the sublime and the pathetic, the uprights of the Druid trilithon already mentioned, with Urizen, the antiintellectual "reason," connecting them. Thus:

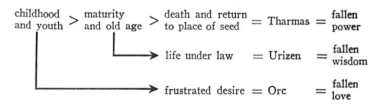

childhood and youth > maturity and old age > death and return to place of seed = Tharmas = fallen power

life under law = Urizen = fallen wisdom

frustrated desire = Orc = fallen love

WESTERN GATE: FOURFOLD VISION

In *The Marriage of Heaven and Hell*, Blake presents the revolutionary vision of man as a self-centered anxious ego sitting on top of a rebellious desire, and he associates the emancipating of desire with the end of the world as we know it. The Proverbs of Hell say: "He who desires but acts not, breeds pestilence." Putting desire into action does not lead to anarchy, for the fires of Orc are "thought-creating": what it does lead to is an apocalypse in which "the whole creation will be consumed and appear infinite and holy, whereas it now appears finite & corrupt." But when we read other works of Blake, we begin to wonder if this "Voice of the Devil" tells the whole story. Blake certainly means what he says in *The Marriage of Heaven and Hell*, but that work is a satire, deriving its norms from other conceptions. As we read further in Blake, it becomes clear that the emancipating of desire, for him, is not the cause but the effect of the purging of reality. There was some political disillusionment as Blake proceeded—the perversion of the French Revolution into Napoleonic imperialism, the strength of the reactionary power in Britain, the continued ascendancy of the slave-owners in America, and a growing feeling that Voltaire and Rousseau were reactionaries and not revolutionaries were the main elements in it—but although this leads to some changes in emphasis in later poems, there is no evidence that he was ever really confused about the difference between the apocalyptic and the historical versions of reality.

Blake dislikes any terminology which implies that there are two perceivers in man, such as a soul and a body, which perceive different worlds. There is only one world, but there are two kinds of things to be done with it. There is, first, what Blake calls the natural vision, which assumes that the objective world is essentially independent of man. This vision becomes increasingly hypnotized by the automatic order and tantalizing remoteness of nature, creates gods in the image of its mindless mechanism, and rationalizes all evils and injustices of existence under some such formula as "Whatever is, is right." In extreme forms, this alienating vision becomes the reflection of the death wish in the soul, and develops annihilation wars like those of Blake's own time. Then there is the human vision, which takes the objective world to be the "starry floor," the bottom of reality, its permanence being important only as a stable basis for human creation. The goal of the human vision is "Religion, or Civilized Life such as it is in the Christian Church." This is a life of pure creation, such as is ascribed in Christianity to God, and which for Blake would participate in the infinite and eternal perspective of God. We note that Blake, like Kierkegaard, leads us toward an "either/or" dilemma, but that his terms are the reverse of Kierkegaard's. It is the aesthetic element for Blake which moves in the sphere of existential freedom; it is the ethical element which is the spectator, under the bondage of the law and the knowledge of good and evil.

We begin, then, with the view of an orthodox or moral "good," founded on an acceptance of the world out there, contrasted with the submerged "evil" desires of man to live in a world that makes more human sense. This vision of life turns out to be, when examined, a cyclical vision, completed by the more elaborate cycles just examined. But in addition to the cyclical vision there is also a dialectic, a separating-out of the two opposing human and natural visions. The categories of these visions are not

moral good and evil, but life and death, one producing
the real heaven of creation and the other the real hell
of torture and tyranny. We have met one pole of this
dialectic already in the conception of Satan, or death, as
the only possible goal of all human effort from one point
of view. The other pole is the impulse to transform the
world into a human and imaginative form, the impulse
that creates all art, all genuine religion, all culture and
civilization. This impulse is personified by Blake as Los,
the spirit of prophecy and creativity, and it is Los, not
Orc, who is the hero of Blake's prophecies. Los derives,
not from the suppressed desires of the individual child,
but from a deeper creative impulse alluded to in Biblical
myths about the unfallen state. These myths tell us that
man's original state was not primitive, or derived from
nature at all, but civilized, in the environment of a garden
and a city. This unfallen state is, so to speak, the previous
tree of which contemporary man is the seed, and the form
he is attempting to recreate. Thus:

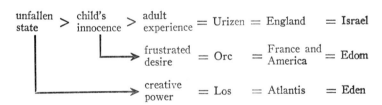

It seems curious that, especially in the earlier prophecies, Los appears to play a more reactionary and sinister
role than Urizen himself. We discover that it is Los, not
Urizen, who is the father of Orc; Los, not Urizen, who

actively restrains Orc, tying him down under Mount Atlas with the "Chain of Jealousy"; and Los who is the object of Orc's bitter Oedipal resentments. In the Preludium to *America*, he is referred to by his alternative name of Urthona, and there it is he and not Urizen who rivets Orc's "tenfold chains." These chains evidently include an incest taboo, for Orc is copulating with his sister in this Preludium. Evidently, as Blake conceives it, there is a deeply conservative element in the creative spirit that seems to help perpetuate the reign of Urizen. In fact certain functions given to Urizen in earlier prophecies are transferred to Los in later ones. According to William Morris, the joy that the medieval craftsman took in his work was so complete that he was able to accept the tyranny of medieval society: similarly, Blake is able to live in the age of Pitt and Nelson and yet be absorbed in building his palace of art on the "Great Atlantic Mountains," which will be here after the "Sea of Time and Space" above it is no more.

This principle that effective social action is to be found in the creation of art and not in revolution is, of course, common to many Romantics in Blake's period. It should not, however—certainly not in Blake—be regarded as a mere neurotic or wish-fulfilment substitute for the failure of revolution. Apart from the fact that the creation of art is a highly social act, Blake's conception of art is very different from the dictionary's. It is based on what we call the arts, because of his doctrine that human reality is created and not observed. But it includes much that we do not think of as art, and excludes much that we do, such as the paintings of Reynolds.

We notice that in *The Gates of Paradise* cycle there is
one point at which there is a break from the cycle, the
plate captioned "Fear & Hope are—Vision." and described
in the commentary as a glimpse of "The Immortal Man
that cannot Die." The corresponding point in *The Mental
Traveller* comes in describing the form ("emanation")
of the life that the Boy has been constructing, just before
it takes shape as the elusive "Female Babe":

> And these are the gems of the Human Soul,
> The rubies & pearls of a lovesick eye,
> The countless gold of the akeing heart,
> The martyr's groan & the lover's sigh.

The curiously wooden allegory is not characteristic of
Blake, but it recurs in *Jerusalem* 12, where the same
theme is under discussion. Evidently, Blake means by
"art" a creative life rooted in the arts, but including what
more traditional language calls charity. Every act man
performs is either creative or destructive. Both kinds
seem to disappear in time, but in fact it is only the
destructive act, the act of war or slavery or parasitism or
hatred, that is really lost.

Los is not simply creative power, but the spirit of
time: more accurately, he is the power that constructs
in time the palace of art (Golgonooza), which is timeless.
As Blake says in a grammatically violent aphorism, the
ruins of time build mansions in eternity. The products
of self-sacrifice and martyrdom and endurance of in-
justice still exist, in an invisible but permanent world

created out of time by the imagination. This world is the genuine Atlantis or Eden that we actually live in. As soon as we realize that we do live in it, we enter into what Blake means by the Last Judgement. Most people do not make this act of realization, and those who do make it have the responsibility of being evangelists for it. According to Blake, most of what the enlightened can do for the unenlightened is negative: their task is to sharpen the dialectic of the human and natural visions by showing that there are only the alternatives of apocalypse and annihilation.

Blake obviously hopes for a very considerable social response to vision in or soon after his lifetime. But even if everybody responded completely and at once, the City of God would not become immediately visible: if it did, it would simply be one more objective environment. The real "heaven" is not a glittering city, but the power of bringing such cities into existence. In the poem "My Spectre around me," Blake depicts a figure like the Boy of *The Mental Traveller* in old age, searching vainly for his "emanation," the total body of what he can love and create, outside himself instead of inside. The natural tendency of desire (Orc) in itself is to find its object. Hence the effect of the creative impulse on desire is bound to be restrictive until the release of desire becomes the inevitable by-product of creation.

The real world, being the source of a human vision, is human and not natural (which means indefinite) in shape. It does not stretch away forever into the stars,

but has the form of a single giant man's body, the parts
of which are arranged thus:

Urizen	= head	= city
Tharmas	= body	= garden
Orc	= loins	= soil or bed of love
Urthona	= legs	= underworld of dream and repose
(Los)		

Except that it is unfallen, the four levels of this world
correspond very closely to the four traditional levels that
we find in medieval and Renaissance poetry. The present
physical world, by the "improvement of sensual enjoyment," would become an integral part of nature, and so
Comus' attempt to seduce the Lady by an appeal to
"nature" would no longer be a seduction or a specious
argument. But the really important distinction is that
for earlier poets the two upper levels, the city and the
garden, were divine and not human in origin, whereas
for Blake they are both divine and human, and their
recovery depends on the creative power in man as well
as in God.

The difference between the traditional and the Blakean
versions of reality corresponds to the difference between
the first and the last plates of the Job illustrations. In
the first plate, Job and his family are in the state of
innocence (Beulah), in a peaceful pastoral repose like
that of the twenty-third Psalm. They preserve this state
in the traditional way, by obeying a divine Providence
that has arranged it, and hence are imaginatively children.
There is nothing in the picture that suggests anything

39

inadequate except that, in a recall of a very different Psalm (137), there are musical instruments hung on the tree above. In the last plate, things are much as they were before, but Job's family have taken the instruments down from the tree and are playing them. In Blake, we recover our original state, not by returning to it, but by recreating it. The act of creation, in its turn, is not producing something out of nothing, but the act of setting free what we already possess.

THE FUTURE OF
LANDOR CRITICISM

Vivian Mercier

I

R. H. Super's review of Landor scholarship and criticism in an earlier volume of the present series demonstrated, by its own excellence as much as by its adverse judgments, how scarce good Landor criticism has always been. Is it not shocking to reflect that Edward Waterman Evans' undergraduate prize essay, published in 1892, remains the *only* book exclusively devoted to a critical study of Landor's work as a whole? And yet the present time is characterized, often with an implied sneer, as an age of criticism. I find it particularly ironic that a writer who devoted not far from half his non-journalistic prose and a goodly portion of his occasional verse to literary criticism (whatever its merit) should be, though not altogether ignored, so casually, and sometimes incompetently, handled by literary critics.

One would have thought that those contemporary poets and critics who have made it their business to revive and illuminate the Tradition of Wit would have brought Landor out of his semi-obscurity and paraded him before us as the "missing link," the true upholder of the continuity of English poetry between Pope and T. S. Eliot, or at the very least, between Johnson and Browning. Ezra Pound, certainly, has paid his respects to Landor in highly Poundian fashion; but Eliot, in *The Use of Poetry and the Use of Criticism* (1933), though he calls Landor "one of the very finest poets of the first part of the nineteenth century," goes on to insist that

"Wordsworth is an essential part of history; Landor only a magnificent by-product."

Cleanth Brooks mentions Landor just once in *The Well Wrought Urn* (1947), and then only to quote a comment of his on Gray's "Elegy." Instead of seeking paradox where it belongs, in Landor's epigrammatic poetry, he looks for it in the "Immortality Ode." Naturally, this provides a greater challenge to Brooks's ingenuity and disturbs the complacency of his readers, who thought Wordsworth had been filed and indexed for all eternity. But must a book on the language of paradox be itself so unrelentingly paradoxical? Might we not have been given at least a paragraph or two on Landor to correct the balance of the chapter on Wordsworth?

It would be tempting to expatiate on I. A. Richards' "Fifteen Lines from Landor" (*Criterion*, 1933), had not Super already dealt with it so magisterially. I would only add that the topographical reference in these lines,

> Though panting in the play-hour of my youth,
> I drank of Avon, too, a dang'rous draught,
>
> (Gebir, Book III, ll. 4-5)

may be taken even more literally than Super proposes. It is not at all irrelevant to picture the youthful Landor swimming in the Avon, losing his breath, and gulping down a dangerous, half-suffocating mouthful of that inspiring stream. *There* is paradox, if you like, especially when this "dang'rous draught" is said in the next line

44

to have "rous'd within the fev'rish thirst of song. . . . "
Draughts do not usually arouse thirst but quench it;
yet it would be a poor critic who could not recognize
the validity of such an ambiguous image: in fairness
to Richards, I should add that he did recognize it.
"Dang'rous," too, is ambiguous, of course. The gulp of
water at first meant physical danger, then later the frightful risks, both moral and physical, that poets incur:
"Toil, Envy, Want, the Patron, and the Jail." Landor's
substantial patrimony failed to save him from most of
these.

Before considering Pound's critical dicta on Landor,
it is worth asking what Landor meant to W. B. Yeats.
The famous lines in "To a Young Beauty,"

> There is not a fool can call me friend,
> And I may dine at journey's end
> With Landor and with Donne,

clearly refer to Landor's oft-quoted boast, "I shall dine
late . . . ," and imply tardy recognition. But Richard
Ellmann, in *Yeats: The Man and the Masks* (1948),
says that Yeats felt a deeper affinity with Landor, locat-
ing himself in the same Phase 17 of the Moon that he
reserves for the deeply divided personalities of Dante,
Shelley, and Landor. The relevant passage in *A Vision*
(1938) runs as follows:

Landor has been examined in *Per Amica Silentia Lunae*.
The most violent of men, he uses his intellect to dis-

45

engage a visionary image of perfect sanity . . . seen always in the most serene and classic art imaginable. He had perhaps as much Unity of Being as his age permitted, and possessed, though not in any full measure, the Vision of Evil.

The passage in *Per Amica Silentia Lunae* amplifies but does not alter the above portrait:

> . . . Savage Landor topped us all in calm nobility while the pen was in his hand, as in the daily violence of his passion when he had laid it down. He had in his *Imaginary Conversations* reminded us, as it were, that the Venus de Milo is a stone, and yet he wrote when the copies did not come from the printer as soon as he expected: "I have . . . had the resolution to tear in pieces all my sketches and projects and to forswear all future undertakings. I have tried to sleep away my time and pass two-thirds of the twenty-four hours in bed. I may speak of myself as a dead man."

Yeats clearly was familiar with the *Imaginary Conversations* and Forster's *Life* and, doubtless, with much of Landor's poetry as well. The three mentions of Landor in Yeats's *Autobiographies* seem to imply a lifelong awareness of his work, but the reference in *Per Amica*, first published in 1917, is almost certainly the fruit of Yeats and Pound's recent joint reading of Landor.

Of the five references to Landor in *The Letters of Ezra Pound 1907–1941* (1950), the most important and the most critical comes from a letter to Iris Barry, dated July 27, 1916:

Yeats and I spent our last winter's months on Landor. There is a whole culture. I don't quite know whether you will like much of it. Perhaps you had better keep it till later. I think it might get a little in the way if you try to gobble it now. It wants leisure and laziness. AND he (Landor) isn't very good as a poet save in a few places, where he is fine, damn fine, *but* he is no use as a model. One has got constantly to be thinking that "this is fine, but this not really the right way to do it."

Not merely those who complain that much of Landor's own criticism is cryptic and frustrating will be baffled by this oracular passage. Fortunately, Pound has provided in *ABC of Reading* (1934) a tiny Landor anthology that helps us to understand what he considered "damn fine." It includes adaptations from Alcaeus ("Wormwood and rue be on his tongue . . . ") and Catullus ("Aurelius, Sire of Hungrinesses!"); "Dirce" ("Stand close around, ye Stygian set . . . "); satirical epigrams on Byron's marriage, Melville's swearing, Macaulay's peerage, Irish discontent, and the Duke of York's statue; the conclusion of the lines to Browning; a poem on the sonnet ("Does it become a girl so wise . . . ?"); the poem on Porson and Bacchus (" 'Twas far beyond the midnight hour . . . "); and, almost inevitably, "Past ruin'd Ilion Helen lives. . . . "

These "exhibits," as Pound likes to call them, are followed by two pages of aphoristic criticism in the Landor manner. I shall try to cull Pound's most significant comments.

"Dirce" is introduced as follows:

> The effect of his severe classical studies never deserts him,
> and the cantabile quality never wholly deserts the verses
> of his shorter poems, even when they are manifestly
> *inscribed*.

(As a gloss on "cantabile," I should mention that Pound
constantly stresses the Greek distinction between verse
written to be spoken and that written to be sung.) After
quoting "Dirce" he adds, "Moral: a man wanting to
conserve a tradition would always do well to find out,
first, what it is," meaning, I presume, that Landor had
done so. Pound then goes on to warn against the dangers
of "preferring 'a manner of writing' to the living language," especially if one's culture is not "as thorough as
Landor's." Many of Landor's longer poems are "inacces-
sible because the language is so far removed from any
speech ever used anywhere."

Pound's view of the *Imaginary Conversations* is unique,
so far as I know, but perhaps none the less valid for that:

> . . . all culture of the encyclopedists reduced to man-
> ageable size . . . and full of human life ventilated, given
> a human body, not merely indexed.
>
> A figure to put against Voltaire. BUT for the Chron-
> ology! . . .
> Voltaire: 1694-1778
> Landor: 1775-1864.
>
> They are mental contemporaries. Landor comes after
> the work is done . . . [and] gathers it up, and if you
> want a handy introduction you have it in his *Conversa-
> tions*. . . .

The remainder of the passage is concerned with this time lag, Landor being behind the times as compared with the French Enlightenment but "so far ahead of his British times that the country couldn't contain him. . . . "

It would be easy to draw a close parallel between Landor and Pound, both as men and as artists; in fact, it has already been drawn by implication on page 18 of Hugh Kenner's *The Poetry of Ezra Pound* (1951). After grouping the modern poet with Ben Jonson, Landor, and Browning, Kenner goes on to list the characteristics that Pound and Jonson have in common: "multi-lingual erudition, . . . orientation toward politics rather than psychology," etc. Almost every word of the description would apply equally well to Landor.

Later in this chapter, I shall have occasion to point out certain critical concepts of Landor's that should appeal strongly to Pound, though one cannot be certain that the latter is aware of all of them. At any rate, enough has been said here to show that Pound regards Landor, with reservations, as part of the "usable past." Indeed, the *ABC of Reading* credits Landor with "driving piles into the mud, and preparing foundations—which have been largely unused by his successors." It is surprising that no contemporary critic except Kenner, a devout Poundian, seems to have taken the hint.

The most sizable body of valid critical judgments rendered on Landor's work by any twentieth-century writer will be found dispersed through the pages of Super's biography, yet I think it is fair to say that the biographer does not regard Landor as his contemporary in any respect. This attitude explains the very great difference in tone between his biography and that by Malcolm Elwin. No doubt because of some emotional or intellectual affinity, Elwin does regard Landor the man as a possible inhabitant of the twentieth century, someone whose political and ethical views still have meaning; on the other hand, I don't recall Elwin's saying anything about the contemporary relevance of Landor's literary ideals. Certainly one finds no mention of Eliot, Yeats, or Pound in *Landor: A Replevin* (1958). Actually, since the writers just mentioned did their most vital work between the two World Wars, the moment of Landor's relevance is already past. Does Landor mean anything to a genuinely post-1945 generation?

Nevertheless, it is the duty—and, I hope, the pleasure—of the scholar and the academic critic to keep always before us "the best that has been thought and said in the world." Therefore, I am going to offer in the remainder of this chapter suggestions for a number of critical approaches to Landor that I think may still prove fruitful—especially those which have the good fortune to coincide with the suggestions already offered by Professor Super.

II

Priority ought surely to be granted to a consideration of Landor's "poetics": those principles, whether explicit or implicit, which governed his own creative work as opposed to his critical judgments of others'. One obvious method of arriving at Landor's implicit principles is the study of his revisions, both in manuscript and in successive editions of his works. I understand that no systematic study of this kind has yet been directed to either the *Imaginary Conversations* or any of the later poetry. Where most of the facts still remain to be established, any deduction from the facts already known would be premature. Stephen Wheeler's preference, in most cases, for the earliest printed versions of the longer poems implies a critical judgment of Landor's more coldblooded revisions that Swinburne, momentarily laying aside his habitual idolatry of the older poet, tends to share. Even if this view is supported by a systematic analysis, more immediate revisions in the original manuscripts—where these exist—may tell an altogether different story.

Landor's most impressive statement on the subject of revision provides one possible standard by which to measure his own practice:

> The first thing a young person who wishes to be a poet has to do, is, to conquer his volubility; to compress in three verses what he had easily thrown off in twelve; and to be an hour about what cost him a minute. (F, VI, 232)[1]

[1] The following abbreviations will be used for citations from these references:

F—*The Works and Life of Walter Savage Landor*, ed. John Forster, 8 vols. (London, 1876). I have used this admittedly unsatisfactory edition for my citations from the prose works because I own a set, by now enriched with marginalia.

S—R. H. Super, *Walter Savage Landor: A Biography* (New York, 1954).

W—*The Poetical Works of Walter Savage Landor*, ed. Stephen Wheeler, 3 vols. (Oxford, 1937).

That Landor often applied this standard to his own work is borne out by the frequent complaints of critics against what they consider his excessive condensation of utterance and suppression of necessary transitions. Indirect confirmation of this principle of revision is supplied by Landor's critical practice in, for instance, the Southey-Landor Conversations and the *Pentameron*. Had Landor had his way, the *Divine Comedy* and Virgil's works would be shorter by several lines, and *Paradise Lost* by several hundred.

Mere length, of course, was for Landor a relatively unimportant criterion; one would expect a study of manuscript revisions to document above all his unrelenting search for *le mot juste*. Unfortunately, Landor himself must have destroyed much the evidence, if we can believe the felicitous quatrain entitled "Verses Why Burnt":

> How many verses have I thrown
> Into the fire because the one
> Peculiar word, the wanted most,
> Was irrecoverably lost.

> (W, II, 472)

Another method of arriving at Landor's implicit poetics is the detailed examination of his prosody and prose rhythm. As Super has noted with due irony, "critics great and small" are very willing to talk about Landor's style but strangely reluctant to study it carefully. He cites Saintsbury as the only exception to this rule; another would be "Vernon Lee," whose weird, wilful article, "The Rhetoric of Landor," reprinted in *The Handling of Words* (1923), might inspire some more disciplined and rational investigation.

Saintsbury's examination of Landor's poetic practice is disappointingly brief and uncommunicative: he dismisses the versification of the longer poems with the comment that it is "almost faultless," adding that "if their faultlessness is saved from being uninteresting, it is chiefly by imagery and phrase." He values the shorter poems much more highly but is content to quote his favorites without prosodic pointing and without clearly indicating where, aside from "the fingering of the measure," their excellence lies. For all that Saintsbury has done to explore it, Landor's prosody may still be considered virgin territory.

Saintsbury devotes a great deal more space, both proportionately and absolutely, to his discussion of Landor's prose rhythm; but it seems to me that he has settled nothing, for two reasons. On the one hand, his quantitative method of scansion is itself highly questionable. On the other hand, he quotes and analyzes only the most self-consciously "poetic" passages from Landor's prose— the subject of almost every one is appropriate to lyric verse, while several were undoubtedly written in conscious emulation of classical, oriental, or Elizabethan eloquence. Such quotations tend to emphasize the sixteenth- and seventeenth-century qualities in Landor, whereas the bulk of his prose, in the *Imaginary Conversations* at any rate, seems to me cast in a late-eighteenth-century mold.

Saintsbury wisely quotes from Landor's most striking pronouncement on prose rhythm, which I give here in full:

> Good prose, to say nothing of the original thoughts it conveys, may be infinitely varied in modulation. It is only an extension of metres, an amplification of harmonies, of which even the best and most varied poetry admits but few. (F, V, 8)

Surely it is just as important to analyze the rhythm of the countless expository passages in Landor—including the fine one just quoted—as to linger over his wilfully purple patches? One of the questions that the specialists should answer is whether Landor's own prose was in fact so "infinitely varied in modulation" as he thought good prose should be. It appears to me exceptionally varied, the cadence constantly adapting itself to subject matter and mood; on the other hand, many readers have thought of it as idiosyncratic and readily identifiable to the point of monotony. I suspect that their criteria were subject matter and emotional tone rather than cadence.

No thorough study of Landor's prose style could afford to overlook his employment of imagery: one takes it for granted in passages where the underlying emotion is lyrical or elegiac, but the point to remember is that it permeates the expository passages also. I opened the *Imaginary Conversations* almost at random in search of an illustration from Landor's literary criticism, and hit upon a page in "La Fontaine and de la Rochefoucault." (F, V, 62) It would take too long to detail all the images in this one speech by La Fontaine; I shall be content with citing two. One refers to Hobbes: "If you call him a sound philosopher, you may call a mummy a sound man." The second concerns La Rochefoucauld: "I consider your *Maxims* as a broken ridge of hills, on the shady side of which you are fondest of taking your exercise: but the same ridge hath also a sunny one." One of these metaphors is used as a weapon in controversy, while the other describes the total effect made by a work of art; neither, to my mind, can be described as either labored or trite. Not every image avoids triteness: there is one on the same page—"the sweetest souls, like the sweetest flowers, soon canker in cities"—which we could easily have done without. Landor thinks naturally in images, however; if one considers the use of imagery out of place in critical discussion, one had better not read Landor at all. Edward Waterman Evans remarked in passing on "the mechanism of Landor's prose—first the simple statement of an idea, then a metaphor illustrative of it." This would imply that Landor's imagery was mere embroidery, not "functional." I don't agree, but any student of Landor's prose style would have to make up his own mind on the question. The poetry raises the same problem, of course. On the vividness and precision of Landor's imagery in both prose and verse there can be only one opinion, I think—a highly favorable one.

Most critics have the gravest doubts concerning Landor's constructive power when it must be applied to any unit longer than the individual line, prose paragraph, or short poem. As we shall see later, his own literary criticism rarely considers larger units than these.

Nevertheless, it would be unfair to criticize the structure of the more discursive among the *Imaginary Conversations* without taking note of his own distinction between conversation and dialogue:

> In Conversation, as in the country, variety is pleasant and expected. We look from the ground before us into the remoter, and much of more than one quality lies between. In Conversation we ought not to be didactic, in Dialogue we may be. . . . (F, V, 162)

Landor has little to say in his occasional prefaces and notes about the structural problems implicit in his longer narrative and dramatic poems. The conclusion of the 1803 Preface to *Gebir* (W, I, 474) provides a summary of the poem that would suggest he had given much thought to the construction of a plot which should be basically simple and yet embrace diversity, and even reversal, within its fundamental unity. Unfortunately, Landor's summary is more coherent than the poem he had actually written. The long, rambling unpublished "Post-script to *Gebir*," first printed in its entirety by Wheeler, contains a few remarks that indicate Landor's conception of the stylistic unity of the poem:

> . . . The language of *Paradise Lost* ought not to be the language of *Gebir*. There should be the softened air of remote antiquity, not the severe air of unapproachable sanctity. . . .
>
> I have avoided high-sounding words. I have attempted to throw back the gross materials, and to bring the figures forward. (W, I, 481)

Landor's attempt "to bring the figures forward" in *Gebir* was far from successful, but I believe it met with better fortune in the *Hellenics* generally, and especially in the 1847 English version of "Corythos." The 652 lines of this poem represent for me Landor's longest sustained flight. The action, though violent, is disposed of as rapidly as possible so that Landor may concentrate on the emotions of the four main characters: Oenone, Corythos, Helena (Helen of Troy), and Paris. The poem begins and ends with Oenone, who sends her son, Corythos, from Mount Ida down to his father, Paris, in Troy. She hopes the young man can warn Paris against the arrows of Philoctetes and win his affection. Helena generously welcomes Corythos, who is drawn to her in spite of himself, and brings him before Paris without any prior explanation. The jealous father kills his son before discovering who he is. Full of remorse, he deserts Helena and is ambushed and fatally wounded at Corythos' tomb; he makes his way to Oenone and dies in her presence after being forgiven by her. She herself dies immediately afterward.

Corythos' murder occupies no more than five lines, the wounding of Paris not much more. In essence, the poem consists of a series of sculptural tableaux, accompanied by moving, yet dignified, speeches full of Greek understatement. It is easy to supply titles for these groups of statuary: Oenone's Farewell to Corythos; Helena and Corythos; Paris at the Tomb of Corythos; Paris' Farewell to Oenone; Death of Oenone. Critics have found parallels to Landor in the Elgin Marbles; a more nearly

contemporary parallel may be found in Flaxman's illustrations to Homer, where the figures also adopt sculptural
poses: it does not seem possible that black-and-white
drawings could contain more white and less black than
his do. (Henry Crabb Robinson recorded Landor's "extravagant . . . praise" of Flaxman.) Nothing is easier
to imagine than a Flaxman drawing of Landor's penulti-
mate tableau:

> "No; I deserve not, seek not, to prolong
> My life," said Paris. "Only let one urn
> Unite us . . me, my Corythos!" He spake
> And held the urn toward her: this she caught,
> Together with the faint and chilly hand
> It had nigh dropt from.

Paris, as we know from earlier lines, is lying on his bier;
Oenone, standing above him, reaches down to take the
urn and his chilly hand. One can almost picture Landor
saying to himself, "What a subject for a sculptor." Though
modern notions of what constitutes a fit subject for sculpture—and even of the true nature of Greek art—differ
sharply from Landor's, we can say, without irony, that
if such a thought crossed his mind, he need not have been
ashamed to admit it. No wonder his visually conceived
poetry appealed to Pound and Richard Aldington (who
wrote an enthusiastic essay on the *Hellenics,* stressing
Landor's "exquisite plastic feeling") in the days of
Imagism.

Landor's powers of construction have been underrated by most critics, though doubtless overrated by Swinburne and Aldington; the latter writes in *Literary Studies and Reviews* (1924):

> Because the poet worked for the architectural qualities of poetry, the "Hellenics" are not easily quotable. Landor's unit is not the line, not the passage, but the poem.

Landor himself contradicted this view—at least so far as his plays are concerned—when, in his old age, he told the actor William Charles Macready, "I have not the constructive faculty. I can only set persons talking; all the rest is chance" (S, 104). Whatever the reasons for Landor's self-belittlement, I think the critics have never fully taken to heart the analogy between his poetry and Greek sculpture that many of them, from De Quincey onward, have rather casually drawn. Stephen A. Larrabee has made the most thorough use to date of this analogy in the relevant pages of his *English Bards and Grecian Marbles* (1943). He shows that the words "sculptural" and "sculpturesque" have been applied to Landor's work rather ambiguously. In speaking of Landor's "sculpturesque faculty," De Quincey

> . . . was thinking . . . not so much of the total effect of Landor's writing—the lucidity and sculptural beauty of the poetry itself, which appeals to the so-called "objective" critics of the early twentieth century—as of the numerous clean-cut or relief-like descriptions of festal processions, storied streets with paneled gates and porticoes, and sculptured vases in his work. In other words, De

Quincey was primarily interested in Landor's classical subject matter, while today critics study his "sculptural" style.

The frame of reference of Larrabee's book made him confine his attention to poems in which Landor describes works of sculpture, whether existing or imaginary. Thus it is never made quite clear that the "living" figures in Landor are also viewed with the eye of a sculptor. A remark by Ernest de Selincourt, quoted by Larrabee, comes closest to the heart of the matter: "We feel the emotion of [Landor's] characters in the pose and gesture of their figures far more than in any words they may speak." To appreciate the justness of this comment, the reader need only look back at my quotation from "Corythos."

If we assume that Landor, consciously or unconsciously, viewed his longer poems in terms of spatial rather than temporal form, as a series of sculptured tableaux, then the brevity or non-existence of narrative links in these works will be simultaneously explained and justified. Are there not Greek friezes which represent the successive stages of a ritual or other dramatic action? If not, we can easily find analogies elsewhere that must have been known to Landor: in Egyptian art, I believe, and certainly in such familiar medieval series as the "Stations of the Cross," "Scenes from the Life of the Virgin," and so on, whether painted or carved. In assimilating his poetry to Greek sculpture, Landor was being classical in more than one respect. The implied analogy between poetry and sculpture was but a small extension of the analogy be-

tween poetry and painting *(ut pictura poesis)* that under-
lies the *Ars Poetica* of Horace.

Landor's art of "bringing the figures forward" imposes
severe limitations upon itself. Scenes of violence are not
dwelt on, obviously because Landor found none in the
Greek sculptures of the Periclean Age. In Larrabee's
words, "Landor's feeling in sculpture was for coldness,
grandeur and restraint." Fables had to be chosen that
would lend themselves to sculptural groupings, often of
a ritual origin.

Not merely the *Hellenics,* but "Crysaor," "The Phoca-
eans," and *Gebir* ought to be analyzed in terms of sculpture, as I have analyzed "Corythos" above. Such an
approach would, I firmly believe, give us a new respect
for Landor's constructive powers. It could not, however,
redeem the verse plays. To say that they are a series of
tableaux is to deny their claim for recognition as drama.

III

Obviously it will be futile to investigate the sources of
Landor's style until we have reached some general agree-
ment about the nature of that style and the poetics
underlying it. However, once the studies outlined in the
preceding section have been carried out, it should be
possible to arrive at some fairly objective judgments
concerning the ancestry of Landor's style, or styles, in
prose and verse. The whole question of his classicism
could then be discussed in a more meaningful way than
it has been hitherto.

On this vexed topic, one point can be made without any danger of subjectivity: Landor almost never translates directly from Greek or Latin. He will translate a fragment from Sappho, perhaps, as in, "Mother, I cannot mind my wheel," but then he will go on to "complete" the poem in a Landorian way. Much as he admires Catullus, he supplies complete translations of only three of the shortest poems; others he translates in part or paraphrases: the famous *Carmen IV* becomes a new poem altogether after the first four lines, which translate the first five of the Latin fairly closely. The erotic overtones in Landor's "The vessel which lies here at last . . . " do not correspond to anything in Catullus' *Phasellus ille* . . . ; if they echo any Latin poem, it is rather Horace, *Odes*, III, 26: *Vixi puellis nuper idoneus.* . . . Hence the astonishing brevity of the section entitled "Translations, Imitations, etc." in Wheeler's edition of the *Poetical Works*. Wheeler does not include any of the numerous poems and dramatic fragments from *Pericles and Aspasia*, presumably because he believed that, aside from scraps of Homer, Sappho, and Hesiod, they were entirely Landor's own. Some are ascribed to poets whose works have in part survived; others to historical characters like Pericles and Alcibiades, who cannot be proved to have written verses at all; still others are supposedly by fictional characters; at least one, "Corinna to Tanagra," is attributed to a historical poetess, none of whose poems survives complete.

In truth, no poet was ever less fitted for translation than the supremely individualistic Landor, who proudly maintained that none of the historical characters in his

Imaginary Conversations and plays ever made a speech that was a matter of historical record. His attempts to imitate English poets, especially Donne, are ludicrously bad; he could not even write a really good parody of Wordsworth, God's gift to English parodists. Landor is a reasonably faithful translator of his own Latin poems only. It is appropriate to recall here Bishop Thirlwall's verdict on Landor's Latin poetry in general, that its "character cannot be illustrated by a comparison with any other Latin poetry, ancient or modern." Once again, whether deliberately or not, Landor had avoided imitation.

Even though there is as yet no full-length study of Landor's English style, it is permissible to regret that no classical scholar whose reading in Latin and Greek matches or surpasses Landor's own has yet devoted an entire book to Landor's classicism. Some of the most interesting comments on the subject to be found in general studies of the classical tradition have been made by J. A. K. Thomson, especially in *The Classical Background of English Literature* (1948), where he expresses an opinion on Landor's prose that I have not seen paralleled elsewhere:

> His prose . . . is more like the best Greek prose than anything produced in the eighteenth century. . . . It was made possible by his knowledge of Greek. It was this which enabled him to produce a less, or at least a more subtly, rhetorical type of sentence than the periods, fundamentally of Roman construction, of Johnson and Gibbon and Burke. . . .

> This was because it had now become possible for men, not professional scholars, to read Greek literature easily enough to perceive and enjoy its qualities. But it was the professional scholars who had created the possibility.

All such critical judgments made in passing tend to be highly subjective; the uniqueness of this tribute to the influence of Greek prose contrasts sharply with the near unanimity of classicists in the opinion that Landor's verse was profoundly influenced by Theocritus and the poets of the Greek Anthology. Nevertheless, one would like to see Thomson's view put to a pragmatic test through the comparison, in terms of sentence structure and prose rhythm, of roughly parallel passages from Landor and selected Greeks.

One purely objective study that only a good Latinist could undertake would put most future critics of Landor in his debt: a detailed survey of Landor's Latin poetry for the benefit of those whose Latin is weak or wanting. The *Poemata et Inscriptiones* (1847) contain eleven longer poems (the *Idyllia Heroica,* including *Gebirus*) and over 260 shorter ones, besides the *Inscriptiones.* The longer poems need to be compared in detail with the English versions of them, while the shorter would doubtless illuminate and often parallel the shorter English poems. Furthermore, they have biographical significance. Elizabeth Nitchie (*Classical Journal,* 1919) says that Landor "preferred the Latin for the expression of his most intimate thoughts and emotions."

The fact that over a hundred poems in the 1847 volume employ Catullus' favorite hendecasyllabic meter provides striking confirmation of the almost unanimous view that Catullus, even more than Horace, was the crucial Latin influence upon Landor's shorter English poems. Indeed, Landor himself makes Asinius Pollio say (F, II, 434) that Catullus' short poems outshine the whole Greek Anthology. More than sixty others are classed as *Iambi*, the appropriate meter for satire, while the remaining hundred *Minora Varia* probably include some imitations of Horace and the elegiac writers. *Poemata et Inscriptiones* is rounded out by an essay on modern Latin poetry and a dedicatory letter to Robert Landor, *Ad Robertum fratrem*, which serves as a preface. The latter, along with the English essays on Theocritus and Catullus, provides a sort of "poetics" of the form that Landor called the "Heroic Idyl," a category that includes most of the *Hellenics*. Super, in his biography (p. 41), has translated some of the essential passages from the letter to Robert:

> People carp at the title of the Idyls, denying that they ought to be called "Heroic." That the ancients thought otherwise is clear not merely by their use of the hexameter or heroic verse-form for them, but by the sort of thing they generally treated. . . . An Idyl is properly a smaller picture of some great picture. From Ovid we might single out very many Idyls. . . .

Landor lists by name the idyls of Theocritus that he considers heroic. He makes the following further comments, not given by Super (my translation):

> Almost all the Idyls of Moschus are heroic. . . . Virgil refused to call his pastorals "Idyls," perhaps for the very reason that they are nothing more than pastorals.

The same theory of the idyl is elaborated at the beginning of Landor's critical essay, "The Idyls of Theocritus," where he defines "Idyl" in English as *a small image of something greater*; he never bothers to explain to the Greekless reader that *eidullion* is a diminutive of *eidos*, "that which is seen, the form, shape, figure." Reading between the lines of the essay on Catullus, we can see that *Carmen LXIII* ("Attis") and *Carmen LXIV* ("The Marriage of Peleus and Thetis") represent for Landor two further examples of the heroic idyl, by virtue of both meter and subject. His own heroic idyls, it is hardly necessary to say, are in blank verse, the true English heroic meter.

The essays on Theocritus and Catullus, along with certain of the *Imaginary Conversations* (for instance, "Lord Chesterfield and Lord Chatham", where Plato's style is one of the topics, illustrated by quotations from the Greek), provide essential insight into Landor's feeling for and knowledge of the classical languages and literature. If one consults the *apparatus criticus* of a modern edition of Catullus, one will find that not all Landor's suggested emendations in the Latin text were capricious. See, for example, his note on line 15 (properly 16) of *Carmen LXIV*, that to *Carmen XCII*, and that to *Carmen XCV*. To revert to Landor's translations and paraphrases from Catullus for a moment, since they first appeared in this essay, I should like to suggest a subject for a brief and illuminating critical study: Take each of these versions of Catullus and compare it with a wholly original poem by Landor on the same subject;

is the treatment similar or different? One might even go on to ask—remembering that any answer is bound to be subjective—which is more classical, the original poem or the imitation?

John Forster sent Landor editions of four in all of the latter's favorite classical authors for detailed treatment in the *Foreign Quarterly Review* (S, 336–37). It is unfortunate that the essays on Pindar and Horace were never written, for we know from Landor's own statements that he consciously tried to imitate the former and delighted in the latter. If Landor could once read Pindar with anything approaching ease, his knowledge of Greek must have been greater than some of his critics are prepared to admit. As J. A. K. Thomson says, Pindar "is a difficult poet, to be read in the original only by scholars." Landor's claim to have read the *Iliad* twice and the *Odyssey* once before encountering *Paradise Lost* is really far less impressive than his claim to have composed *Gebir* "fresh from repeated perusals of Pindar" (S, 42).

In view of my own limited reading in Latin and Greek, I must refrain from adding any more to the vast number of *obiter dicta* on Landor's classicism. One very important general point about "The Classics" must be driven home with all the emphasis at my command, however. Those who have never studied Latin and Greek—and even many who have—tend to talk about classical literature as if it were all of a piece. Nothing could be farther from the truth. Latin literature is at least as different from Greek as English literature is from French, and within each of the classical literatures the range is fully as great as it is in any modern literature—at any rate, before the twentieth century. Pindar differs from Aristophanes as much as Milton does from Congreve; Petronius resembles Virgil as little as Rabelais does Racine. A thorough study of Landor's classicism would take this elementary fact for granted, dividing both verse and prose into a variety of genres: the more serious of the *Imaginary Conversations* would be compared with the works of Cicero and even those of Landor's *bête noire,* Plato; the more Voltairian would be compared with the dialogues of Lucian; no doubt there would be other subdivisions. In classical poetry, the verse form dictates the genre, or vice versa, so that a subjective element would enter into the classification of Landor's English verse. Nevertheless, Landor himself observed some of the classical distinctions, as we have seen in his discussion of the heroic idyl.

In one area, that of the non-satirical epigram, the dullest classicist is more ready to appreciate and understand Landor than the most brilliant critic whose taste has been molded by English Romantic poetry. T. S. Eliot remarked, in his introduction to Ezra Pound's *Selected Poems* (1928), "The reader who does not like Pound's epigrams should make very sure that he is not comparing them with the *Ode to a Nightingale* before he condemns them." Pound, like Landor, was trying to revive the Greek tradition of epigram found in the *Palatine Anthology,* better known as the Greek Anthology; but it will always be difficult, for those who know English literature

68

only, to realize that an epitaph may also be an epigram—indeed, *must* be one according to the earliest definition of "epigram," which is "an inscription." In spite of all that Eliot and so many others have written to make us appreciate the "serious wit" of Donne or Jonson, there will still be readers who balk at Landor's "Dirce" as too frivolous for an epitaph:

> Stand close around, ye Stygian set,
>   With Dirce in one boat conveyed!
> Or Charon, seeing, may forget
>   That he is old and she a shade.

The classicist, unperturbed, would simply file this under "epigrammata" and produce a number of analogues for comparison.

Instead of resounding generalizations about Landor's classicism, we should then find ourselves confronted by a series of particular judgments: in *this* poem Landor shows a debt to *this* branch of classical tradition, in *that* poem, to *that*. It is also salutary to remember that Landor quoted with apparent approval Shelley's explanation of how Keats was able to write "Hyperion" without knowing Greek—"because he *was* a Greek" (F, IV, 478). Nor should we forget Landor's lines, "To the Author of *Festus* on the Classick and Romantick," which discuss the illusory nature of the distinction between romantic and classical:

> The classical like the heroick age
> Is past; but Poetry may reassume
> That glorious name with Tartar and with Turk,
> With Goth or Arab, Sheik or Paladin,
> And not with Roman and with Greek alone.
>   The name is graven on the workmanship. . . .

This argument is not invalidated by the fact that the aging Landor went on to grant classical rank to Scott's *Marmion* and Felicia Hemans' "Casabianca" as well as to Shakespeare, Milton, and the author of *Festus* himself, Philip James Bailey.

IV

From the classical sources of Landor's style it is natural to pass to the modern. As far as these sources are English, the only safe course is to leave the final verdict to the prosodists, the students of prose rhythm, and the practitioners of the new discipline of stylistics. Landor provides a worthy challenge to them all. To my mind, the last word has not yet been said on even the much-canvassed topic of Milton's influence on *Gebir*. Super (p. 42) has clearly made up his mind against the importance of any such influence:

> As for the reviewer's charge that his language was Miltonic, that he borrowed "too many phrases and epithets from our incomparable Milton," Landor's reply was unanswerable and remains so: "I challenge him to produce

them." The most careful student of the subject [R. D. Havens] has been able to find almost nothing Miltonic about the poem.

This is impressive testimony, but let us look at what I have always considered the three most haunting lines in *Gebir* (Book III, lines 85–87):

> Twilight broods here, lull'd by no nightingale,
> Nor waken'd by the shrill lark dewy-winged,
> But glowing with one sullen sunless heat.

Are these Miltonic or not? William Bradley, in *The Early Poems of Walter Savage Landor* (1914), cites *Paradise Lost*, IV, 771, "there lull'd by nightingales." He also quotes, with some justification, from *P.L.*, I, 62–63, " . . . yet from those flames/ No light but rather darkness visible." Landor's Underworld is not too different from Milton's Hell in respect of light and heat. On the other hand, "Shrill lark" seems unique to Landor, though not quite alien to the lark in "L'Allegro" that "singing startles the dull night." Only a specialist could tell us whether the rhythm of these lines is exactly paralleled anywhere in Milton, but I will hazard the comment that it does not sound *un*-Miltonic, especially in the third line.

After reading almost all the *Imaginary Conversations,* I am left with a very strong impression that Landor's middle style in prose, especially when speaking in his own person, is remarkably close to Dr. Johnson's. I am not referring to the Johnson of *Rasselas* but to the later

Johnson of the *Lives of the Poets* and the conversations in Boswell's *Life*. I found valuable support for this intuition in one of the footnotes to "A Satire on Satirists" (W, III, 382), where Landor writes:

> Many have ridiculed, and with no little justice, the pompous diction of Johnson on ordinary occasions; and some have attempted to depreciate his imitations of Juvenal. But among our clippers and sweaters of sterling coin, not one will ever write such vigorous verses as those on Charles the Twelfth, or such vigorous prose as the Lives of Savage and Dryden.

Anybody who wishes to judge for himself whether Landor can imitate the Doctor's conversational style is free to turn to the Conversations between Johnson and John Horne (Tooke). Again, the whole question must be settled by the specialists, if at all. Were we to claim an influence for every prose writer whom Landor praises, even among the moderns alone, we should provide the ingredients for a rare witches' brew. Voltaire and Rousseau, Gibbon and Goldsmith, would bubble side by side —and to some extent they do. A style so varied in its moods and rhythms as Landor's may well be a synthesis of the most diverse influences. In a blank-verse poem on Gibbon of no fewer than 74 lines, Landor propounds a theory of matching prose style with subject matter that he undoubtedly followed himself at times:

> Words have their proper places, just like men.
> I listen to, nor venture to reprove,

Large language swelling under gilded domes,
Byzantine, Syrian, Persepolitan. . . .

(W, II, 423)

There is a passage in the Conversation between the Abbé
Delille and Landor where the latter, speaking in his own
person, contrives to praise Gibbon and Voltaire simultaneously for excellence in the prose territories that they
have made peculiarly their own. It is reasonable to suppose that he learned something from each. I have deliberately mentioned only eighteenth-century names in this
paragraph because Saintsbury and J. A. K. Thomson,
among others, have stressed Landor's seventeenth-century
antecedents. But enough of this guesswork.

V

Studies of Landor's stylistic influence upon his contemporaries and successors offer the same pitfalls and
opportunities as do studies of the influences operating
upon him. There are phrases and whole poems in Yeats
that I privately classify as Landorian, but who would
agree with me? To escape once and for all from this
particular critical quagmire, I wish to suggest a project
for the pure scholar. It may prove to have critical significance, or it may not; it may indicate an influence exercised by Landor upon some of his younger contemporaries, or it may not. The project is this: a thorough investigation into Landor's career as a collector of paintings,

and an attempt to assess his knowledge of the history of painting. More daring spirits may wish to go further and assess his taste in painting and his influence (if any) on the taste of Browning, the Pre-Raphaelite Movement, and later aesthetic currents. Forster and others made humorous remarks about the poor quality of Landor's pictures, but the geese of one generation sometimes prove swans to the next and vice versa; it would be interesting—but in all probability depressing—to learn what paintings hung on John Forster's walls. Super and Elwin have done something to correct the false impression left by Forster on this matter, but a great deal still remains to be discovered.

A footnote in Super's biography will send the alert reader to Tancred Borenius' *Pictures by the Old Masters in the Library of Christ Church, Oxford* (1916). The twenty-six pictures in the Christ Church collection, presented jointly by Miss C. E. Landor and Miss Duke, are not the only ones acquired by Landor that can still be traced; for Elwin says that others remain in the possession of the Landor family. Nevertheless, they form a worthwhile collection in themselves. All belong to the Florentine and Sienese schools, none dating from later than 1500. According to Borenius,

> The most remarkable of the pictures of the Landor-Duke Gift are the Madonna, by a Florentine artist of about 1350 (No. 8) ; the Virgin and Child, from the school of Lorenzo Monaco (No. 19) ; the little altar-piece by Neri di Bicci (No. 31) ; the Madonna and Saints, by Sano di

Pietro (No. 72); the beautiful little Crucifixion by Giovanni di Paolo (No. 73); and the Madonna with Angels, by Guidoccio Cozzarelli (No. 74).

The last three paintings are also taken note of by Bernard Berenson in *Central Italian Painters*. Borenius includes monochrome illustrations of the six Landor-owned paintings listed above, and one other, a Crucifixion of the Florentine School, *ca.* 1500. He comments on the added charm and value possessed by a collection reflecting the personal taste of an art lover who was in advance of his time, and states unequivocally that "Landor . . . is known to have been one of the pioneers in the appreciation of the Italian primitives."

For a number of years, I have assumed that Leigh Hunt, by virtue of the description in his *Autobiography* of the frescoes in the Campo Santo at Pisa, which he first saw in 1822, was the earliest conscious literary forerunner —as opposed to an unconscious forerunner like the Keats of "The Eve of St. Agnes"—of the Pre-Raphaelite Brotherhood. That is to say, he was a Pre-Raphaelite before Pre-Raphaelitism was dreamed of, althought the first version of the *Autobiography* was not published until 1850. I now begin to wonder whether Hunt really appreciated what he had seen at Pisa before he made Landor's acquaintance. At any rate, Landor and Hunt developed a taste for Italian painting of the Trecento and Quattrocento almost simultaneously. Landor was the first to reach Italy and also the first to live in Pisa, so the priority doubtless justly belongs to him.

75

On the one hand, a student of art history ought to trace and catalogue as many as possible of the paintings once owned by Landor and to gather together the opinions of them expressed by competent authorities such as Berenson; on the other hand, a literary scholar should assemble every scrap of Landor's writing on the subject of painting, including the few relevant *Imaginary Conversations*. Such factual material would supply the basis for a considered judgment of Landor's knowledge and taste in this branch of the fine arts. Specialists in Browning, Dante Gabriel Rossetti, and others may be able to add evidence of Landor's influence upon the artistic tastes of his successors. Fresh research may yield further evidence about the origins of Landor's knowledge and taste, in so far as the latter was not a matter of native endowment; Super suggests that Landor may have first acquired his great love for paintings under the tutelage of Isaac Mocatta, who died in 1801, when Landor was only twenty-six. There should also be scope for at least a short critical study examining how this almost lifelong enthusiasm for painting affected Landor's choice and employment of imagery.

VI

It may seem perverse that, having begun this essay with some suggestions for an approach to Landor's poetics, I should at this late stage broach the question of his critical principles. To assume, however, that a writer's poetics coincide with his critical principles is to be guilty

of "the intentional fallacy." Landor's principles as a
creative writer are best arrived at inductively, whereas
we may, with reservations, take his own word for his
critical theories.

In speaking of Landor's critical principles, I find myself
somewhat at odds with Stanley T. Williams. In his admirable essay, "Walter Savage Landor as a Critic of Literature" (*PMLA*, 1923), he says that Landor, as a literary
critic, had "ideals but few principles. . . . We look in vain
. . . for a method or a body of criteria." I think he is
being too severe on Landor; for one thing, the latter had
a method, even if Williams does not approve of it: close
verbal criticism. A defense of this method and a statement of related principles will be found in that little
masterpiece, the Alfieri-Salomon Conversation:

> There are those who would persuade us that verbal criti-
> cism is unfair, and that few poems can resist it. The truth
> of the latter assertion by no means establishes the former:
> all good criticism hath its foundation on verbal. Long
> dissertations are often denominated criticisms, without one
> analysis; instead of which it is thought enough to say:
> "There is nothing finer in our language . . . we can safely
> recommend . . . imbued with the true spirit . . . des-
> tined to immortality, &c."
> A perfect piece of criticism must exhibit *where* a work
> is good or bad; *why* it is good or bad; in what degree it
> is good or bad; must also demonstrate in what manner
> and to what extent the same ideas or reflections have come
> to others, and, if they be clothed in poetry, why, by an
> apparently slight variation, what in one author is medioc-
> rity, in another is excellence. (F, IV, 277)

77

I could also have quoted Porson's half-joking curriculum for the education of critics (F, IV, 19). The method outlined above is one that Landor followed again and again, especially in the *Pentameron*, the Southey-Landor Conversations on Milton, those between Southey and Porson on Wordsworth, and that between Barrow and Newton on Bacon's *Essays*. It is a method that can very easily become tiresome and is, furthermore, as Williams says, "a transference of the scholia of classical criticism to English literature." Nevertheless, Landor's verbal criticism is perfectly valid, in my opinion; the chief objection to the method lies in its incompleteness: it rarely considers units larger than the word, the phrase, or at best the sentence.

Yet words are basic to literature; furthermore, as Pound has tirelessly emphasized, they are basic to politics and a healthy national life, also. Landor expresses this view with extraordinary vividness, force and brevity in the Hare-Landor Conversation:

> When the tongue is paralyzed, the limbs soon follow. No nation hath long survived the decrepitude of its language. (F, V, 101)

If we accept this principle, the passionate discussion of lexicography and orthography between Johnson and Horne Tooke becomes central rather than merely eccentric.

But it is false to assert that Landor never considers the larger structural elements of a work of art. An outstanding instance to the contrary occurs early in the first

Southey-Landor Conversation. The passage is too long to quote in full, but the heart of it may be given:

> Both in epic and dramatic poetry it is action, and not moral, that is first demanded. The feelings and exploits of the principal agent should excite the principal interest. The two greatest of human compositions are here defective: I mean the *Iliad* and *Paradise Lost*.

Landor, using Southey as his mouthpiece, does not make the error of calling Satan the hero of Milton's poem,

> . . . unless, as is usually the case in human life, he is the greatest hero who gives the widest sway to the worst passions. It is Adam who acts and suffers most, and on whom the consequences have most influence. This constitutes him the main character; although Eve is the more interesting, Satan the more energetic, and on whom the greater force of poetry is displayed. The Creator and his angels are quite secondary. (F, IV, 434)

Landor is here upholding the principles of unity of action and unity of protagonist in a manner worthy of Aristotle, however often he may have violated them in his own work.

Landor's essay on Catullus, which consists mainly of scholia, ends with a determined attempt to state what constitutes "might, majesty and dominion" in poetry. We are told that the "four things requisite . . . are creativeness, constructiveness, the sublime, the pathetic." Alas, he never adequately defines these four terms, although we can disentangle some implied definitions from the pages which follow (F, VIII, 419–23); in Williams' phraseology, these are "ideals" rather than "principles." The whole passage, furthermore, deviates from its lofty aims into an unpleasant attack on Wordsworth and a loyal glorification of Southey. Landor's critical principles, here and sometimes elsewhere, are at war with his critical practice. Let him that is without sin among us cast the first stone.

Valuable as Williams' study is, then, it need not be considered the last word on Landor as a literary critic. Working along the lines I have sketched above, one could put forward a case for Landor as a moderately consistent literary theorist; or, failing that, at least as one who remained faithful to a critical method that can never become entirely obsolete. Furthermore, I should like to see Landor's critical methods and principles compared with those of his contemporaries and immediate predecessors. They might be found quite similar to Samuel Johnson's, though very different from Coleridge's. Viewed from this aspect, Landor does not appear, as he does from so many others, entirely unique.

VII

One area of Landor studies, namely, research into the sources of his subject matter, has been deliberately neglected in the preceding pages, on the grounds that it has little to do with criticism and, sometimes, even with Landor. Much of the mindless research into the "sources" of *Gebir* actually deals with those of Clara Reeve's *The*

Progress of Romance, from which Landor borrowed the fable of his poem. Nevertheless, Super has made us keenly aware that some already existing research into the sources of the *Imaginary Conversations* has great importance for Landor criticism. It shows that Landor characteristically modified the known views of historical characters, sometimes in quite subtle ways, to make them conform with his own; more than that, he succeeded in making them his mouthpieces for commentary on the literary and political controversies of his own time.

In fact, Landor's outlook is fundamentally ahistorical and aligns him with the eighteenth century rather than the history-obsessed nineteenth; as Stanley T. Williams has noted, "he judged Pindar and Wordsworth each *per se;* one would think he was a contemporary of both." For all his Marxism, Bernard Shaw undoubtedly shared Landor's archaic, essentially neo-classical attitude toward history, though I have searched in vain through the lavish index of *Prefaces by Bernard Shaw* (1934) for a reference to Landor. The discussion of nationalism and protestantism between Warwick and Cauchon in Scene IV of *Saint Joan* is a true Imaginary Conversation, as are the entire first act of *In Good King Charles's Golden Days* and large portions of Shaw's other "historical" plays, such as *The Man of Destiny* and *Caesar and Cleopatra.* Shaw and Pound, so unlike in many respects, rival each other as Landor's two chief heirs in the twentieth century, even if Shaw never acknowledged his heritage.

We must never lose sight of this gift of Landor's for transforming almost all that he touches into something uniquely individual. While stressing the paradoxical contrast between Landor's life and his art, Yeats might well have noted a further paradox: Landor, the writer most steeped in tradition of all his generation, was sometimes original to the point of eccentricity. Furthermore, there is merit in Elizabeth Barrett Browning's equally paradoxical suggestion that Landor was "of all living writers . . . the most Greek, because preëminently and purely English" (F, I, 362). The best criticism of Landor will define his uniqueness and distinguish carefully between his valid individualism and his merely cranky and self-indulgent oddity.

Some of the best Landor criticism may be termed implicit, since it involves the multiple acts of choice that bring to birth a good anthology. To my mind, Sidney Colvin's *Selections from Landor* (verse and prose) in the "Golden Treasury Series" (1882) outshines all the rest; whereas Havelock Ellis' *Imaginary Conversations and Poems* in "Everyman's Library" (1933) decidedly brings up the rear, if only because of its brief and feeble selection from the poetry. E. K. Chambers' *Landor: Poetry and Prose* (1946), a text for English secondary schools, occupies an honorable middle ground between Colvin and Ellis. J. B. Sidgwick's brief selection *The Shorter Poems of Walter Savage Landor* (1946) shows taste and provides some useful annotation for the general reader; but the introduction contains some appalling errors of fact, including the description of *Gebir* as a massive verse drama. Ernest de Selincourt's *Imaginary Conversations: A Selection* in "The World's Classics" (1915) stresses the historical and dramatic aspects of the *Conversations* to the neglect of the critical and discursive ones, but this very fact shows that the editor made his selection according to a principle; furthermore, all the entries appear to be given in their entirety. Colvin included a small number of dramatic Conversations complete, and then culled aphorisms and paragraphs from the "reflective and discursive" ones, whereas Ellis hacked and hewed pretty much at random.

Anthologies are pretty toys—no doubt every good Landorian would like to compile his own—but they do not in the end promote the cause of Landor. As several critics have noted, the great obstacle to Landor's fame is that no single poem and no compact body of work is indissolubly associated with his name by the ordinary reader or, at least in America, by even the college graduate. The *Imaginary Conversations* are simply too numerous for familiarity, while Landor's poetry has never found a permanent niche in the English literature survey courses and textbooks. To my mind, the volume entitled *The Hellenics and Gebir of Walter Savage Landor* (1907), which used to be available in the "Temple Classics" series, was the most strategic presentation of Landor ever attempted. To associate Landor with such a limited and relatively homogeneous body of work seems the only way to win him an enduring reputation among readers who are neither poets nor specialized scholars. From that point to the survey textbooks would be a very short step indeed.

But one can imagine what that maverick Landor would feel about such a public relations campaign. Although publicity and public relations were infants in his day, he recognized them for what they were, and would have strangled them in their cradles if he could. Partly by accident, partly by design, he managed to keep the masses in ignorance of his work during his lifetime. Why should we endeavor to thwart his will today? It was still possible, at the time and place where I went to college, for an English major to have the delight and glory of discovering contemporary authors for himself. In America, at least, this is now a thing of the past. Should we not continue to hold in reserve a few "neglected" writers like Landor, who can be freshly discovered by the choice spirits of each new generations? Only if we do this can the "unsubduable old Roman" continue to make good his magnificent boast: "I shall dine late; but the diningroom will be well lighted, the guests few and select."

This much more I would add: everything has been done for Landor's verse that can be done, except of course the publication of a reasonably-priced complete edition in one volume, and it therefore seems unlikely that the well-read person's estimate of this aspect of Landor will change markedly in the near future; on the other hand, it is generally accepted that we still need a critically edited and thoroughly annotated text of the *Imaginary Conversations*; once this has been provided, there is a real possibility of radical change in our estimate of the *magnum opus*. I assume that the annotation of this ideal edition would show clearly how much each dialogue owes to historical sources and how much to the personality of Landor; in that case, we ought at last to be able to discover the true analogue or analogues of this body of work that has so long defied classification. Unless I am greatly mistaken, we should be forced to conclude that Landor was neither a Plato *manqué* nor a Lucian *réussi,* neither a belated Voltaire nor an early "prose Browning"—to borrow Oscar Wilde's phrase about Meredith. We should see instead that the learning, the discursiveness, the search for a truly conversational style, the self-revelation (so covert in most of Landor, so overt in his counterpart), all link the *Imaginary Conversations* to the *Essais* of Montaigne. Without rereading all of Montaigne, I should not care to say how far this analogy can be stretched; certainly in respect to self-knowledge no comparison is possible. But is there any English prose writer other than Landor who can be set beside Montaigne without seeming either narrow in range of interest and knowledge or anemic in personality? Coleridge? Hazlitt? De Quincey? Carlyle? Ruskin? Arnold? Shaw? Is there one among them who would not shrivel when set beside Montaigne—as Joseph Scaliger does in the brief Conversation between him and "the old man of the mountain" (F, IV, 294–98). Apart from this dialogue, I find no trace in Landor of any conscious debt to the French writer, nor do I suspect much direct influence. I envisage them as setting out from the same point—the Greek and Latin classics—and arriving at the same end, but by utterly different though equally eccentric paths. And I certainly do not think it absurd to hope that Landor may yet reach a standing among English prose writers at least distantly comparable to that of Montaigne among French ones.

THE HISTORICAL IMPORTANCE
OF CERTAIN "ESSAYS OF ELIA"

Geoffrey Tillotson

I

Englishmen who study nineteenth-century English literature are usually aware that scholars have been doing these things better across the Atlantic, that we English have been asleep while the huntsmen have been up in America. Some amends, however, are now being made, though there is still not much to report as far as Lamb goes. Not that he has been quite neglected since that moment in 1887 when Leslie Stephen called him "our finest critic of some of the more important English literature,"[1] and that moment in 1903 when the author of *Shakespearean Tragedy* pronounced him "the best critic of the nineteenth century,"[2] for Mr. Edmund Blunden has always admired him and has said so in thoughtful essays and books; and the Bulletin of the Charles Lamb Society began its career in 1935.[3] I must confess that in my own case it was an accident that drew me back to him—a fortunate accident if only because it enabled me to see that for anyone working in the mid-

[1] *Men, Books, and Mountains* (London, 1956), p. 23.

[2] A. C. Bradley, *Oxford Lectures on Poetry* (London, 1909), p. 105.

[3] Cf. C. A. Prance, Lamb Society *Bulletin*, No. 165 (1962), p. 367: "If one were asked to name the living writer who had done most for the memory of Charles Lamb, the reply would undoubtedly be Edmund Blunden. As far back as 1928, he was writing of Leigh Hunt, with many references to Lamb, and the following year he edited an edition of *The Last Essays of Elia*. Looking around my bookshelves I can see, without much searching, nearly a dozen volumes by Edmund Blunden which are of Lamb interest, from books devoted solely to Elia to volumes of essays which have a single essay on him or merely passing mention—even an essay on John Skelton starts off with a Lamb reference!"

nineteenth-century field Lamb is as important as Wordsworth and Coleridge, Keats and Shelley, Jane Austen
and Scott. His essays were of the very mind of his successors, whose work in poetry and the novel we are coming
to value more truly. We know how much Dickens admired
him, and one proof lies in the perceptive remark of
Gissing's, in *The Immortal Dickens:* he holds that the
"Parliamentary Sketch," in *Sketches by Boz,*

> contains an admirable portrait, that of the parliamentary
> butler, which (as might be said of one or two things in
> the book) rather reminds one of Charles Lamb, and in-
> deed would not be unworthy of him.[4]

(It is as if Ben Jonson were writing of the debt of the
young Shakespeare to Marlowe.) Thackeray also admired
the essays, as did Charlotte Brontë, and Browning, and
Le Fanu; and though Mrs. Gaskell does not seem to
mention them, it is inconceivable that her genius did not
recognise its kinship with his.

I take it that the essays are irremovable masterpieces
in their own right, but I am looking at some of them here
mainly as a reminder that Lamb's work in this particular
field is vital to our proper understanding of the great
things that followed in the mid–nineteenth century.

II

The method used in "A Bachelor's Complaint of the
Behaviour of Married People" is mainly Lamb's inven-

[4] *Op. cit.* (London. 1925), p. 38.

tion. When reading that complaint, we notice two things
—what is said and what is implied. What is said is both
sound and new. All of us, whether married or single, have
found the behaviour of married couples objectionable, on
occasion at least, and the charges brought against them,
which we have been dimly aware of as invited, we all
agree to be valid once they are stated:

> I cannot say that the quarrels of men and their wives
> ever made any great impression upon me, or had much
> tendency to strengthen me in those anti-social resolutions,
> which I took up long ago upon more substantial consider-
> ations. What oftenest offends me at the houses of married
> persons where I visit, is an error of quite a different
> description;—it is that they are too loving.
>
> Not too loving neither: that does not explain my mean-
> ing. Besides, why should that offend me? The very act of
> separating themselves from the rest of the world, to have
> the fuller enjoyment of each other's society, implies that
> they prefer one another to all the world.
>
> But what I complain of is, that they carry this preference
> so undisguisedly, they perk it up in the faces of us single
> people so shamelessly, you cannot be in their company a
> moment without being made to feel, by some indirect hint
> or open avowal, that *you* are not the object of this prefer-
> ence. Now there are some things which give no offence,
> while implied or taken for granted merely; but expressed,
> there is much offence in them. If a man were to accost
> the first homely-featured or plain-dressed young woman
> of his acquaintance, and tell her bluntly, that she was not
> handsome or rich enough for him, and he could not marry
> her, he would deserve to be kicked for his ill manners;
> yet no less is implied in the fact, that having access and
> opportunity of putting the question to her, he has never

yet thought fit to do it. The young woman understands this as clearly as if it were put into words; but no reasonable young woman would think of making this the ground of a quarrel. Just as little right have a married couple to tell me by speeches, and looks that are scarce less plain than speeches, that I am not the happy man,—the lady's choice. It is enough that I know I am not: I do not want this perpetual reminding.

This is a sample of some half-dozen of the bachelor's ideas, all devastatingly true, and expressed for the first time. Ideas on the same general subject had been plentiful in the late seventeenth-century comedies that Lamb liked so much, but not these particular ideas. We are both delighted and profited. And we are delighted further because of the dry way in which married people are shown to be ridiculous—it would take a long time to draw out the sly and complex implications of the following, for example:

> The excessive airs which those people give themselves, founded on the ignorance of us unmarried people, would be more offensive if they were less irrational. We will allow them to understand the mysteries belonging to their own craft better than we who have not had the happiness to be made free of the company: but their arrogance is not content within these limits. If a single person presume to offer his opinion in their presence, though upon the most indifferent subject, he is immediately silenced as an incompetent person. Nay, a young married lady of my acquaintance, who, the best of the jest was, had not changed her condition above a fortnight before, in a question on which I had the misfortune to differ from her, respecting the properest mode of breeding oysters for

the London market, had the assurance to ask, with a sneer, how such an old Bachelor as I could pretend to know any thing about such matters.[5]

We agree with all that he says, and we sympathize with him and give him all credit for subtlety of mind and for a sort of tart humor. And yet, what he omits to say is more interesting still, for his tone is often edgy. It is evident from his complaint that, without knowing it, he is envious. We hear him speak his admirable, mannered prose, but the raised tone of his voice, unmistakably suggested in the cold print, gives him away:

It is enough that I know I am not: I do not want this perpetual reminding.

And the ending of this paragraph:

The display of superior knowledge or riches may be made sufficiently mortifying; but these admit of a palliative. The knowledge which is brought out to insult me, may accidentally improve me; and in the rich man's houses and pictures,—his parks and gardens, I have a temporary usufruct at least. But the display of married happiness has none of these palliatives: it is throughout pure, unrecompensed, unqualified insult.

Or the assumed contempt of his term for children:

But what I have spoken of hitherto is nothing to the airs which these creatures give themselves when they come, as they generally do, to have children. When I con-

[5] Oysters were in demand as aphrodisiacs, and the joke is the better for her likely ignorance of this.

sider how little of a rarity children are,—that every street
and blind alley swarms with them,—that the poorest people
commonly have them in most abundance,—that there are
few marriages that are not blest with at least one of these
bargains . . .

And this, still about children:

> If they were young phoenixes, indeed, that were born but
> one in a year, there might be a pretext. But when they
> are so common——
>   I do not advert to the insolent merit which they
> assume with their husbands on these occasions. Let them
> look to that. But why *we,* who are not their natural-
> born subjects, should be expected to bring out spices,
> myrrh, and incense,—our tribute and homage of admir-
> ation,—I do not see.

And we have sensed this bottled-up but escaping envy in
the sentence that begins the "essay" and forms its first
paragraph:

> As a single man, I have spent a good deal of my time in
> noting down the infirmities of Married People, to console
> myself for those superior pleasures, which they tell me
> I have lost by remaining as I am.

We can see how Lamb's method here differs from what
comes nearest to it in the earlier literature. When one of
Shakespeare's villains—Richard III or Iago—soliloquizes,
he speaks of himself, and is confident that he is producing
a certain effect on his hearers. That effect is not quite
what he thinks. Then there are a few letters written to

the periodical essayists—for example, that of Misellus to the *Rambler*. Misellus is a new author who informs us that he has "been cautious, since the appearance of my work, not to give myself more premeditated airs of superiority, than the most rigid humility will allow," and proceeds to complain of the way he suffers for his greatness:

> If I knock at a door, no body is at home; if I enter a coffee-house, I have the box to myself. I live in the town like a lion in his desert, or an eagle on his rock, too great for friendship or society, and condemned to solitude by unhappy elevation and dreaded ascendency.[6]

Richard, Iago, and Misellus mistake the effect their speeches produce. Richard expects complete admiration and gets something else besides; Iago assumes that his case is unanswerable; Misellus expects sympathy and gets ridicule. But all of them speak of themselves. Lamb's method is to make the Bachelor speak of other people, and speak interestingly of them, and yet to interest us most in what we gather about himself. And this is the method of some of the most famous of Browning's dramatic monologues—as, for example, "My Last Duchess" and "Soliloquy of the Spanish Cloister." "My Last Duchess" is the brilliant thing it is because of the difference between what the speaker thinks he is conveying and what he is conveying without knowing it. The duke assumes that we are being properly impressed by the immemorial splendors of his house and line, whereas our

6 *Rambler,* No. 16.

servile admiration is changing by degrees into something very different—into horror at his cruelty, which is also, perhaps, his criminality. The sum total of his exhibition represents, so he thinks, the mind of a monomaniac who has something to say that is well worth saying; he speaks well about things he knows will interest us. But we come to see that below the aesthetic smugness, below the pride, stretches the black pool of an evil moral character, perhaps undiscovered by its possessor—his conscious mind may be all the mind he has. The same method of literary construction had been used in "A Bachelor's Complaint," and in "Mrs. Battle's Opinions on Whist."

III

One of the most profound essays is "Witches and Other Night Fears." It contains the best extended account in our literature of child psychology (on several of its sides, not merely the horrific) that exists before Dickens. Lamb is one of the first writers to discover the child's psyche as a substantial matter for literature. His essay serves to show that the subject as Lamb discovered it qualifies for treatment in prose. Lamb discovers the child's psyche for what it is, not for what it is conveniently believed to be by the sentimental and the avuncular. Indeed, there cannot have been many of his many successors in this field who have dared to tell autobiographical truths so little to the author's credit. Clearly as a *British* child Lamb was a failure.

Take, for instance, this paragraph. Lamb has been describing how Stackhouse's illustrated *History of the*

Bible fascinated him as a child, and has told us that, forbidden to handle the volumes, he could not forget the picture—"That detestable picture!"—of "The witch raising up Samuel, which I wish I had never seen":

> I was dreadfully alive to nervous terrors. The night-time solitude, and the dark, were my hell. The sufferings I endured in this nature would justify the expression. I never laid my head on my pillow, I suppose, from the fourth to the seventh or eighth year of my life—so far as memory serves in things so long ago—without an assurance, which realized its own prophecy, of seeing some frightful spectre. Be old Stackhouse then acquitted in part, if I say, that to his picture of the Witch raising up Samuel —(O that old man covered with a mantle!) I owe—not my midnight terrors, the hell of my infancy—but the shape and manner of their visitation. It was he who dressed up for me a hag that nightly sate upon my pillow—a sure bed-fellow, when my aunt or my maid was far from me. All day long, while the book was permitted me, I dreamed waking over his delineation, and at night (if I may use so bold an expression) awoke into sleep, and found the vision true. I durst not, even in the day-light, once enter the chamber where I slept, without my face turned to the window, aversely from the bed where my witch-ridden pillow was.—Parents do not know what they do when they leave tender babes alone to go to sleep in the dark. The feeling about for a friendly arm—the hoping for a familiar voice—when they wake screaming—and find none to soothe them—what a terrible shaking it is to their poor nerves! The keeping them up till midnight, through candle-light and the unwholesome hours, as they are called,—would, I am satisfied, in a medical point of view, prove the better caution.—That detestable picture, as I have said, gave the fashion to my dreams—if dreams

they were—for the scene of them was invariably the room in which I lay. Had I never met with the picture, the fears would have come self-pictured in some shape or other—

Headless bear, black man, or ape—

but, as it was, my imaginations took that form.—It is not book, or picture, or the stories of foolish servants, which create these terrors in children. They can at most but give them a direction. Dear little T[hornton] H[unt] who of all children has been brought up with the most scrupulous exclusion of every taint of superstition—who was never allowed to hear of goblin or apparition, or scarcely to be told of bad men, or to read or hear of any distressing story—finds all this world of fear, from which he has been so rigidly excluded *ab extra,* in his own "thick-coming fancies"; and from his little midnight pillow, this nurse-child of optimism will start at shapes, unborrowed of tradition, in sweats to which the reveries of the cell-damned murderer are tranquillity.

Crabbe (in the chapter on "Prisons" in *The Borough*) had already encouraged doubts on the comparison made in the last sentence of this passage; and Thackeray (in "Going to See a Man Hanged") and Dickens (in *Oliver Twist*) were to show it to be untrue. But these do not detract from the status of the child's terrors. The truth of Lamb's account of his own horrors (I am assuming that the essay is autobiographical) is evinced by two things in particular: (1) the detail of the mantle—it is shown billowing wildly in the engraving, and we all remember that horror is worst when its hugeness is concentrated in a detail; and (2) the picture, nowadays at least, would not seem to be more than mildly disturbing—in other words Lamb, as he well knew, contributed horror from his own capacity to create it. If not shaped by Stack-house's illustrator, his horror would have come, as he says, "self-pictured"; and in "Old Benchers of the Inner Temple" he writes:

> In those days [when he was a child] I saw Gods, as "old men covered with a mantle" [that mantle again!], walking upon the earth [in the form of old benchers]. Let the dreams of classic idolatry perish,—extinct be the fairies and fairy trumpery of legendary fabling,—in the heart of childhood, there will, for ever, spring up a well of innocent or wholesome superstition—the seeds of exaggeration will be busy there, and vital—from every-day forms educing the unknown and the uncommon.

Proust was to hold that the child's disposition to love creates its own objects; and Miss Elizabeth Bowen has asked if this is not also true of his disposition to fear.[7] Lamb loved the old authors—he damned posterity, and elected to write for antiquity—and yet his firmest psychological links are with his successors. It is interesting that on the less gruesome occasions recalled by "Old Benchers" he should have called his superstition "innocent and wholesome." He would have stood by those epithets even when concerned with witches and other night fears; for I shall shortly come to quote his remark from the essay under discussion that "credulity . . . is the child's strength." Penetration into obscurity, understanding and wisdom—we do not often meet these qualities together on this theme, nor meet them worded so exactly and sharply. It is interesting to compare Wordsworth, whose chief

7 Introduction to Sheridan Le Fanu's *Uncle Silas* (1947), p. 21.

writing on childhood, in *The Prelude*, remained unpublished for thirty years after Lamb's essay. His account differs from Lamb's in two main respects. It allows a place in a child's experience for pleasant dreams. As an instance of this, there is that unfinished passage that was intended at one time for *The Prelude*, and of which his editors give the following account:

> when in my bed I lay
> Alone in darkness, I have seen the gloom
> Peopled with shapes arrayed in hues more bright
> Than flowers or gems, or than the evening sky;
> Processions, multitudes in wake or fair
> Assembled, puppet shews with tru[m]pet, fife,
> Wild beasts, and standards waving in the [field?].
> These mounting ever in a sloping line
> Were foll[ow]ed by the tumult of the shew
> Or horses [   ]
> These vanishing, appeared another scene—
> Hounds, and the uproar of the ch[ase?], or steeds
> That galloped like the wind through standing corn.
> Then headless trunks and faces horrible,
> Then came a thron[g] of forms all [   ]
> Unutterably, horribly arranged
> In parallel lines, in feature and in look
> All different, yet marvellously akin;
> Then files of soldiery with dazzling arms
> Still mounting, mounting upwards, each to each
> Of all these spectres every band and cl[ass?]
> Succeeding with fa[n]tastic difference
> And instant, unimaginable change.
> [   ] phantoms [   ]

On the evidence of this, there was nothing in Wordsworth's experience to warrant his using the word "hell,"
which Lamb could not refrain from using. No doubt
Lamb's mind lacked the power to control the nightmare
as Wordsworth's stronger mind managed to; and so, perhaps, for all its abnormal sensitiveness, it is nearer the
normal mind of childhood. The Wanderer's experience
over horrific book illustrations has nothing of the horror
of Lamb's over those milder ones in Stackhouse. The
Wanderer had "read, and read again"

> A straggling volume, torn and incomplete,
> That left half-told the preternatural tale,
> Romance of giants, chronicle of fiends,
> Profuse in garniture of wooden cuts
> Strange and uncouth; dire faces, figures dire,
> Sharp-kneed, sharp-elbowed, and lean-ankled too,
> With long and ghostly shanks—forms which once seen
> Could never be forgotten![8]

And in the second place, the horrors of Wordsworth's
childhood were partly induced by moral transgression.
This comes out very clearly from the account of the stealing of the boat in the first Book of *The Prelude*. Again,
Lamb's account is more representative of the experience
of the normal child in allowing terror to exist apart from
guilt.

Preceding the passage I have quoted from "Witches
and Other Night Fears" is another, equally remarkable,

---

[8] *The Excursion*, i, 178 ff. I am grateful to Miss Carol Landon for
calling my attention to this parallel between Lamb and Wordsworth.

which introduces the Stackhouse incident. Here is the latter part of it:

> Stackhouse is in two huge tomes—and there was a pleasure in removing folios of that magnitude, which, with infinite straining, was as much as I could manage, from the situation which they occupied upon an upper shelf. I have not met with the work from that time to this, but I remember it consisted of Old Testament stories, orderly set down, with the *objection* appended to each story, and the *solution* of the objection regularly tacked to that. The *objection* was a summary of whatever difficulties had been opposed to the credibility of the history, by the shrewdness of ancient or modern infidelity, drawn up with an almost complimentary excess of candour. The *solution* was brief, modest, and satisfactory. The bane and antidote were both before you. To doubts so put, and so quashed, there seemed to be an end for ever. The dragon lay dead, for the foot of the veriest babe to trample on. But—like as was rather feared than realised from that slain monster in Spenser—from the womb of those crushed errors young dragonets would creep, exceeding the prowess of so tender a Saint George as myself to vanquish. The habit of expecting objections to every passage, set me upon starting more objections, for the glory of finding a solution of my own for them. I became staggered and perplexed, a sceptic in long coats. The pretty Bible stories which I had read, or heard read in church, lost their purity and sincerity of impression, and were turned into so many historic or chronologic theses to be defended against whatever impugners. I was not to disbelieve them, but—the next thing to that—I was to be quite sure that some one or other would or had disbelieved them. Next to making a child an infidel, is the letting him know that there are infidels at all.

Credulity is the man's weakness, but the child's strength. O, how ugly sound scriptural doubts from the mouth of a babe and a suckling!

And Lamb ends this paragraph by recounting the accident ("a fortunate piece of ill-fortune") that removed the book from his fascinated grasp. Again, one does not know which to admire more—the power to perceive or the power to understand. Once more, one cannot but compare Lamb with his betters, compare and prefer. One recalls how Wordsworth and Coleridge—and Newman after them— were for humbling the adult mind to the pitch of wishing it superstitious. There is more wisdom in Lamb's distinction: "Credulity is the man's weakness, but the child's strength."

IV

The essay ends with one of those long codas where, as not infrequently in Lamb's essays, the tension is eased, or the mood lifted or depressed to a different level. Up to now, we have been attending to the child, though always from the point of view of maturity—the man has been remembering the child and his double interest in himself, and it has been kept before us by means of a series of short inserted comparisons, one of which (about credulity) I have just quoted. But now at the close, we abandon the child and take a look at what remains in the adult of the child's great power of gruesome imagination. The turn affords an opportunity that Lamb has the genius to take.

He takes it partly by means of a poem recently published by his friend, Barry Cornwall, "A Dream," which has the appended note: "This is merely the recollection of an actual dream." The dream that the poem recounts is a long one of the sublime sort, in which great places and people appear to the poet in succession. Barry Cornwall is not a bad poet—he unfolds his visions with grace and authority. Presumably some of his first readers believed him when he claimed to have experienced a dream so remarkable. But there is always the suspicion of humbug in such things, and, indeed, Barry Cornwall admitted as much when, in the *Poetical Works* of 1822, he changed the title to read "A Vision," and the headnote less offhand: "This is little more than. . . . " Ordinary people do not dream dreams of this kind, and they cannot fail to suspect that unless adult dreams are desperately encouraged by opium (De Quincey) or heavy suppers (Mrs. Radcliffe) or strong tea (Le Fanu) they take very much more humdrum forms. The sympathies of most readers will be with Lamb and the use he makes of Barry Cornwall's poem. He claims very little for his own dream. Though it began in grandiose fashion, it ended in a way that no poet of this time—unless he were that uncommon thing at this date, a poet who could freely alternate or interpenetrate the comic and sublime—would have dared to describe. Indeed, Lamb shows Barry Cornwall's poem to resemble a great bubble only too liable to puncture at the touch of a household pin. The application of the pin makes for brilliant comedy. But we cannot help seeing that Lamb's account—modest, anti-romantic, and, indeed, anti-poetic—has a poetical quality that is much

in advance of Barry Cornwall's, for all his grandiosity.
This is the conclusion of Cornwall's poem:

> And then I heard the sullen waters roar,
> And saw them cast their surf upon the strand,
> And then, rebounding toward some far-seen land,
> They washed and washed its melancholy shore,
> And the terrific spirits, bred
> In the sea-caverns, moved by those fierce jars,
> Rose up like giants from their watery bed,
> And shook their silver hair against the stars.
> Then, bursts like thunder—joyous outcries wild—
> Sounds as from trumpets, and from drums,
> And music, like the lulling noise that comes
> From nurses when they hush their charge to sleep,
> Came in confusion from the deep.
> Methought one told me that a child
> Was that night unto the great Neptune born;
> And then old Triton blew his curled horn,
> And the Leviathan lashed the foaming seas,
> And the wanton Nereides
> Came up like phantoms from their coral halls,
> And laughed and sung like tipsy Bacchanals,
> Till all the fury of the ocean broke
> Upon my ear.————I trembled and awoke.[9]

And so to Lamb's use of it:

> My night-fancies have long ceased to be afflictive. I
> confess an occasional night-mare; but I do not, as in early

[9] *Dramatic Scenes and Other Poems*, (1819), pp. 131 f.

youth, keep a stud of them. Fiendish faces,[10] with the extinguished taper, will come and look at me; but I know them for mockeries, even while I cannot elude their presence, and I fight and grapple with them. For the credit of my imagination, I am almost ashamed to say how tame and prosaic my dreams are grown. They are never romantic, seldom even rural. They are of architecture and of buildings—cities abroad, which I have never seen, and hardly have hope to see. I have traversed, for the seeming length of a natural day, Rome, Amsterdam, Paris, Lisbon—their churches, palaces, squares, market-places, shops, suburbs, ruins, with an inexpressible sense of delight—a map-like distinctness of trace—and a day-light vividness of vision, that was all but being awake.—I have formerly travelled among the Westmoreland fells—my highest Alps,—but they are objects too mighty for the grasp of my dreaming recognition; and I have again and again awoke with ineffectual struggles of the inner eye, to make out a shape in any way whatever, of Helvellyn. Methought I was in that country, but the mountains were gone. The poverty of my dreams mortifies me. There is Coleridge, at his will can conjure up icy domes, and pleasure-houses for Kubla Khan, and Abyssinian maids, and songs of Abara, and caverns,

Where Alph, the sacred river runs[*sic*],

to solace his night solitudes—when I cannot muster a fiddle. Barry Cornwall has his tritons and his nereids gambolling before him in nocturnal visions, and proclaiming sons born to Neptune—when my stretch of imaginative activity can hardly, in the night season, raise up the ghost of a fish-wife.[11] To set my failures in somewhat a mortify-

[10] The phrase is taken from Wordsworth's "Her Eyes Are Wild," line 23.

[11] Cf. Browne, *The Garden of Cyrus,* chap. v. *ad fin.*

ing light—it was after reading the noble Dream of this
poet, that my fancy ran strong upon these marine spectra;
and the poor plastic power, such as it is, within me set to
work, to humour my folly in a sort of dream that very
night. Methought I was upon the ocean billows at some
sea nuptials, riding and mounted high, with the customary
train sounding their conchs before me, (I myself, you may
be sure, the *leading god,*) and jollily we went careering
over the main, till just where Ino Leucothea should have
greeted me (I think it was Ino) with a white embrace, the
billows gradually subsiding, fell from a sea-roughness to
a sea-calm, and thence to a river-motion,[12] and that river
(as happens in the familiarization of dreams) was no
other than the gentle Thames, which landed me, in the
wafture of a placid wave or two, alone, safe and inglorious,
somewhere at the foot of Lambeth palace.

This is masterly comedy. It is also a display of the very
imagination Lamb disclaims, for there is, as in the poems
of his beloved Pope, more power of imagination in its
half-comic, half-beautiful scene than in scenes purely
beautiful by poets less great than Keats and Tennyson.
Lamb's imagination—that is, his power to make pictures,
what he here calls his "plastic" power—has never been
given its due. He has been taken too much at his own
evaluation. In his maturity, he lost, he says, his power
of "seeing ghosts," but his apostrophe to Death is one
of the most gruesome in our literature:

Some have wooed death——but out upon thee, I say,
thou foul, ugly phantom! I detest, abhor, execrate, and
(with Friar John) give thee to six-score thousand devils,

12 Cf. Polonius, *Hamlet,* Act II, Scene ii, lines 146 ff.

as in no instance to be excused or tolerated, but shunned as a universal viper; to be branded, proscribed, and spoken evil of! In no way can I be brought to digest thee, thou thin, melancholy *Privation,* or more frightful and confounding *Positive!*

V

The preceding extract is from "New Year's Eve," a characteristic essay, which sounds the Elian instrument through much of its compass—for as well as the apostrophe to Death, it contains the human wisdom of

> I would scarce now have any of those untoward accidents and events of my life reversed. I would no more alter them than the incidents of some well-contrived novel.

Like "Witches and Other Night-Fears," the essay deals in reminiscence, with all that that implies of a preceding past and a resultant—or at least a subsequent—and contrasting present. It is really about the death of the old year, and only becomes a toast to the birth of the new because of a trick of grinning optimism all the more creditable for being performed against the grain. Up to that point, there have been some half-indulgent references to those cheerful souls who think of the occasion only as an excuse, and a good one, for a celebration. But Lamb, or Elia to be exact, has no option but to join them at last, however grim the path to that welcome collapse.

The eve of the New Year is occasion for a heart-searching for Elia as it is for us all, in proportion as we care to think about it. The virtue of the essay consists in the exhausting of this profound and universal annual topic, and the doing so, as ever, in prose that has that classic quality of being unimprovable. Of the many things to remark, I select the following, in which use is made of "Elia," the fictitious name that seems to have been pronounced "Elīa" (and so to have sounded almost like "a liar"), and which, in any event, was made up from the letters of "a lie":

If I know aught of myself, no one whose mind is introspective—and mine is painfully so—can have a less respect for his present identity, than I have for the man Elia. I know him to be light, and vain, and humorsome; a notorious * * * ; addicted to * * * * : averse from counsel, neither taking it, nor offering it;— * * * besides; a stammering buffoon; what you will; lay it on, and spare not; I subscribe to it all, and much more, than thou canst be willing to lay at his door——but for the child Elia—that "other me", there, in the back-ground—I must take leave to cherish the remembrance of that young master—with as little reference, I protest, to this stupid changeling of five-and-forty, as if it had been a child of some other house, and not of my parents. I can cry over its patient small-pox at five, and rougher medicaments. I can lay its poor fevered head upon the sick pillow at Christ's, and wake with it in surprise at the gentle posture of maternal tenderness hanging over it, that unknown had watched its sleep. I know how it shrank from any the least colour of falsehood.—God help thee, Elia, how art thou changed! Thou are sophisticated.[13]—I know how honest, how courageous (for a weakling) it was—how religious, how imaginative, how hopeful! From what have I not fallen,

13 Recalling *Lear,* Act III, scene iv, line 105.

if the child I remember was indeed myself,—and not some dissembling guardian, presenting a false identity, to give the rule to my unpractised steps, and regulate the tone of my moral being!

The two Elias, man and boy, are looked at by another intelligence that is external to them both. This intelligence would seem to be that of Lamb himself, and yet we cannot allege this confidently in face of the preface to *Last Essays*, which describes "the first person" as Elia's "favourite figure"—the preface was written by Lamb himself, but signed "By a Friend of the Late Elia." What is in process in the passage I have quoted is a "dialogue of the mind with itself," but it is expressed as in a play with three persons present on the stage together. And yet all the persons are one. We see, then, how far Lamb has gone toward putting the authorial "I" to use, making it contribute toward a method. He hit on that method, no doubt, because of his liking for mystifications—it is one of the many traits of character he shared with Pope and Swift. He begins "Christ's Hospital Five and Thirty Years Ago" with the bland deception of "In Mr. Lamb's 'Works,' published a year or two since, I find a magnificant eulogy of my old school. . . ." Hit on for the general purposes of mystification, Lamb came to see its general value as a method—it enables the reminiscent author to combine the intimacy of confession with the freedom open to the writer of fiction. We are becoming increasingly aware how much this sort of "I" meant to the novelists who followed Lamb, and even when they were writing in forms other than the novel. They also

follow Lamb in giving out the "I" as aged and rumina-
tive, and also as unheroic. They, like him, have dreams
of the sort that take place somewhere at the foot of
Lambeth Palace.

VI

To characterize Lamb's mind as shown in the essays,
we should have to invoke something between the mind
of novelist, critic, and poet—something like the mind of
a seventeenth-century metaphysical poet added to that
which George Eliot employed when writing *Theophrastus
Such*. I have indicated his power as a poet. To write a
great novel, more is required than to write a *Theophrastus
Such*. When that fine book was published, somebody
remarked that it "was a higher order of book and *more
difficult to write* than a novel," and the view aroused
George Eliot's amused contempt: "Wait long enough,
and every form of opinion will turn up."[14] In addition
to the powers to create personages and ideas—powers
that are amply displayed in *Theophrastus Such*—the
novelist needs the power to engage personages in an action
that springs both from their own nature, from that of
other imagined personages, and from the nature of things.
Lamb evinced no such additional powers, though Wordsworth urged him to write a novel.[15] His plays, interesting
as they are, are on too small a scale to affect the present

14 *Letters,* ed. G. S. Haight (New Haven, Conn. and Oxford, 1954–56),
VII, 165.

15 Edmund Blunden, *Charles Lamb and His Contemporaries* (Cambridge, 1937), p. 149.

issue; and the tale about roast pig is little more than anecdote, though it is well invented. But he did have a power of creating personages, and complex ones. The Bachelor, whose complaint we examined, was created whole. We know his physical height; we can discern the pain he is made to feel:

> Every long friendship, every old authentic intimacy, must be brought into their [the wives'] office to be new stamped with their currency . . . You may guess what luck generally befalls such a rusty piece of metal as I am in these *new mintings*.

We can see the sensitiveness of what affections come his way in the details he gives of their tokens:

> . . . A dog, or a lesser thing,—any inanimate substance, as a keep-sake, a watch or a ring, a tree, or the place where we last parted when my friend went away upon a long absence, I can make shift to love, because I love him, and any thing that reminds me of him. . . .

And we note that in his complaint it is mainly the woman who comes in for the blame. Then, again, Mrs. Battle is so much richer a personage than one who merely put cards first. She is potentially a personage in a novel; we can imagine her in wider action. Her fully worked-out preference for whist over all other games places her in a larger world than the recreational drawing room. "Chance . . . is nothing, but when something else depends upon it;" and "Man is a gaming animal. He must be always trying to get the better of something or other"—remarks

like these belong to the total world drawn on by novels.
The method by which she is presented is that of the
apologia, as it is the method later used for Bishop
Blougram—for Browning's postscript in his own person
makes the monologue into something different and nearer
Lamb's essay. And in both instances, the materials are
drawn from deep in human nature as a whole, and so
could serve, *mutatis mutandis*, to plead the primacy of
other courses of life. It might be thought that because
Lamb is sometimes engaged in special pleading, he then
gives a distorted picture of things. The truth is quite the
reverse. In "Old China," for instance, he argues a preference for being skimped for money over having enough
of it. We agree that there is something in it. But there
is the whole truth in what he says about poor folk. Bridget
is speaking:

> You are too proud to see a play anywhere now but in
> the pit. Do you remember where it was we used to sit,
> when we saw the Battle of Hexham, and the Surrender of
> Calais, and Bannister and Mrs. Bland in the Children in
> the Wood—when we squeezed out our shillings a-piece to
> sit three or four times in a season in the one-shilling gallery
> —where you felt all the time that you ought not to have
> brought me—and more strongly I felt obligation to you
> for having brought me—and the pleasure was the better
> for a little shame—and when the curtain drew up, what
> cared we for our place in the house, or what mattered it
> where we were sitting, when our thoughts were with
> Rosalind in Arden, or with Viola at the Court of Illyria?
> You used to say, that the gallery was the best place of all
> for enjoying a play socially—that the relish of such exhibi-
> tions must be in proportion to the infrequency of going—

that the company we met there, not being in general
readers of plays, were obliged to attend the more, and did
attend, to what was going on, on the stage—because a
word lost would have been a chasm, which it was impossible for them to fill up. With such reflections we consoled
our pride then—and I appeal to you, whether, as a woman,
I met generally with less attention and accommodation,
than I have done since in more expensive situations in the
house? The getting in indeed, and the crowding up those
inconvenient staircases, was bad enough,—but there was
still a law of civility to women recognised to quite as great
an extent as we ever found in the other passages—and
how a little difficulty overcome heightened the snug seat,
and the play, afterwards! Now we can only pay our
money, and walk in. You cannot see, you say, in the gal-
leries now. I am sure we saw, and heard too, well enough
then—but sight, and all, I think, is gone with our poverty.

Though his occasion for saying such things is one that
invites special pleading, he gives us the object squarely,
and so is as useful as any writer who has the strength of
mind to write disinterestedly. Novelists write so. They
represent life as it is; and this is what Lamb's essays
do, though they may be pretending to do something
else. In the mid-nineteenth century, there was a strong
movement toward taking truth as the first virtue of a
fiction writer; and among its predecessors, Lamb stands
prominent.

VII

He deserves in his own right all the attention we can
give him. It is high time we forget the charges our fathers

brought against him because it is high time we came
to see that they concern only his imitators. Up to now,
what these later essayists got from him has been the
only ground advanced for his historical importance—or
for his notoriety—which is like condemning Shakespeare
because he set up so many tragedy writers in the nineteenth century. If now and again Lamb indulges a fancy
that is not so nimble, fiery, and delectable as, say, Swift's,
we must allow that he alternates the use of fancy with
the use of a strong and subtle intellect. He may begin
an essay with a thing like this, which though effective
in its own day, has not enough in it to remain so:

> I have no ear.
> Mistake me not, reader. . . .

but he continues it with such a thing as the analysis of
what the experience of music means to a man who cannot understand it. The subjects he chooses are usually
complex, as is that item in psychology, though it might
be truer to say that his genius was the sort that discovered complexity latent in ordinary things.

I mentioned above that there was a poet in Lamb. He
did, in fact, write poetry in meter, and some of the results
are admirable. But his most remarkable poetry is em-
bedded in his prose. Some of it is the poetry of fancy, but
in that description of the dream, and in a score or two
of comparable passages there is poetry of a deeper sort,
which we should be the more ready to allow because we
have recently returned to admire and marvel at the
poetry of Pope. It is poetry that is flexible in its opera-

tion—of the sort that Hazlitt discerned in the *Rape of the Lock*, and did not know whether to laugh or cry over. It mixes beauty and commonplace, richness and dinginess, and those two things which, according to Thackeray, make humour when combined—wit and love.

LEIGH HUNT AND THE END
OF ROMANTIC CRITICISM

Stephen F. Fogle

If the Preface to the second edition of *Lyrical Ballads* stands at the beginning of a new age of criticism, so the appearance of Leigh Hunt's long essay "An Answer to the Question 'What is Poetry?,'" which opens his book *Imagination and Fancy* in 1844, closes the same period. Wordsworth's essay has a respectable ancestry in the history of criticism, but it is its quality of manifesto rather than its traditionalism that still gives it importance. It is the first large-scale attempt to set down the principles of a new age of poetry and poets, and it looks to the future rather than the past. Hunt's essay belongs to a period that is already closing, and is a summing-up and explanation, a charting of ground already won, rather than an attempt to explore the future.

The work is Hunt's most important critical production, the most extended piece of theoretical critical writing of a man who had been a practicing critic for nearly forty years of journalism of one sort or another. Commencing with his theatrical criticism for *The News* in the first decade of the century, Hunt had very seldom been without some newspaper connection, some means of expressing an opinion upon literary matters. As one looks back over this long stretch of practical criticism, a strange dichotomy emerges. Hunt is frequently brilliant in his judgments, and yet there is very little statement of principles. He knows what he likes, and he can tell us why he likes it, demonstrating over and over again his vivid personal reaction to the play he is seeing, the poem he is reading. Yet there is no reference to a governing set of principles.

The most kindly and appreciative of recent writers upon Hunt, the late C. D. Thorpe, says,

> . . . However impressionistic Hunt's criticism may appear to be, he was fundamentally neither slipshod in his methods nor random in his judgments. He had principles and he made constant application of them. Put these principles together and you recognize an aesthetic of sound and substantial outline.[1]

Yet Professor Thorpe is driven to reconstruct these principles from Hunt's practical criticism, since there is never a clear statement of them that can be quoted and discussed. One must say that Hunt "is presumably thinking" of the imagination in a certain way, that he "comes very near" to stating what he believes the imagination to be.[2]

> There is in him virtually nothing of the close psychological and metaphysical analysis which we find in Coleridge. For the kind of literary philosophizing at which Coleridge was such a master and in which he was so much at home, Hunt had small talent and even less taste. When he approaches analytical formulation he rarely holds himself firmly enough to his last to come out with clear and full presentation. What he says is excellent so far as it goes, but, on more abstract issues, it has a habit of glancing off or coming to a stop before the full blow is struck.[3]

[1] Clarence D. Thorpe, "An essay in Evaluation: Leigh Hunt as a Man of Letters," in *Leigh Hunt's Literary Criticism*, ed. L. H. and C. W. Houtchens (New York, 1956), p. 56.

[2] *Ibid.*, p. 52.

[3] *Ibid.*, p. 53.

It is very probable that the reason Hunt put off the statement of critical principles of his own is that he was incapable of formulating them consistently and coherently, of making definitions that should be comprehensive enough to include everything he liked and that should equally exclude from serious consideration everything that he found intolerable. One of the difficulties, of course, is that he is not always completely consistent; some of the poetry he read moved from one of these categories to the other. Also, when attempting to assess Hunt's criticism of a contemporary poet, it is always wise to attempt to reconstruct what Hunt's personal relations with that poet were at the time he was writing the criticism. It is not that he was consciously or venally attempting to use the power of the press as a weapon in personal vendettas, but that he had no strong critical system, no set of abstract rules, to which he could refer judgment. Thus his personal disappointment in Byron's treatment of him infected his judgment of Byron's poetry for a time. His shifting attitude toward Wordsworth in the 1840's needs to be considered not only as literary criticism but also against the background of Wordsworth's having been given, in 1843, the laureateship for which Hunt had been almost openly maneuvering since Victoria's accession.

Then, too, Hunt's own taste changed over the years. His attitude changed as he read more in the literature of the world and as he acquired more and more knowledge of the entire work of the poet he was considering. Originally unsympathetic with many of the writers of his own time, he became one of the most appreciative critics, a tireless propagandist for the work of those he believed in. This development can be traced by a brief glance at his early career. His own first book, *Juvenilia*, a book of poems, many of them school exercises, was published in 1801, the same year as the actual appearance of the second edition of *Lyrical Ballads*. It is an insipid volume, thoroughly derivative in its imitations and translations, preserving some interest in the present day only through the quaintness of its list of subscribers. It is asking too much that Hunt, at seventeen, should have been aware of Wordsworth and Coleridge, even though Hunt, too, was a Bluecoat Boy, educated at Christ's Hospital, and acquainted at least with the legend Coleridge had left behind him in the school.

When, a few years later, he came to review the productions of the London theaters for his brother's paper *The News* and later for *The Examiner*, Hunt's critical method was by no means clear. It is easy to see why these reviews were successful and made his reputation, for they are both well-written and informal, the application of the manner of the personal essayist to the performances of the London stage. But it must have puzzled the performers to know how to please this critic. He was a man of taste, but of a highly personal taste, often even capricious. His reviews of performances as performances are brilliant because he was fascinated by acting, and is able to convey to his reader the movement and personality of the actor upon the stage and to suggest how various effects are obtained. The editors of *Leigh Hunt's Dra-*

matic Criticism, 1808-1831 feel that he gave an impetus to the course of Romantic criticism by "his adoption of romantic criteria in certain reviews for the *Examiner*." [4] But these criteria are not consistent and, in general, must be quarried out of the implications of the review by the diligent reader. Also, while there are "certain romantic criteria," there are also attitudes that are in direct contradiction to them. Anything less like the new Romantic criticism of Shakespeare than Hunt's willingness to excise the Fool from *King Lear* as "now out of date" would be hard to find.[5]

The various versions of *The Feast of the Poets* indicate Hunt's indecisiveness as a critic in his early years. The piece occupied ten pages of *The Reflector's* fourth and final issue in March, 1812, was revised for separate publication in 1814, and then was reissued the following year, with alterations in both text and notes. The tone of the poem is rather cheaply satiric, and may have been meant to capitalize on the popularity of Byron's *English Bards and Scotch Reviewers*. Apollo comes down to earth to give a banquet to poets at a tavern. Various guests are announced, among them "Bob, Billy, and Sam," the Lake poets. Wordsworth and Coleridge are quickly disposed of, not permitted to linger at the select feast for four poets, although Southey stays. By the final version of the poem, the feast has been enlarged to eight guests and includes both Wordsworth and Coleridge, the first of whom has

[4] *Leigh Hunt's Dramatic Criticism: 1808-1831*, ed. L. H. and C. W. Houtchens (New York, 1948), p. viii.
[5] *Ibid.*, p. 15.

become, in the preface, "the first poet of the day." The changes in the notes to the poem between the 1814 and 1815 editions indicate Hunt's changing attitude toward Wordsworth. In 1815, he is ranked with Milton and Spenser, has one hundred times the genius of Southey, but is still subject to scolding and instruction from Leigh Hunt. Whatever the future fame of Wordsworth, good or bad, after the 1815 edition of *The Feast of the Poets*, Hunt could safely claim to have predicted it.

Yet it is within a few years following this poem that Hunt rendered his greatest contributions to practical criticism: the recognition of merit in the work of Keats and Shelley, at a time when such recognition was an act of real discovery. To have brought out in *The Examiner*, one of the most influential papers of the day, the first published work of John Keats, and to have used its power to assist both Keats and Shelley is an act of prescience from which nothing can detract.

It was in such work that Hunt was able in the next three decades to serve the cause of literary criticism rather than in abstract statements of principles. His championing of Keats and Shelley in the highly controversial book *Lord Byron and Some of His Contemporaries*, in 1828, went largely unnoticed because of the virulence of his attack upon Byron; but he was to continue at almost every opportunity through the 1830's to quote from them, to write about them, to tell the public what it had neglected. That his power of recognition had not atrophied or deserted him is borne out by his devoting space in four issues of *The Tatler* in 1831 to the poetry of the young Alfred and Charles Tennyson, praising both but singling out Alfred as the better poet.

Yet, when Hunt turns to abstractions, he becomes softly sentimental, taking refuge in easy personifications that attract attention to their own picturesque quality rather than to the idea to be expressed. For example, in the introduction to an article, "Words for Composers," published in the *Musical World* in 1839, Hunt wrote:

> While Music utters divine inarticulate cries out of the pure heaven of feeling, charming the senses of all, but suggesting distinct imaginations to few, Poetry charms the senses less, but has the power of making all distinctly partake of her imaginations: and Painting has the divine power of saying: "You shall behold with the eyes of sense what my sister Music makes you hear and my sister Poetry makes you think of, and what we all three of us feel."[6]

It is hard to believe that any writer who had thought long and seriously on the principles of literary criticism could have used "imaginations" in the way it is used in the passage above.

In 1844, Hunt's major critical pronouncement, *Imagination and Fancy*, appeared. It was Hunt's sixtieth year, and for forty years he had been earning his living by his pen. He had turned his hand to every sort of hack work, driven by the necessity of providing for his large family, presided over by his improvident, eccentric, and alcoholic

---

[6] Cited in Louis Landré, *Leigh Hunt: Contribution à l'histoire du Romantisme anglais* (Paris, 1936), II, 139 n.

wife.[7] He had written plays, a novel, poems, short pieces of every description, but no extended work of literary criticism. By now, his work was largely one of popularization, of introducing the new middle-class reading public to established authors. His method of composition now was to quote and comment, to bring together separate essays from his own past works, to translate, to introduce, to make graceful paraphrases. He could take his readers on gentle and gossipy rambles through the suburbs of London and in the byways of literature, but he apparently could not produce an original work of any length. Even the *Autobiography* of 1850 was to be largely a skillful rehashing of materials he had already at hand.[8] Similarly, such works as *A Book for a Corner* or *Readings for Railways*, with their oddly deprecatory titles, were aimed frankly at the lending libraries.

Imagination and Fancy was not written in response to a request from a publisher; it had been written and compiled as one of the endless projects with which Hunt busied himself in the quest for money. Failing to dispose of it immediately, Hunt pawned the manuscript, borrowing forty pounds upon it as security, from Thomas Powell, a city clerk and literary dilettante. It was Powell who negotiated the sale of the book to Smith, Elder and

[7] See Carl R. Woodring, *Victorian Samplers: William and Mary Howitt* (Lawrence, Kan., 1952), p. 117. See also the caricature of Mrs. Hunt as Mrs. Skimpole in Dickens' *Bleak House*.

[8] For a discussion of the materials included in the *Autobiography*, see *Leigh Hunt's Autobiography: The Earliest Sketches,* ed. Stephen F. Fogle, ("University of Florida Monographs, Humanities Series," No. 2 [Gainesville, Fla., 1959]), pp. vi–viii.

Company, and thus initiated the longest period of literary success that Hunt had ever experienced.[9] The work was not, then, the result of long deliberation, a carefully planned statement of a critical position. It was, like many of the other books Hunt was turning out at the time, a rather hastily written drawing-together of old notions, many of them still in the form in which they had previously appeared. The comments on Keats's "Eve of St. Agnes," for example, had been used earlier but were too good to be thrown away and forgotten.

The wonder is that the work is as good as it is. It was an immediate financial success, a second edition appearing in 1845, a third in 1846, and a fourth in 1852. After Hunt's death it was reprinted in four separate editions before the end of the century. And in the meantime, it had been pirated and gone through a number of editions in the United States. In short, the book swiftly became a standard item, the first work of Hunt to achieve anything like permanent approval. In 1846, he tried again, for the same publisher, with *Wit and Humour*, a book that disappeared fairly swiftly; and a third production, *Action and Passion*, never went beyond the stage of discussion.

The immediate circumstances of 1844 were favorable for a success by Leigh Hunt. There had been a long slow growth in his reputation, rising again from the nadir it had reached in 1828 with the scandals surrounding *Lord Byron and Some of His Contemporaries*. His personal

9 George Smith, "In the Early Forties," *Cornhill Magazine*, ser. 3, IX, 583.

charm, his wide acquaintance among literary men, his friendliness to the younger men who were slowly making their own reputations, and the very fact of his growing older and becoming a sage, as well as the consciousness that the world had dealt harshly with a man who deserved better—all predisposed the public and the press to like his new book.

But the permanent success of the work is owing to qualities in the book itself. It sums up the four decades that preceded it, using all the terms that had been either introduced or redefined by the great Romantic critics. Hunt, however, is using these terms for the emotional aura that surrounds them, and all precision of meaning is lost.

Certainly one of the characteristics of the writing of the first quarter of the nineteenth century is the struggle to take words in common usage and to give them a special, heightened sense. Wordsworth's term *joy*, used in several senses in *Tintern Abbey*, undergoes further refinement of meaning; and by the time it is picked up and used climactically by Coleridge in *Dejection: An Ode*, it has been charged with so much meaning that it is a philosophical term with an emotional connotation rather than simply a label for one emotion, the antonym of *sorrow*. Wordsworth's original version of the passage in the *Prelude* (Book IV, lines 323 ff.), which describes his first dedication as a poet, is an example of an almost mystical use of the verb *to be*, of the attempt to charge a simple word with more meaning than could be readily comprehended by the ordinary reader. We may look upon the changes as the compromise of an early Victorian poet with his own youth; in the original passage the simple words had managed to convey an intensity far beyond their usual force. Coleridge's attempts to invent and give currency to new critical terms that would be more accurate than anything in contemporary usage are remembered as fascinating examples of the way in which his mind worked rather than as permanent additions to the critical vocabulary. Yet he took two terms that had been commonplaces of previous criticism and charged them with such meaning that they have never been quite the same since. We may look upon his invented word, *esemplastic*, as an oddity, needing to be glossed each time it is used, but *imagination* and *fancy* have been permanently changed for every student of literature.

The very title of Hunt's book looks back to Coleridge, but for Hunt *imagination* and *fancy* are catchall terms, not qualities to be carefully discriminated one from the other, each being made by careful scrutiny to yield up every nuance of which it is capable. For Hunt they are familiar, approved words that can be made to include everything he wishes to say. The first paragraph of the opening essay manages to include not only these but very nearly every other of the critical terms used by his great predecessors.

> Poetry, strictly and artistically so called, that is to say, considered not merely as poetic feeling, which is more or less shared by all the world, but as the operation of that feeling, such as we see it in the poet's book, is the utterance of a passion for truth, beauty and power, embodying and illustrating its conceptions by imagination and fancy, and

modulating its language on the principle of variety in uniformity. Its means are whatever the universe contains; and its ends, pleasure and exaltation. Poetry stands between nature and convention, keeping alive among us the enjoyment of the external and spiritual world: it has constituted the most enduring fame of nations; and, next to Love and Beauty, which are its parents, is the greatest proof to man of the pleasure to be found in all things, and of the probable riches of infinitude.

One can only wonder what the average Victorian made of this. To an educated reader of a half century earlier, one may believe it would have been incomprehensible. In the interim, almost every one of the abstractions with which the passage is crowded had undergone heavy modification or expansion of meaning. Even so, however, there is the appearance of statement without the statement's ever being clearly made. What are we to make of the long modifying interruption between subject and verb? A paraphrase might run thus: "Poetry, if we mean poetry written down instead of just a vague condition of mind, which we all share more or less, . . . " But then the sentence goes on to repeat the notion. "Poetry, thus defined as utterance, is utterance. . . . "[10] There follows the torrent of terms in which lies the heart of this definition of poetry: "truth," "beauty," "power," "imagination," "fancy," and "variety in uniformity." We have met them all before, under circumstances where they meant more to us. "Truth" and "beauty" juxtaposed like this are in-

[10] "Utterance" here is probably a reminiscence of John Stuart Mill's statement, "Poetry is the expression or uttering forth of feeling" ("What is Poetry?" in *Early Essays* [London, 1833] p. 208).

escapably Keats. "Power" is presumably eventually from Wordsworth's distinction in the *Prelude* between the literature of knowledge and the literature of power, but probably in this instance through De Quincey's "Letters to a Young Man whose Education has been neglected." "Imagination" and "fancy" come of course primarily from Coleridge, and the "principle of variety in uniformity" owes a good deal both to Coleridge and to Wordsworth's "Dissimilitude in similitude" in the Preface to *Lyrical Ballads*.

It is not reasonable to insist upon a single, exclusive source for each of these terms; the very words themselves are not uncommon. However, each of these words had acquired from the great Romantics a heightened meaning, which has been lost here; the very piling up of terms in this passage has worn them threadbare. That they are all set down here together, that it is this cluster of words rather than another, is proof that something has happened in the world of criticism since 1800.

In his continuation, Hunt falls from the new terminology of the nineteenth century into the conventional rhetoric of critical commonplaces: "ends" and "means" are set up in an easy antithesis, but the means are "whatever the universe contains," and the ends are "pleasure and exaltation," the latter term a substitution for the "instruction" which might have been expected. After more antitheses ("nature and convention," "the external and the spiritual"), the paragraph ends with one of those personifications that are regularly a danger signal in Hunt. To make Poetry the child of Love and Beauty (not apparently the beauty that was juxtaposed with truth in the opening sentence) is to create a family group that defies analysis or at least turns it aside. The relation of these three abstractions to each other has been defined according to a sentimental pattern, which must not be pursued beyond its surface. One would like to ask what the exact qualities of Love and Beauty are that are reproduced in their child Poetry—or, remembering his earlier "Words for Composers," Poetry's sisters, Music and Painting.

After his initial paragraph, Hunt goes on to discuss the parts of his original definition, sometimes in considerable detail. Having puzzled the average reader with his opening riddle, he shows us that all these hard words are really very simple indeed. One difficulty, which Hunt does not avoid, is that, having set out to show us that one term is meant in a special sense, he must go on and define, for the sake of symmetry, what does not need definition. For example, "Poetry is a passion, because it seeks the deepest impressions, and because it must undergo, in order to convey, them." One may doubt that the reader knew a great deal more about the nature of passion as an identification for poetry after reading this, but at least some explanation was needed. But the following statement, "It is a passion for truth, because without truth the impression would be false or defective," seems at first glance hardly worth the space it takes. And yet its very flatness and poverty are revealing. Is this all that Hunt makes of Keats's *truth*? Is it possible that for Hunt, Keats's use of *truth* is a simple antithesis to *untruth*? At any rate, he passes on immediately to his next point. "It [Poetry] is a passion for beauty, because its office is to exalt and refine by means of pleasure, and because beauty is nothing but the loveliest form of pleasure." Here at least is a suggestion of the traditional defense of poetry as a moral agent, since the notion of refining is brought in where we would expect either instruction or improvement to be mentioned.

One other danger signal appears in this passage for the experienced reader of Hunt. As one reads work after work, volume after volume, one begins to notice that one set of words, the verb *love*, and the adjectives and adverbs which can be derived from it—*lovely, lovelier, loveliest, lovesome*—regularly play an odd part. It is not merely that they are used vaguely to indicate approval, but that they indicate a special type of sentimentality, which is apparently connected with Hunt's weakness for easy personification. When we are told that "beauty is nothing but the loveliest form of pleasure," are we to understand that *loveliest* means *most intense*? Is the adjective simply a device to avoid defining *beauty* as being the *most beautiful* form, and thus defining a word in terms of itself? Or is there a kind of personification concealed here? Is Hunt thinking of *Beauty* as a female figure in a masque?

The next part of the definition concerns power, which is "impression triumphant, whether over the poet, as desired by himself, or over the reader, as affected by the poet." At first glance, it is hard to know what to make of *impression* here, since our usual use of impression as something rather vaguely felt and not intellectually understood would weaken this passage into nonsense. For such an impression to be triumphant over both poet and reader could be only a situation to be deplored rather than celebrated. Leaving aside the difficult question of the poem's differing effect upon its author and its readers, one can best explain this definition by a glance back to what is probably its source. De Quincey was to publish his famous distinction between the literature of knowledge and the literature of power in its definitive form only in his review essay of an edition of Pope in 1848, four years after Hunt's book was published. But he had stated his ideas as early as 1823, in the third of the "Letters to a Young Man whose Education has been neglected." "The true antithesis to knowledge, in this case, is not *pleasure*, but power. All that is literature seeks to communicate power; all that is not literature, to communicate knowledge." In the note to this passage, De Quincey gives us a clear statement of the special usage of the term by his own contemporaries, and his notion of the source of that special usage.

> For which distinction, as for most of the sound criticism on poetry, or any subject connected with it that I have ever met with, I must acknowledge my obligations to many years' conversation with Mr. Wordsworth. Upon this occasion it may be useful to notice that there is a rhetorical use of the word "power," very different from the analytic one here introduced, which, also, is due originally to Mr. Wordsworth and will be found in no book before 1798; this is now become a regular slang term in London con-

versation. In reference to which, it is worth notice that a critic, speaking of the late Mr. Shelley, a year or two ago, in the most popular literary journal of the day, said, "It is alleged that there is power in Mr. Shelley's poetry; now, there can be no power shown in poetry, except by writing good poems" (or words to that effect). Waiving, however, the question of Mr. Shelley's merits, so far is this remark from being true, that the word was originally introduced expressly to provide for the case where, though the poem was *not* good from defect in its *composition,* or from other causes, the stamina and matériel of good poetry as fine thinking and passionate conceptions, could not be denied to exist.[11]

Whatever one may think of De Quincey's defining *power* partly in terms of *stamina*, this is far clearer than Hunt's *impression triumphant* and seems to explain it. The *impression* of the poem would then be the force felt to be in its concept but not carefully worked out in the composition. Hunt is maintaining that any good poem must have a vital concept behind it, whether that concept is well presented or not; or perhaps it would be better to say that the concept, or *impression*, behind a poem must of itself be vital, no matter how well worked out technically the composition may be. This explanation of *impression* explains how it can be triumphant "over the poet, as desired by himself, or over the reader, as affected by the poet." But again Hunt has been a faulty translator of others' ideas. As stated in *Imagination and Fancy*, the notion of power as a quality of poetry is confused and misleading.

[11] De Quincey, *Works* (Edinburgh, 1863), XIII, 55.

The same process of weakening critical terms and rendering them less effective has also hurt the use of *imagination* and *fancy*. Doubtless, Hunt felt them to be key terms, or he would not have used them as the title of his book. Familiar in the criticism of the eighteenth century, they had undergone such a change at the hands of Coleridge that the old usages seemed of historical interest only. But for Hunt the change has not been complete; his definition is a mixture of the new and the old.

> It [Poetry] embodies and illustrates its impressions by imagination, or images of the objects of which it treats, and other images brought in to throw light on those objects, in order that it may enjoy and impart the feeling of their truth in its utmost conviction and affluence. It illustrates them by fancy, which is a lighter play of the imagination, or the feeling of analogy coming short of seriousness, in order that it may laugh with what it loves, and show how it can decorate it with fairy ornament.

It is clear that imagination can be used to embody as well as to illustrate, that fancy can be used only to illustrate, and that imagination exists on more than a single level, since it employs images of the objects treated and also images to throw light on those objects. The truth is that Hunt had all along felt a difficulty in the term. As early as 1820, in an essay "On the Realities of the Imagination," he had used the word as a plural to mean things apparent or supposed and not actual, and had then confounded his term with the usual literary usage of it. Later in the 1844 essay, he manages to make his distinction between fancy and imagination clearer than here at the beginning. Fancy is here a "lighter play of the imagination"; it comes "short of seriousness." And then the weakness for easy personification shows itself again, and again, typically, involving the word *loves*, so that the definition is lost in sentimentality. Later, after Hunt has defined no less than seven levels of imagination, from the very simplest to the most complex, he is driven to limiting Fancy, the "younger sister of Imagination": "Imagination belongs to Tragedy, or the serious muse; Fancy to the comic." It is only in works of mixed genre that both can be found.

> The terms were formerly identical, or used as such; and neither is the best that might be found. The term Imagination is too confined: often too material. It presents too invariably the idea of a solid body;—of "images" in the sense of the plaster cast cry about the streets. Fancy, on the other hand, . . . has rarely that freedom from visibility which is one of the highest privileges of imagination.

Again, one wonders what the early Victorian reader, in search of self-improvement, made of such a passage. There seems a clear contradiction between the charge that imagination is too material and that one of its highest privileges is freedom from visibility. The gradation of seven (why seven, rather than six, or eight, or even nine?) levels of the imagination is too lengthy to be quoted; but it is a little startling to have the final and presumably the highest of these described as being "apparently of the vaguest kind." Hunt adds to the confusion by quoting an example from Coleridge's *Christabel* and adding praise for the use of the letter *l* by which this imaginative effect is achieved.

The final section of his original compact definition of poetry deals with the principle of variety in uniformity. As suggested earlier, this is Wordsworth's dissimilitude in similitude, and for once Hunt has hit upon the happier term. His discussion of this principle leads him, as it had led Wordsworth in the Preface to *Lyrical Ballads,* into a defense of verse as against prose. But Hunt carries the argument further than Wordsworth and completely rejects any notion that "poetry need not be written in verse at all." "The opinion is a prosaical mistake," and "verse is necessary to the form of poetry." This would seem a complete reversal of the earlier Romantic position that the correct antithesis is between verse and prose rather than between poetry and prose, if it were not for Hunt's immediate reservation, "I do not mean to say that a poet can never show himself a poet in prose." His next step however is to praise verse and reject all arguments for a great prose poem, coming to the conclusion that "every poet is a versifier; every fine poet an excellent one."

It is in the remaining third of the essay, where he is discussing and illustrating this point, that Hunt is at his best. The real enthusiasm that he brought to the reading of poetry made him a good anthologist, and in his comments upon the lines he has selected, he is almost always able to communicate the pleasure he himself has found. When he speaks of the technical means by which a poet obtains an effect, he speaks with authority; it is only on matters of broad principle that Hunt is likely to be an unsure guide.

After the initial essay, indeed, Hunt's book must have given real pleasure to the contemporary reader. It may even be that the befuddlement produced by the initial essay was looked upon as part of the general reader's money's worth. This was the stodgy bolus of instruction, after which the genteel reader was free to enjoy the sweets of the anthology. For Hunt chooses interesting passages, and his comments are brief. There may be a little too much instruction, and the present-day editor would hardly dare to signalize lines and even individual words as especially happy strokes by placing them in italics. Hunt's raptures, his "loveliest's" and "exquisite's," may come too frequently, but he has chosen well.

Imagination and Fancy remained Hunt's only attempt at an extended critical work. If the Preface to *Lyrical Ballads*, appearing in early 1801, marks the beginning of a critical era, the essay "An Answer to the Question 'What is Poetry?'" marks at least a transition from the time when literary criticism could be looked upon as "the creation of profound, informing, and transforming ideas about literature and life"[12] to a time when the first impact of the minds that had created the ideas was lost and the ideas themselves were coarsened and devitalized to become the commonplaces of a new generation. Hunt's was an imitative rather than a truly creative mind, and, in criticism at least, his imitation was occasionally nearly a misrepresentation of the original.

[12] Mary M. Colum, *From These Roots* (New York, 1938), p. 6.

THOMAS DE QUINCEY

Douglas Grant

Thomas De Quincey liked anecdotes, for their own sake and for their use as telling illustrations, and he himself became the subject of many. How often the story of his setting fire to his hair at the candle flame, and tranquilly patting it out when advised by his affectionate daughters, experienced in his eccentricities, has been repeated to illustrate him in the role of the lovable, harmless, and semi-domesticated scholar. But more typical of his character were the stories current in Edinburgh during his later years, when he was residing in or near the city— of his habit of taking long nocturnal rambles among the streets or through the countryside, carrying a patent lamp to light him out of difficulties. Such an appearance among the neighboring hills, David Masson speculates, must have been "a trial to the nerves of the hardiest belated tramp, or other night-bird, with any dread of the supernatural. . . . " But, Masson continues—and he had had the advantage as a young man of knowing his subject— De Quincey himself "was perfectly fearless of night-bird or demon. Night was his natural element."[1]

One of the most remarkable of his nocturnal walks was made by De Quincey many years earlier than his life in Edinburgh, in 1807, after his first encounter with S. T. Coleridge—in itself one of his most famous anecdotes, and among the best known in English literature. Coming from Nether Stowey, where he had failed to meet Coleridge, after years of reverential anticipation, De Quincey

---

1 David Masson, *De Quincey* (London, 1881), p. 109.

at last ran him down in the streets of Bridgewater. Coleridge was standing under a gateway, deep in reverie, but De Quincey knew him at once by his eyes: " . . . His eyes were large, and soft in their expression; and it was from the peculiar appearance of haze or dreaminess which mixed with their light that I recognised my object."[2] The Coleridge of De Quincey's encounter was the Coleridge returned from Malta, with his life "to all appearance blighted,"[3] but his conversational powers were still unimpaired. He talked at De Quincey all evening, "and in the course of this performance he had delivered many most striking aphorisms, embalming more weight of truth, and separately more deserving to be themselves embalmed, than would easily be found in a month's course of select reading."[4] De Quincey listened; he was coldly introduced to Mrs. Coleridge; he was solemnly warned against an addiction to opium; and with his admiration and curiosity at last gratified, he set off in a state of high intellectual excitement to walk through the night to Bristol. Such a walk:

> The roads, though, in fact, a section of the great highway between seaports so turbulent as Bristol and Plymouth, were as quiet as garden-walks. Once only I passed through the expiring fires of a village fair or wake: that interruption excepted, through the whole stretch of forty miles from Bridgewater to the Hot-wells, I saw no living creature but a surly dog, who followed me for a mile along a

2 Thomas De Quincey, *Works* (2nd ed.; Edinburgh, 1863), II, 52.
3 *Ibid.,* p. 66.
4 *Ibid.,* p. 60.

park-wall, and a man, who was moving about in the half-way town of Cross. The turnpike-gates were all opened by a mechanical contrivance from a bedroom window; I seemed to myself in solitary possession of the whole sleeping country. The summer night was divinely calm; no sound, except once or twice the cry of a child as I was passing the windows of cottages, ever broke upon the utter silence; and all things conspired to throw back my thoughts upon that extraordinary man whom I had just quitted.[5]

The meeting with Coleridge had several consequences, the most immediate being De Quincey's anonymous and generous "loan" of three hundred pounds to Coleridge to set his mind free for the prosecution of a great work; and, of more lasting significance, his accompanying Mrs. Coleridge to the Lakes in October, 1807, and his meeting with the true "god of his idolatry," Wordsworth, with whom he had first corresponded as long ago as 1803 but whom he had never yet found the courage to face.

De Quincey's purpose in opening a correspondence with Wordsworth in 1803 was that he might have "the satisfaction of recollecting that I made one effort at least of obtaining your notice." The *Lyrical Ballads*, he went on, had "singly afforded" him infinitely more than "the whole aggregate of pleasure I have received from some eight or nine other poets that I have been able to find since the world began."[6] He prided himself on being one of the earliest of those initiated into the mystery of the new

---

[5] *Ibid.*, p. 67.

[6] Quoted in Horace Ainsworth Eaton, *Thomas De Quincey: A Biography* (New York, 1936), p. 95.

poetry, and when he ran away from Manchester Grammar School in 1802, the Lake District was the quarter to which he first turned; but the idea of presenting himself to Wordsworth under such circumstances was sufficient to send him in another direction. And "oftentimes on moonlight nights," during the terrible months in London that concluded this set of adventures, his "consolation was (if such it could be thought) to gaze from Oxford-street up every avenue in succession which pierces through the heart of Marylebone to the fields and the woods; and *that*, said I, travelling with my eyes up the long vistas which lay part in light and part in shade, '*that* is the road to the north, and therefore to [Grasmere], and if I had the wings of a dove, *that* way I would fly for comfort.'"[7] He asserted himself to be the only admirer of Wordsworth and Coleridge in Oxford, during his years at the university (1803–1808), and one of the two readers of Walter Savage Landor's *Gebir* in the whole of England, the other being Robert Southey.[8]

De Quincey may have exaggerated, though not unduly, the uniqueness of his response to the new poetry, but the influence of Wordsworth and Coleridge upon his life and opinions was fundamental. His meeting with Wordsworth in 1807 put them on an intimate footing, and he had arrived to stay with the family at their new house at Allan Bank by November of the following year. The Wordsworth children took him to their hearts, and

[7] *Confessions of an English Opium-Eater* (4th ed.; London, 1826), p. 83.

[8] See Eaton, *Thomas De Quincey*, pp. 113–14, and De Quincey, *Works*, VIII, 289.

Dorothy was especially fond of him. He was shortly able to make himself useful to Wordsworth himself by going to London to see the manuscript of the *Convention of Cintra* through the press in the spring of 1809; and though such a duty required someone far less discursive than De Quincey, the misunderstandings involved in the prolonged correspondence between London and Grasmere did not immediately disturb the harmony between the poet and his disciple. Upon his return to the Lakes in 1809, he moved into Dove Cottage, the Wordsworth's old home, under Dorothy's superintendence, and in those surroundings, which remarkably satisfied the vision that had haunted his nocturnal wanderings in London in 1802, he lived alone until his marriage to Margaret Simpson in 1817, an event that did nothing to improve relations with his by now critical neighbors, the Wordsworths.

When De Quincey first took up residence in Dove Cottage, Coleridge was living at Allan Bank and conducting *The Friend*. He was in the habit of seeing De Quincey almost daily and of borrowing from his extensive library, inscribing the books so borrowed with their owner's name and the title of "Esquire." The "Esquire" was later to cause De Quincey some embarrassment, since it might have appeared, he thought, to have been self-conferred; but it does indicate the gentlemanly state of leisured and scholarly retirement in which he seemed to the rest of the world to live. The books Coleridge borrowed were German books, and in this study, as in poetry, De Quincey was in advance of the taste of his age, German being still an unusual accomplishment. His other languages were chiefly classical; it goes without saying, in view of his grammar school education, that he was a good Latinist, but he prided himself especially upon his Greek and was inclined to boast of his prowess in it as a boy. He had a further interest besides metaphysics and literature, and, as a child of his time, politics—that of political economy; but it was not until 1818 that he read Ricardo's *Principles* and put it down after the first chapter with the exclamation, "Thou art the man!"[9]

We have, then, to imagine him during these years as engaged in such studies. The object of his meditations, in so far as they were directed, was the "slow and elaborate toil of constructing one single work, to which I had presumed to give the title of an unfinished work of Spinosa's—viz., '*De Emendatione Humani Intellectûs.*' "[10] Under no conceivable circumstances, could this vast projected work have been written, not least because De Quincey was by this time a confirmed opium eater, deeply experienced in its pains and pleasures, and addicts, as he remarked, "though good fellows upon the whole, never finish anything."[11]

The story of De Quincey and opium is one of the best known in English literature; whoever reads has read *The Confessions of an English Opium-Eater*, first published in Taylor and Hessey's famous *London Magazine* in 1821. He wrote it at a time when the utter eclipse of his private affairs forced him from sheer necessity to put his multifarious knowledge to some immediate use and embarked

[9] *Works*, I, 255.
[10] *Ibid.*, p. 254.
[11] *Ibid.*, XI, 108.

him on a career of journalism, in which he continued until his death. The *Confessions* was a sensation and earned him the sobriquet of "the Opium Eater."

Why the *Confessions* should have been such a success upon its publication as articles, and as the small book into which they were promptly collected, can be appreciated more clearly by studying it in its original form rather than in the revised and enlarged text that De Quincey prepared in 1856 for the edition of his collected works. The later version is naturally the one for general reading since it contains much additional matter, descriptive and auto-biographic, that could not be disregarded, and is itself the best example of his elaborate, mature style. But the very fact that the original had, in De Quincey's own words, been "written hastily," and had, therefore, perforce passed over "a succession of secondary incidents,"[12] meant that it had a comparative directness of presentation and simplicity of style that greatly helped it to make an immediate effect. The revision was, in a sense, addressed to those who were already accustomed to De Quincey's literary character—who were preconditioned to appreciate him.

The *Confessions* was originally more a narrative and less an exercise in "impassioned prose": a strange and distressing narrative, describing how a youth "of gentle blood" ran away from school, wandered into Wales, there to subsist for a time on "blackberries, hips, haws, etc.,"[13] made his way through uncertain stages to London, consorted with rogues and prostitutes, endured cold and

[12] *Ibid.*, I, xi.
[13] *Confessions*, p. 33.

hunger, and, upon his surprising translation to Oxford, was induced to take opium for the relief of toothache, taking it eventually over a course of years, in extraordinary quantities, with a startling effect upon his dreams. But a summary cannot explain the impact made by the *Confessions*, which lay not in the facts alone, but in the subtle but pronounced contrast between them and De Quincey's manner. How was the sordid realism of the London adventures, for example, to be reconciled with the fastidious language and sensibility of their description? That Ann, his companion of those months, should have been acknowledged without apology as a woman of the streets was disconcerting; but more disturbing still was her saintly translation in the dream climax to a visionary figure at the center of the religious mystery of the universe:

> The scene was an Oriental one; and there also it was Easter Sunday, and very early in the morning. And at a vast distance were visible, as a stain upon the horizon, the domes and cupolas of a great city—an image or faint abstraction, caught perhaps in childhood from some picture of Jerusalem. And not a bow-shot from me, upon a stone, and shaded by Judean palms, there sat a woman; and I looked; and it was—Ann! She fixed her eyes upon me earnestly; and I said to her at length: 'So then I have found you at last.' I waited: but she answered me not a word. Her face was the same as when I saw it last, and yet again how different! Seventeen years ago, when the lamp-light fell upon her face, as for the last time I kissed her lips (lips, Ann, that to me were not polluted), her eyes were streaming with tears: the tears were now wiped

away; she seemed more beautiful than she was at that time,
but in all other points the same, and not older. Her looks
were tranquil, but with unusual solemnity of expression;
and I now gazed upon her with some awe, but suddenly
her countenance grew dim, and, turning to the mountains,
I perceived vapours rolling between us; in a moment all
had vanished; thick darkness came on; and, in the twin-
kling of an eye, I was far away from mountains, and by
lamp-light in Oxford-street, walking again with Ann—
just as we walked seventeen years before, when we were
both children.[14]

Equally perturbing was his whole attitude toward opium-
eating. While seeming to deplore it, his impatience with
all earlier writers on the subject as pretenders; his arro-
gant reckoning up of the enormous amount of the drug
that he was at length able to consume safely; and his
apparently disingenuous admission that he used it at
one time for the sake of its pleasures, suggested that his
attitude toward it was either genuinely amoral, or adopted
for the purpose of discomfiting the reader. The tone of
his address is ironic and mocking—even intimidating—
from the moment of his description of his first purchase
of the drug:

The druggist, unconscious minister of celestial pleasures!
—as if in sympathy with the rainy Sunday, looked dull and
stupid, just as any mortal druggist might be expected to
look on a Sunday: and, when I asked for the tincture of
opium, he gave it to me as any other man might do: and
furthermore, out of my shilling, returned me what seemed

[14] *Ibid.,* pp. 177–78. The passage was hardly changed when *Confessions*
was revised.

to be real copper half-pence, taken out of a real wooden drawer. Nevertheless, in spite of such indications of humanity, he has ever since existed in my mind as the beatific vision of an immortal druggist, sent down to earth on a special mission to myself.[15]

And the equally famous passage in which he describes the scene of his later confirmed indulgence is troubled by the same undercurrent of incongruous facetiousness. Picture a remote cottage set in a winter landscape; a glowing fire and a family tea table: picture these, he advises, but paint, too, on the table, a decanter, into which

> you may put a quart of ruby-coloured laudanum: that, and a book of German metaphysics placed by its side, will sufficiently attest my being in the neighbourhood; but, as to myself,—there I demur.[16]

His attitude toward the drug was hard to determine. His great friend and fellow "Lakist," John Wilson—"Christopher North" of *Blackwood's*, who introduced him as a contributor to that periodical—used to call him a "hedonist" in "playful reproach";[17] and the same charge was brought against him much less playfully by Coleridge, who accused him, in De Quincey's own paraphrase, of having "resorted to opium in the abominable character of an adventurous voluptuary, angling in all streams for variety of pleasures."[18] De Quincey angrily rejected Cole-

15 *Ibid.*, p. 89.
16 *Ibid.*, p. 142.
17 *Works*, I, 251 n.
18 *Ibid.*, p. 3.

ridge's accusation; but while undoubtedly correct in insisting that he, too, had been driven to the drug by a physical pain at least equal to Coleridge's, he lacked Coleridge's moral inhibition in its use and deliberately exploited the increased power it conferred "of dealing with the shadowy and the dark."[19] Had he not done so we should not have had the *Confessions*.

The *Confessions* was a study in addiction, but, as De Quincey averred, the "pompous dreams and dream sceneries . . . were in reality the true objects—first and last—contemplated" in it.[20] He found that opium immeasurably heightened his apprehension of the world about him, and by timing his doses he could enjoy to the full his sense of the vastness and populousness of London, and of the raptures of music. But neither of these pleasures was caused by opium. He relished music as a child, and his first impression of London was as sharply remembered and as accurately detailed as those that form such an arresting part of the *Confessions*. "The great length of the streets in many quarters of London," he wrote in *Autobiographic Sketches*, with reference to his visit in 1800,

> . . . the continual opening of transient glimpses into other vistas equally far-stretching, going off at right angles to the one which you are traversing; and the murky atmosphere which, settling upon the remoter end of every long avenue, wraps its termination in gloom and uncertainty; all these are circumstances aiding that sense of vastness

[19] *Ibid.,* XI, III.
[20] *Ibid.,* I, 13.

and illimitable proportions which forever brood over the aspect of London in its interior.[21]

De Quincey is one of the earliest and the finest of the nineteenth-century poets of the metropolis.

But it is for its dream visions that the *Confessions* is famous. There are, as De Quincey said, "in fact, two classes of temperaments as to this terrific drug—those which are, and those which are not preconformed to its power."[22] His imagination was certainly "preconformed": his "dreaming tendencies" were, he elsewhere insisted, "constitutional, and not dependent upon laudanum."[23] The dreams are most fully developed in the 1856 edition, but the prose of the original exemplifies best the lesson De Quincey had learned from Wordsworth, that "it is in the highest degree unphilosophic to call language or diction 'the *dress* of thoughts'; and what was it then that he would substitute? Why this: he would call it 'the *incarnation* of thoughts.' Never, in one word, was so profound a truth conveyed."[24] De Quincey's style, at its best, is such an "incarnation"; but he also held, and expressed in another paper, the view that "style has an *absolute* value, like the product of any other exquisite art, quite distinct from the value of the subject about which it is employed, and irrelatively to the subject."[25] The revising and augmenting of the *Confessions* was under-

[21] *Ibid.*, XIV, 184.
[22] *Ibid.*, XI, 110.
[23] *Ibid.*, XIV, 6.
[24] *Ibid.*, X, 273.
[25] *Ibid.*, VIII, 93.

taken too much in the light of his second and lesser truth, and De Quincey himself was not always happy that he had not spoiled the original effect. "Sometimes, for instance," he wrote, "a heavy or too intricate arrangement of sentences may have defeated the tendency of what, under its natural presentation, would have been affecting."[26]

Today's taste would immediately endorse De Quincey's opinion; but however ready we may be to class as "artificial," and therefore to condemn, the great prose voluntaries (such as "The Daughter of Lebanon," on which De Quincey's fame with earlier readers greatly depended), we must also acknowledge and admire, if only as an exercise, the skill with which the music and manner of the seventeenth century are invoked and consciously rivalled. The harmonies of Milton are never out of mind, —the poet in whom only, De Quincey claimed, "first and last, is the power of the sublime revealed,"[27] augmented by the others of that "Pleiad," as he calls them: "Donne, Chillingworth, Sir Thomas Browne, Jeremy Taylor, Milton, South, Barrow . . . a constellation of seven golden stars, such as no literature can match in their own class."[28] The De Quincey of the *Confessions* would be as difficult to match in his.

When De Quincey wrote the general Preface to his collected works in 1856, he divided his writings into three classes, drawing upon his famous distinction between

26 *Ibid.*, I, xii-xiii.
27 *Ibid.*, VI, 319.
28 *Ibid.*, I, 54.

the literature of knowledge and the literature of power. The distinction—for which, on his own avowal, he was indebted to Wordsworth, but in which he had also been anticipated by Hazlitt[29]—is based essentially on the distinction drawn by the German transcendentalists between the reason and the understanding. "All that is literature," he had written in 1832, in the third of his "Letters to a Young Man whose Education has been neglected," "seeks to communicate power; all that is not literature, to communicate knowledge."[30]

Of all his works, De Quincey himself put into the category of literature only the *Confessions* and the *Suspiria de Profundis*. These were, he claimed, to the best of his knowledge, "modes of impassioned prose ranging under no precedents . . . in any literature."[31] But the rest of his works did not, therefore, fall entirely into the other, the inferior category. There existed a third, the literature of amusement—writing, he argued, that "may or may not happen occasionally to reach a higher station, at which the amusement passes into an impassioned interest."[32] And he cites as an example of this mode the *Autobiographic Sketches*.

De Quincey's theory of the two literatures is by now imbedded as a commonplace in English criticism, but we need not accept it in order to recognize that such works

[29] See M. H. Abrams, *The Mirror and the Lamp* (New York, 1958), pp. 142–43.
[30] *Works,* XIII, 55.
[31] *Ibid.,* I, xvii.
[32] *Ibid.,* p. x.

as the *Autobiographic Sketches* do share in the "impassioned interest" of the *Confessions*. Several of the "visionary" scenes in the *Sketches* are among his finest writing. The deaths of his sister Elizabeth and of his father, who had returned home from abroad to die, both occurring in the summer, a season when death is the "more profoundly affecting" because of "the tropical redundancy of life in summer, and the frozen sterilities of the grave,"[33] dominate the opening of the work and carry us immediately, through a "chorus of restless images, or of suggestive thoughts," [34] into the mysterious intellectual solitudes of his imagination. How little such passages were literary fabrications but were truly symbolic of his deepest nature is suggested by his dying words, which seem to have been addressed to the composite image of both Elizabeth and Ann: "As the waves of death rolled faster and faster over him, suddenly out of the abyss we saw him throw up his arms, which to the last retained their strength, and say distinctly, and as if in great surprise, 'Sister! sister! sister!' " [35]

We should also have to include in this third category, "The English Mail-Coach," which makes briefly the same progression as the *Confessions*, from the real to the visionary—from his early delight in coaching and in the experience of speed to a dream-fugue based on those recollections—and which illustrates yet again another of

[33] *Ibid.*, XIV, 12.
[34] *Ibid.*, p. 35.
[35] Quoted in Eaton, *Thomas De Quincey*, p. 506.

the creative principles underlying his finest work: "One part of the effect from the symbolic is dependent upon the great catholic principle of the *Idem in alio*. The symbol restores the theme, but under new combinations of form or colouring; gives back, but changes; restores, but idealizes."[36] The autobiographical writings are the best illustration of this principle, as they are of the concept of power, and the impersonal essays are usually memorable to the degree that they resemble them in intention and execution. The "Revolt of the Tartars," which concludes with the famous passage describing the arrival of the barbaric horde, maddened by fear and thirst, on the frontiers of China, is entirely successful for this reason; and there are occasional flights of similar quality elsewhere—the somber opening of "On War," for instance, and the description of Caesar's encounter with the ghost at the crossing of the Rubicon in the lengthy "Caesars," which else belongs to the literature of knowledge.

De Quincey's most famous exercise in criticism, "On the Knocking on the Gate in Macbeth," is intimately related to the *Confessions* and the other examples of the literature of power. Its acute perception is autobiographical to the extent that it sprang from his intense and typical interest in the subject of murder, and, specifically, in the horrific Williams murders of 1812, which he brilliantly described in an appendix to his clever and facetious essay "On Murder Considered as a Fine Art." The knocking on the door by the servant girl in the Williams case irresistibly reminded him of the not dissimilar moment

[36] *Works*, XIV, 27.

in *Macbeth;* and by relating the two, he was able to throw an uncannily brilliant light on the dramatic impact of the incident in the play and sharpen our appreciation of Shakespeare's imagination. The essay admirably supports in part his assertion that for an "absolute and philosophic criticism . . . we must have a good psychology."[37]

De Quincey's great reputation as a critic has been gained largely on the strength of this essay, but it is hardly deserved by the rest of his criticism; in fact, criticism bulks surprisingly small among his miscellaneous works. Even Wordsworth, whom he revered most after Milton, is discussed as a poet in only one paper, "On Wordsworth's Poetry," which is principally on *The Excursion*, and memorable rather for indicating how well De Quincey might have written on his subject had he taken the time, rather than for its own achievement—in spite of some acute asides, as, for instance, when he observes that the earlier short poems are "generally scintillating with gems of far profounder truth [than *The Excursion*]. I speak of that truth which strengths into solemnity an impression very feebly acknowledged previously, or truth which suddenly unveils a connection between objects hitherto regarded as irrelate and independent."[38] The essays on Shelley and Keats are, in his own words, "slight impromptus";[39] the one on Hazlitt, kinder and shrewder than one might have expected, given the political and religious antipathies of the two men; and the study of

[37] *Ibid.,* V, 234.
[38] *Ibid.,* V, 259.
[39] *Ibid.,* p. i.

159

Charles Lamb is biographical rather than critical, though he notices acutely that "his character lies" in his writings "dispersed in anagram."[40]

So much for De Quincey as a critic on his contemporaries. Among the earlier English poets, it is Pope who most attracts his attention. "I admire Pope in the very highest degree," he wrote, "but I admire him as a pyrotechnic artist for producing brilliant and evanescent effects out of elements that have hardly a moment's life within them."[41] He has nothing of effect to say about the novel, which is hardly surprising when his own most ambitious attempt in that form, *Klosterheim*, is so unconvincing. As his daughter remarked, he was out of sympathy with the novel since Mrs. Radcliffe: "He could make nothing of the modern novel with its pictures of real life."[42] His general critical papers, such as the one on "Style," are the most rewarding, and especially those on classical themes. He displays both his knowledge and his perception in the essay on the "Theory of Greek Tragedy"; and the one on "Antigone," prompted by a production of the tragedy in Edinburgh in 1845, is, however digressive, equally fine. But, in general, his best criticism is casual, and takes the form of asides that express succinctly the ideas that had struck an intellectual of exceptional sensibility, wide reading, and independence of mind. They occur everywhere among his writings, and were delivered by chance and scarcely ever developed—

[40] *Ibid.*, VIII, 112.
[41] Ibid., XII, p. 26
[42] Quoted in Eaton, *Thomas De Quincey,* p. 223 n.

such, for example, as his remark on Donne, whom he classified as a "rhetorical" rather than a "metaphysical" poet: "Few writers have shown a more extraordinary compass of powers than Donne; for he combined what no other man has ever done—the last sublimation of dialectical subtlety and address with the most impassioned majesty." [43]

The principal weakness of De Quincey's miscellaneous essays lies in his constitutional inability to set a straight course and come deliberately to a point. He tried to excuse himself by pleading the exigencies of journalism. "It is my misfortune," he once wrote, "to have been under the necessity too often of writing rapidly, and without opportunities for after-revision." [44] But anyone who follows his journalistic career in H. A. Eaton's admirable biography must be astonished that at times of the direst need he should have written the most elaborate and courteous letters of explanation and apology to his editors rather than have pursued the actual matter in hand. The real explanation of affairs was given by Coleridge in his illuminating comment on the quality of De Quincey's mind, that it was "anxious yet dilatory, confused over accuracy, and at once systemmatic and labyrinthine." [45]

De Quincey himself was perfectly aware of how he tended to wander from his subject, often spilling his irrelevant information into inflated footnotes. "This digression," he remarked mockingly on one occasion, "is

[43] *Works,* X, 39.
[44] *Ibid.,* XIII, 61.
[45] Quoted in Eaton, *Thomas De Quincey,* p. 159.

. . . I am afraid, too long by half; not strictly in proportion. But don't mind *that*. I'll make it all right, by being too short upon something else, at the next opportunity; and then nobody can complain."[46] His best general papers are, consequently, those whose subjects either warranted digressions, or provided a ready-made sequence for him to adhere to—such papers as his satirical, high-spirited, and thoroughly Tory account of Dr. Parr, "Dr. Samuel Parr; or, Whiggism in its Relations to Literature"; or his charmingly discursive and wisely urbane "Letters to a Young Man whose Education has been neglected." In the same category, his review of Richard Bentley's life allowed him scope for his delight in scholarship and character and held him to a chronology; and so did his essay on "The Last Days of Kant," where the need to work from a German original was an additional discipline. In fiction, he was only successful in the "Spanish Military Nun," where the picaresque form and the exotic setting of South America gave him all the license he required.

These papers display what is De Quincey's especial attraction as a miscellaneous essayist, his informal style. The attention of critics of English prose has been naturally turned to the great, impassioned, rhetorical flights of his prose-poems; but the bulk of his work had necessarily to be written at a far lower pitch, and he himself thus described his ordinary manner: " . . . My way of writing is rather to think aloud, and follow my own humours, than much to consider who is listening to me."[47] He

46 *Works,* IV, 268.
47 *Confessions,* p. 145.

aimed to achieve the effects of conversation, and his conversation, which was almost as monological as Coleridge's, was described by one of his young admirers in words that could be as well applied to his usual prose: "It was in fact an exquisite and transient emanation from the intellectual and moral nature of the man, enhanced in its effect by the rare beauty of his language, and the perfectly elegant construction of every phrase and sentence that he uttered."[48] The style can vary from elaborate contempt to judicious enthusiasm; from scorn for Parr to praise of Herodotus; but the diction is always natural and the rhythms harmonious. On Parr, he wrote:

> There was labour, indeed, and effort enough, preparation without end, and most tortuous circumgyration of periods; but from all this sonorous smithery of harsh words, dark and pompous, nothing adequate emerged—nothing commensurate, but simply a voluminous smoke . . . to me there seemed always to settle a smoke symbolical upon the whole sum of the Doctor's life.[49]

And on Herodotus, he is as euphonious as he is acute:

> Antiquities or mythology, martial institutions or pastoral, the secret motives to a falsehood which he exposes, or the hidden nature of some truth which he deciphers—all alike lay within the searching dissection of this astonishing intellect, the most powerful lens by far that has ever been brought to bear upon the mixed objects of a speculative traveller.[50]

[48] Quoted in Eaton, *Thomas De Quincey*, pp. 442–43.
[49] *Works*, V, 33.
[50] *Ibid.*, VIII, 164–65.

If "The Caesars" or "The Essenes" are still read, it is for the sake of the style.

But none of the miscellaneous essays, not even the best, will be read again with the popular attention that they once commanded; the exception being the studies of Coleridge, Wordsworth, and Southey, which are collected under the title of "Recollections of the Lakes and the Lake Poets." They most emphatically pass on occasion into "an impassioned interest." The "Recollections" will remain one of the most important sources not only for an understanding of several passages in the lives and characters of the poets themselves, but also of the type of sensibility they at first attracted and their effect upon it, in the person of De Quincey. Though he once inveighed against anecdotes, protesting that "*All* anecdotes . . . are false," and that "all dealers in anecdotes are tainted with mendacity,"[51]—a suspicion that has often fallen on De Quincey himself—he collected many of the most telling kind about his early friends and quondam idols, and introduced them into his narrative with considerable effect. A reader of the "Recollections" is unlikely to forget the spectacle of Coleridge, when he was housed in the offices of the *Courier* newspaper, shouting downstairs for his solitary attendant, Mrs. Brainbridge: " 'Mistress Brainbridge! I say, Mistress Brainbridge!' was the perpetual cry, until I expected to hear the Strand, and distant Fleet Street, take up the echo of 'Brainbridge!' "[52] Nor will he

[51] *Ibid.,* IV, 265.
[52] *Ibid.,* II, 98.

have failed to notice the sly relish with which De Quincey tells how undistinguished Wordsworth's appearance was from the back—so undistinguished that even Dorothy Wordsworth was once driven to exclaim in pained surprise, " 'Is it possible,—can that be William? How very mean he looks!' "[53] By the time he came to write these essays, he was to an extent disillusioned with his subjects —especially with Wordsworth—for, as he observed pathetically, "seldom, indeed, is your own silent retrospect of close personal connections with distinguished men altogether happy."[54] His memories may have become in consequence occasionally touched with malice, but the "Recollections" are still the truthful impressions of a remarkable and searching mind.

De Quincey acutely observed, in the course of discussing Lamb, that there is "in modern literature a whole class of writers, though not a large one, standing within the same category [as Lamb]; some marked originality of character in the writer becomes a co-efficient with what he says to a common result; you must sympathize with this *personality* in the author before you can appreciate the most significant parts of his views."[55] The observation could be applied to De Quincey himself to the extent that he has become identified with the character he first assumed in print, that of the Opium Eater. The identification is misleading if it suggests that his genius was the

[53] *Ibid.,* II, 140.
[54] *Ibid.,* V, 235.
[55] *Ibid.,* VIII, 111.

result of a drug, but luckily perceptive if it is taken to indicate that his reputation must finally depend upon the *Confessions* and those related writings, which fall together under the heading of "power." They are among the most original prose writings in English—the work of a solitary who, viewed symbolically, took "the very greatest delight in nocturnal walks."[56]

[56] *Ibid.*, II, 228.

HAZLITT ON THE
DISINTERESTED IMAGINATION

Kathleen Coburn

By a paradox, two of the works by which Hazlitt set most store are perhaps among the most completely forgotten in his twenty volumes; certainly they are not referred to either for authority on their subjects or in corroboration of Hazlitt's high standing as literary critic and supreme prose stylist in his kind. *On the Principles of Human Action* was his first completed work, published in 1805; the third and fourth volumes of his life of Napoleon Bonaparte appeared a few months before his death in December, 1830. The "metaphysician" he thought himself to be, the passionate social critic and moralist in him, the strenuous thinker, the close reasoner wearing himself and his friends out with arguments and anger, endearing though he may be for his idealism, is less to us now than the ardent playgoer, the reviewer, the journalist, the table-talker, the conversationist, the familiar essayist.

Yet can such a man, especially the critic, be so altogether wrong about his own work? Was it merely a wrong guess about the tastes of posterity? No work from such a mind can be valueless, and works such as these should reveal some of the mainsprings of his writing. A sympathetic look at them should discover at the very least some of the sources of that intensity and conflict which subsist in all our impressions of his temperament and interests, and in any survey of his work as a whole.

Numerous impressions come from his contemporaries who found in their own feelings toward the man and his works ambivalences difficult to stabilize. Lamb first of all, Charles Cowden Clarke at the close, Leigh Hunt,

Byron, Crabb Robinson, Wordsworth, Southey, Benjamin Haydon, Perry of the *Chronicle*—those who had no doubts about his powers, but reservations about his opinions, arguments, his personal life, his malice, even his venom, constitute a long list of eminent names. His logic and the durability of his pronouncements were often in question, but not his passionate love for literature, painting, and great men, nor his burning concern for the human condition. It is not necessary here to remind ourselves in detail of the attacks on and defenses of Hazlitt, but Coleridge's well-known description of him in a letter to Thomas Wedgwood in 1803 (Hazlitt was 25 years old) is apposite to our purpose:

> William Hazlitt is a thinking, observant, original man, of great power as a Painter of Character Portraits, & far more in the manner of the old Painters, than any living Artist, but the Object must be *before* him / he has no imaginative memory. So much for his Intellectuals.—His manners are to 99 in 100 singularly repulsive—: brow-hanging, shoe-contemplative, *strange* / —he is, I verily believe, kindly-natured—is very fond of, attentive to, & patient with, children / but he is jealous, gloomy, & of an irritable Pride—& addicted to women, as objects of sexual Indulgence. With all this, there is much good in him—he is disinterested, an enthusiastic Lover of the great men, who have been before us—he says things that are his own in a way of his own—& tho' from habitual Shyness & the Outside & bearskin at least of misanthropy, he is strangely confused & dark in his conversation & delivers himself of almost all his conceptions with a Forceps, yet he says more than any man, I ever knew, yourself only excepted,

that is his own in a way of his own—& oftentimes when
he has warmed his mind, & the synovial juice has come
out & spread over his joints, he will gallop for half an
hour together with real Eloquence. He sends well-headed
& well-feathered Thoughts straight forwards to the mark
with a Twang of the Bow-string.—If you could recom-
mend him, as a Portrait-painter, I should be glad. To be
your Companion he is, in my opinion, utterly unfit. His
own Health is fitful.—I have written, as I ought to do, to
you most freely imo ex corde / you know me, both head
& heart, & will make what deductions, your reason will
dictate to you.[1]

Coleridge's epitaph for Hazlitt (used also for various
other persons) has often been quoted.

Obit Saturday, Sept' 18, 1830.

W. H.   Eheu!

Beneath this Stone doth William Hazlitt lie.
Thankless for all, that God or Man could give,
He lived like one who never thought to die,
He died like one who dared not hope to live.

It is less known that when he wrote it in his notebook
(No. 47), he added, "With a sadness at heart, and an
earnest hope, grounded on his misanthropic strangeness
when I first knew him, in his 20 or 21st year, that a

1 *The Collected Letters of Samuel Taylor Coleridge,* ed. E. L. Griggs
(Oxford, 1956), II, 990–91.

something existed in his bodily organism that in the sight of the All-merciful lessened his responsibility—& the moral imputation of his acts & feelings."[2]

This was dated September 18, 1830, the day of Hazlitt's death. Four days later, in an unpublished fragment of *Table Talk*, H. N. Coleridge reports Coleridge as saying —and here Hazlitt the writer appears to be under discussion rather more than Hazlitt the man—"I certainly always did say there was something original and powerful about Hazlitt at a time that Poole and Wordsworth were quite incredulous about it. I still think there was by nature, but the Devil that was in him—the brutal savagery of mind—prevented any development." Have Coleridge's words any meaning?

Hazlitt's earliest attempts at literary articulation were made when he was fifteen years old, and just about to enter Hackney College. He went to the school in October, 1793, with a draft of a first section of an essay on "political rights and general jurisprudence," i.e., his *Project for a New Theory of Civil and Criminal Legislation.* This was the work, he said later, that first induced him to think for himself. It was a natural consequence of his Unitarian surroundings, his father's life and influence, the early Burke, and all the voices effective with the angry young men of the 1790's—Price, Priestley, Tom Paine, the young Mackintosh, Mary Wolstonecraft, and Godwin. The trials of Horne Tooke, Thelwall, and Holcroft, and the influence of yet greater minds, were still to come. Though completed late in life, the essay was never finished in its early

[2] British Museum, Add MS47542 fl^v (Notebook 47).

form. It had taken its origin, characteristically enough, in contention and rebellion; but it was more shallowly rooted in the climate of opinion around him and in his upbringing than his next precocious attempt which was more clearly directed by the deeper drives of his own temperament and genius.

An Essay on the Principles of Human Action: Being an Argument in favour of the Natural Disinterestedness of the Human Mind. To which are added Some Remarks on the Systems of Hartley and Helvetius was his first completed work published by J. Johnson of St. Paul's Churchyard. It was begun after what he later came to regard as a harmful period of over-intense study, in 1796, when he was about to abandon formal schooling and to dash all parental hopes of his becoming a Unitarian parson like his father; he toiled over it until 1805, when it was published anonymously. The full title suggests the ardent concern for his subject, the sincerity and conviction behind the idealism with which many a young writer hovers over the exact wording of his first title page. And for Hazlitt some of these words remained the important words, from this schoolboy essay to his four-volume *The Life of Napoleon Buonaparte* (1828–30): *principles, human action, argument, natural disinterestedness,*— these from first to last, in every sort of piece, on politics, poets, the theater, art exhibitions, economics, comic writers, contemporaries, were the liberating, and also at times, the limiting terms.

The Essay on the Principles of Human Action now reads as rather less a work of "originality" than it did to Coleridge, who so described it in a footnote to his second

Lay Sermon (1817). In defense of the "Natural Disinterestedness of the Human Mind," Hazlitt attacks the doctrines of self-love, enlightened or otherwise. In the background are Rousseau, the Bishop Butler of the *Sermons*, the Hume of the *Treatise*, Shaftesbury, Berkeley's *Essay on Vision*, and James Ussher's *Theory of the Human Mind*, not to mention Hartley and Helvetius.

The argument itself is trite, circular, ill-defined in its terms, wholly on a rationalist level, and without the psychological awarenesses already developing in the nineteenth century and, contrary to Coleridge, to deepen later in Hazlitt's own writings. The essay shows, however, that his first interest was ethical rather than psychological, and that he had not read much, if any, Kant. Broadly the argument is:

> If we admit that there is something in the very idea of good and evil, which naturally excites desire or aversion, which is in itself the proper motive of action, which compels the mind to pursue the one and to avoid the other by a true moral necessity, then it cannot be indifferent to me whether I believe that any being will be made happy or miserable in consequence of my actions, whether this be myself or another. I naturally desire & pursue my own good, in whatever this consists, simply from my having an idea of it sufficiently warm and vivid to excite in me an emotion of interest, or passion; and I love and pursue the good of others, of a relative, of a friend, of a family, a community, or of mankind for just the same reason.
> . . . In this sense self-love is in its origin a perfectly disinterested, or if I may say so, *impersonal* feeling. The

174

reason why a child first distinctly wills or pursues his own good is not because it is *his,* but because it is *good.*[3]

Or again:

I can only abstract myself from my present being and take an interest in my future being in the same sense and manner, in which I can *go out of myself* entirely and enter into the minds and feelings of others.[4]

Clearly the whole question of what "moral necessity" is, what is "natural" and what acquired, abnormal, individual, irrational, or in some sense *non*-necessary, is here begged. And to boot, as he says with youthful disingenuousness, "There is nothing in the foregoing theory which has any tendency to overturn the fundamental distinctions between truth and falsehood, or the common methods of determining what these are: all old boundaries and landmarks remain just where they were."[5] Philosophically speaking, this is our difficulty; they are just where they were. There is here indeed no new method for determining truth and falsehood, for distinguishing true benevolence and concealed self-interest. What he himself described as his "incorrigible attachment to a general proposition" had landed him in a position that could be used by the most ardent royalist defender of Louis XVI; he had described "a system which founds [he said in a letter to his father

[3] *The Works of William Hazlitt,* ed. P. P. Howe (London, 1930–34), I, 12. All references to Hazlitt's works are to this edition.
[4] *Works,* I, 39.
[5] *Ibid.,* I, 28.

in 1796] the propriety of virtue in its coincidence with the pursuit of private interest,"[6] yet all the while he hopes for and trusts to its general application by the forces sympathetic to the French Revolution.

When in 1807 he abridged Abraham Tucker's *Light of Nature* and wrote his Preface to the *Abridgement*, the theme of disinterestedness versus self-love was still preoccupying him and he was eager to improve some statements in the *Principles*, and especially to gainsay the notion that our motives are "blind mechanical impulses" derived only from associated feelings. He comes close to saying—but does not quite say it—that our motives are not all subconscious, but that a distinction can be made between involuntary (subconscious) and voluntary (conscious) ones. He singles out Tucker's essay on consciousness for special praise, and is enthusiastic about the chapters on morality, vanity, education, and death. He signs the *Abridgement* as by "The Author of An Essay on the Principles of Human Action," clearly the work by which he hopes and expects to be known.

That the subject was an enduring (and sometimes scarcely a not lightly endured) one all his life can be seen throughout the twenty volumes of his works, peppering with asides the literary criticism, or, for better and for worse, driving him to large moralistic themes.

It comes out with significant vividness in a late essay on "Self-Love and Benevolence," first printed in the *New*

[6] Quoted by P. P. Howe in *The Life of William Hazlitt* (London, 1949), p. 45.

Monthly Magazine for 1828. That essay, like the state of Hazlitt's mind, is in the form of a debate, though the more it changes the more we have the same thing. "The imagination or understanding is no less the enemy of our pleasure than of our interest. It will not let us be at ease till we have accomplished certain objects with which we ourselves have no concern but as melancholy truths." The negative aspects of his equation of self-interest and disinterestedness are more apparent, plainly, than they were twenty-five years before. But the same arguments about the nature of personal identity, the possibilities of awareness of the self in the future, and of other selves, goes on. And *imagination* has now in the discussion become a more important word.

> A. . . . The imagination on which you lay so much stress is a part of one's-self.
>
> H. I grant it: and for that very reason, self-love, or a principle tending exclusively to our own immediate gratification or future advantage, neither is nor can be the sole spring of action in the human mind. . . . Imagination is another name for an interest in things out of ourselves, which must naturally run counter to our own.[7]

The capacity for imagination depends entirely for Hazlitt on feeling. It is not "the whole soul" called "into activity," "a synthesizing and magical power," though it does discover "the hitherto unapprehended relation of things." "Those who have the largest hearts have the soundest

[7] *Works,* XX, 170.

understandings," he maintains in another late essay ("Belief, whether Voluntary?"); "and he is the truest philosopher who can forget himself."[8]

The most remarkable and unexpected defense of the equation of self-interest and public devotion, illustrating the hold the belief had on Hazlitt's faith and his need to preach it, occurs in his *Buonaparte*.[9] Hazlitt's Preface, suppressed in the original edition by his publishers, and later concealed by Hazlitt in the first chapter of his third volume, was, in 1828–30, naturally a defense for writing a biography of Bonaparte at all. He admires the man, whose first virtue was that as the "child and champion of the Revolution" he was a "thorn in the side of Kings." He was also a glorious figure, and succeeded by what Hazlitt valued above all things, "personal merit." And not least among his merits was the disinterested conception, in contrast with the Bourbon view that "millions were made for one," of one having been made for the millions —namely himself, saviour of liberty for the many. He was, Hazlitt argues, not entirely a free agent; "there was but one alternative between him and that slavery, which kills both the bodies and souls of men." France "required a military dictator to repress internal treachery and headstrong factions, and repel external force." It was George III and English interference with French liberty, "the

---

[8] *Ibid.*, p. 369

[9] *The Life of Napoleon Buonaparte* (*The Works of William Hazlitt*, Vols. XIII–XV). Subsequent references to this work will be made in the text.

pressure from without that caused the irregularities and conflicts within" (Chapter III). The horrors of the revolution arose out of the Coalition of Allied Powers against France, not the Coalition out of the horrors (Chapter V); and similarly, the rupture of the Peace of Amiens was owing to English snobbery and George III's insane refusal to treat with an "upstart." He argues that the French would never have prepared for invasion of England if England had minded her own business. Had she not seized French shipping in English ports, British subjects would not have been detained in France; and so on through the whole dire calendar of events. The initiative in wrongs is English, from motives of self-aggrandizement in the court and the ruling class (Chapter XXXII).

More interesting than the interpretations of episodes, undocumented as they are, the asides of a political and moral sort convey Hazlitt in his passionate quiddity. To choose but two: In the account of Corsica as Napoleon's background, in Chapter II, there is a diversionary attack on Malthusianism as "a paradox founded neither on facts, nor reasoning, but which has gained converts because it serves as a screen for the abuses of power and to shift the responsibility for a number of evils existing in the world from the shoulders of individuals on the order of Providence or on the mass of the people"; or in Chapter III, there is a five-page digression on a subject of early interest to Coleridge as well as Hazlitt, "the relative social efficacy of printing and organized religion." "The French Revolution might be described as a remote but inevitable result of the invention of the art of printing."

The incorrigible tendency he noticed in himself to generalize on the human situation often proceeds less out of social observation or abstract theorizing than out of immediate personal feeling. To quote the first chapter, "Friendship and good will are often neither conciliated by benefits nor effaced by injuries, but seem to depend on a certain congeniality of temper or original predilection of mind."[10] And there is something touching in the identification with his hero shown in his account of Napoleon's destruction of a youthful essay on "What are the sentiments most proper to be cultivated, in order to render men happy," because, says Hazlitt, "the style of the work was highly romantic and extravagant, abounding in sentiments of liberty suggested by the warmth of a fervid imagination, at a moment when youth and the rage of the times had inflamed his mind, but too exalted (according to his own account of the matter) ever to be put into practice."[11] So his hero had a smack of the writer about him, at least in youth. But it is the man of action who exemplifies the possibility of disinterestedness on a grand scale; not a man of letters, not an artist, qualifies for such a biography. With Bonaparte, private ambition and public beneficence, both written large, were the same thing, in spite of admitted personal weaknesses. And it is in the various subtle analyses of Bonaparte's weaknesses, for all his power, that Hazlitt shows himself at his paradoxical best.

[10] *Works,* XIII, 21.
[11] *Ibid.,* XIII, 12.

. . . Excess of strength always inclines to a degree of weakness. . . . He sometimes seemed disposed to mistake the number and extent of the means that he called into existence and the clearness and comprehension with which he arranged them . . . for the final success of his measure. . . . The very boldness and strength of will which are necessary to great actions must often defeat them; for a high spirit does not easily bend to circumstances or stoop to prudence. Whatever were his own resources, he could not always command the co-operation of others; yet his plans were on too large a scale not to require it. . . .

Neither can I think so poorly of my countrymen (with all my dissatisfaction with them) as to suppose that even if Buonaparte had made good his landing, it would have been all over with us. He might have levelled London with the dust, but he must have covered the face of the country with heaps and *tumuli* of the slain, before this mixed breed of Norman and Saxon blood would have submitted to a second Norman Conquest. Whatever may be my opinion of the wisdom of the people, or the honesty of their rulers, I never denied their courage or obstinacy. They do not give in the sooner in a contest for having provoked it.[12]

It is for such aphoristic pronouncements we can still extract pleasure from a work no longer read for its main contention, or its recounting of events. Hazlitt's passionate belief in Napoleon's disinterestedness scarcely concerns us now; his arrows in his asides sometimes, as Coleridge noticed, unerringly find their mark in the

12 *Ibid.,* XIV, 210.

wider panorama of the human condition and its hidden pulsations.

The older the nineteenth century got, and the more he talked with Lamb and Coleridge, the more Hazlitt must have recognized—and did recognize as his lectures on the Elizabethans show—the importance of imagination. In the essay already referred to on "Self-love and Benevolence," the imagination "or understanding" [*pace* Coleridge!] "is no less enemy of our pleasures than of our interest." It will not let us be at ease till we have accomplished certain objects with which we ourselves have no concern but as melancholy truths.

The ability to sublimate the self, go out of oneself, became, perhaps was from first to last, for Hazlitt a kind of touchstone. In *A View of the English Stage,* for instance, actors are judged by it. It was the source of the superiority of Kean's Sir Giles Overreach over Kemble's, or rather of the utter failure of the latter's interpretation. "Was this Sir Giles Overreach? . . . Mr. Kemble wanted the part to come to him, for he would not go out of his way to the part. . . . He is chiefly afraid of being contaminated by too close an identity with the character he represents. This is the greatest vice in an actor, who ought never to bilk his part." Kean, on the other hand, when he plays Hamlet, "by an art like that of the ventriloquist . . . throws his imagination out of himself, and makes every word appear to proceed from the very mouth of the person whose name he bears." [13]

[13] *Ibid.,* V, 185, 303.

It is the burden of Hazlitt's attacks on most of those whom he dislikes, either as men or in their works, that they do not lose sight of themselves in their goals and productions. "We do not think our author [Wordsworth] has any very cordial sympathy with Shakespear. How should he? Shakespear was the least of an egotist of any body in the world." [14] This from the portrait of Wordsworth in *The Spirit of the Age*. But when he steps aside from some other theme, goes out of his way to glower with disapproval, the murderous fit is really on him—as if he would smash an idol for its feet of clay. In *A View of the English Stage*, he strikes out at both Wordsworth and Southey without mentioning them by name, but by inference contrasting them with Milton:

> "*We* have no less respect for the memory of Milton as a patriot than as a poet. Whether he was a *true* patriot, we shall not enquire: he was at least a consistent one. He did not retract his defence of the people of England; he did not say that his sonnets to Vane or Cromwell were meant ironically; he was not appointed Poet-Laureate to a Court which he had reviled and insulted; he accepted neither place nor pension."

He goes on in this review of *Comus* (ducking to a footnote because, no doubt, the degree of irrelevancy was too great even for his wrath to countenance) to berate Wordsworth for omitting from his collected poems of 1815 "The Female Vagrant" and including the sonnet

[14] *Ibid.,* XI, 92.

183

addressed to George III.[15] Or again, in the *Lectures on the English Poets*, on Burns, Wordsworth is scored for "moralising on" "the scenes of many-coloured life," not, like Burns, "entering into them." [16]

One can go on indefinitely in the literary and dramatic as well as in the social and political criticism turning over examples, as central theme or as digression, as particulars or generalities. "The love of fame differs from mere vanity in this, that the one is immediate and personal, the other ideal and abstracted. . . . The love of nature is the first thing in the mind of the true poet: the admiration of himself the last. A man of genius cannot well be a cox-comb; for his mind is too full of other things to be much occupied with his own person." [17] The passage, in the lecture "On the Living Poets," continues grandly if repetitiously, dealing with Raphael, Titian, Shakespeare, Kean, Milton, Chaucer, before he descends to the for-gotten reputation-seekers of his own day, as well as to those to whom he does pay genuine tribute. But it is the vortex of all his whirling attacks on Wordsworth and Southey, whom chiefly he cannot resist attacking, that for all their preachments on the subject of imagination, they did not exercise it morally speaking. In his view, therefore, they are fair game, as hypocritical, self-centered, vain, and sycophantish.

There is nothing new in suggesting that Hazlitt's con-demnation of his enemies, especially of perhaps the only

[15] *Ibid.*, V, 233.
[16] *Ibid.*, p. 131.
[17] *Ibid.*, p. 144.

two he ever hated and who hated him, was essentially moral and not literary. What may not, perhaps, have been hitherto widely supported is the argument here that the moral condemnation takes its origin at the point where Hazlitt's need to believe in the possibility of disinterestedness, as a solution of conflict between private and altruistic feelings, is masked by a concept, a word almost, that is a sledge in his hand rather than a light on the subject. He had even less notion of "the egotistical sublime," than of "negative capability."

Hazlitt's criticism is often held to be a collection of more or less brilliant fragments. He himself said in the Preface to his *Characteristics*, "There is only one point in which I dare even allude to a comparison with Rochefoucault—*I have no theory to maintain*; and have endeavoured to set down each thought as it occurred to me, without bias or prejudice of any sort." [18] It was true. There is no consistent theory of life based on a scientific, or theological, or metaphysical, or any of the systematic disciplines (with the vices as well as the virtues of such freedom); yet the subjects of concern remain passionately the same, robustly and ingeniously tackled with spontaneous feeling, without benefit of Aristotle, Kant, or contemporary science.

De Quincey said he was ignorant:

> Hazlitt had read nothing. Unacquainted with Grecian philosophy, with Scholastic philosophy, and with the recomposition of these philosophies in the looms of Germany

[18] *Ibid.*, IX, 165.

during the last seventy and odd years, trusting merely to the untrained instincts of keen mother-wit—whence should Hazlitt have had the materials for great thinking? . . . The very reason for Hazlitt's defect in eloquence as a lecturer is sufficient also as a reason why he could not have been a comprehensive thinker. . . . Hazlitt was not eloquent, because he was discontinuous. No man can be eloquent whose thoughts are abrupt, insulated, capricious, and (to borrow an impressive word from Coleridge) non-sequacious. Eloquence resides not in separate or fractional ideas, but in the relations of manifold ideas, and in the mode of their evolution from each other. It is not indeed enough that the ideas should be many, and their relations coherent; the main condition lies in the *key* of the evolution, in the *law* of the succession. . . . Hazlitt's thoughts were of the same fractured and discontinuous order as his illustrative images—seldom or never self-diffusive; and *that* is a sufficient argument that he had never cultivated philosophic thinking.[19]

The statement as a whole is exaggerated and false, but it contains truth. The wide reading can be demonstrated; the thinking, whether philosophical or not, was undoubtedly fragmented by conflicts unresolved by philosophy, or science, or theology, and fostered even by an apparent need to believe, till the end of his life, in the possibility of the disinterestedness of men. That creed or compulsion dictated his career, his choice of masters and idols, of enemies and friends, of subjects and his attitude toward them. It is a source of his limitations and also of much

[19] "Charles Lamb's Works," *De Quincey's Works,* ed. David Masson (London, 1897), V, 231–32.

that draws us in admiration to his lectures. Lectures his works largely are. Coleridge is thought of as the great talker, the monologuist among nineteenth-century writers, but Hazlitt's work depends even more on the speaker-audience relation; the raised voice, the admonitory tone, the aside, changes of pace, the being carried along by a whirl of similitudes repeated with a difference. At his best, he is the eyewitness, reporting with powers of observation and acumen we envy but by which we are reduced to a knowledge secondhand. He does not invite us to intimacy, like Lamb, nor to self-exertion, like Coleridge. He tells us what to think, as convincingly as he knows how, and we may take it or leave it, according to our abilities. The style bears the scars (and enjoys the elevation) of the podium; it shows too, the urgent sense of a public, the willingness to pay the price of self-exposure, perhaps the preacher's need for it.

He reports himself as saying to Northcote, in 1830, the last year of his life, "the hardest lesson seems to be to look beyond ourselves." [20] The double irony is that he whose lifelong desire it was to believe in that possibility did not really manage to find it in the best imaginations of his own age, and did not achieve it himself, though he struggled with the conflict between the appearance and the reality with a candor that must move all who recognize it. There is a sense in which he did not need to achieve it. For by another irony, what we most value in Hazlitt are those inward recognitions by which he

[20] *Works,* XI, 212.

illuminates those experiences of literature and art that engage his real, and not an outward or theoretical, interest. Yet there is a continuity in his views, if only of irritation and conflict. The moralistic Puritan background of his idealism was inadequate, in any systematic sense, to the magnitude of the reconcilations demanded of the men of his age. Nor had Hazlitt the scientific knowledge—or even, perhaps it is not too much to say, the scientific curiosity—nor the philosophic range and training, to build a system. Theology had early been rejected. There remained the literary and moral engagement, dependent on a capacity for independent literary pleasure, and on an integrity unsurpassed for candor and rashness. When he is free to exercise and expand in his incomparable love and understanding for literature, and to unleash his wit, whether enthusiastic or malicious, he discharges the first and highest duties of a critic. He enhances our enjoyment of literature, and in the very act of so doing, creates a critical literature difficult to overestimate. When the gospel of disinterestedness becomes the whip for his prejudices and private conflicts, this youthful admonition to himself can reduce his work to a series of brilliant aphorisms or digressions, sometimes perverse or extreme, lacking largeness—lacking, in fact, disinterestedness. The question is, is it really any the worse for that, or is not its very absence sometimes the source of his critical strength?

POEMS OF
JOHN CLARE'S SANITY

Ian Jack

If Clare had never lived it would have been tempting to invent him, for he conforms remarkably to the romantic stereotype of The Poet. He was very poor: he was uneducated: he was a passionate lover: he described the scenes of external nature with extraordinary fidelity: and for many years of his life he was mad. The fact that his career as a published poet opened auspiciously does not destroy the general pattern, for his early poems were praised for the wrong reasons while his major poetry went largely without recognition. Imagine a poet who wins early success because of his humble origins; who comes to London and meets Hazlitt and Lamb and other contributors to Taylor and Hessey's brilliant *London Magazine;* and who goes on to produce a second collection of poems and then a third, in which he shows conclusively that he has many of the gifts of a distinguished poet. Imagine the reading public, attracted by the idea of a Peasant Poet, receiving the first volume with an enthusiasm that it hardly deserved and then swiftly losing interest, so that the high merit of the third collection escapes notice. Set these incidents in time so that the publication of the third collection takes place during the poetry slump that followed Byron's death. Imagine the poet producing a halfhearted final volume a few years later. Imagine him, "awkward at every art of rising in the world,"[1] impulsive and emotional, gradually losing his balance and drifting into madness. Imagine him living

[1] *The Athenæum,* No. 1964 (June 17, 1865), p. 806c.

on as an inmate of a lunatic asylum to which he was admitted "after years addicted to Poetical prosings," and surviving to the age of seventy, sometimes worse and sometimes better, scribbling poetry intermittently and subject to recurrent delusions that he was Byron, or Nelson, or a famous prize fighter. Imagine his death passing almost unnoticed in the heyday of Tennyson and Browning. What sequel would one expect? That some modern scholar (perhaps), moved by the story of his life, and fascinated by this example of the phenomenon of the mad poet, should explore the manuscripts and hold up the poems that they contain to the admiration of modern readers with the suggestion that here is a poet who deserves to be read again, and that it is above all the poems written during his madness that give him the right to be reconsidered.

All this is true of Clare. Just as his life had two periods, so his reputation has had two phases. He was famous in 1820: today he is famous again: but for different reasons. In 1820 he was praised as an example of the ability of Genius to dispense with education and write agreeable poetry about the life of a village. Today he is praised above all for his asylum lyrics.

There is no doubt that some of Clare's finest poems were written after he had been certified. Few English poems have the curious resonance of "I am: yet what I am" or "I lost the love of heaven above." Yet before Clare was a mad poet, he was a sane poet; and it has been overlooked that one of the four collections of verse that he himself published is greatly superior to the other three, and that his reputation may rest as securely on the poems contained in this volume as on anything that he wrote in the later years of his life. He should be remembered not only as the author of *Poems of John Clare's Madness* (to cite the title of Mr. Grigson's collection), but also as the author of *The Shepherd's Calendar*, a volume published by Taylor and Hessey in 1827 that should have added luster even to their distinguished imprint.

That he is not is partly due to Professor J. W. Tibble. Although Professor Tibble has done a great deal for Clare, neither in *John Clare: A Life*, which he and Anne Tibble published in 1932, nor in *John Clare: His Life and Poetry*, a later study that appeared in 1956, is there any clear acknowledgment of the superiority of *The Shepherd's Calendar*. In itself, this is a failure of critical discrimination. What is still more unfortunate is that the editorial procedure that Professor Tibble adopted in his *Poems of John Clare* [2] helped to obscure the superiority, and indeed the identity, of Clare's finest book. Although these two stout volumes contain some 860 or 870 poems, they by no means constitute a complete edition. "In the present edition are gathered together for the first time the bulk of the poems published during Clare's lifetime and after his death," Professor Tibble remarks in the Introduction. "To these 560 poems," he continues, "300 previously unpublished have been added." This is remarkably vague and ambiguous: readers who have jumped to the conclusion that what Professor Tibble gives us is the complete

---

[2] *The Poems of John Clare,* ed. J. W. Tibble (London 1935).

body of Clare's published work, together with selections from his unpublished poems, are hardly to be blamed. The fact that Professor Tibble elsewhere refers to his edition as Clare's *Collected Poems* [3] even suggests that he may have changed his plans at some point during the preparation of the edition. In any event, Professor Tibble omits a considerable number of the poems that Clare himself included in his four collections. There are two poems in *The Shepherd's Calendar* (for example) that are not to be found in his edition at all.[4]

It is equally regrettable that Professor Tibble's editorial procedure leads him to disperse the contents of Clare's greatest volume. Instead of giving us Clare's four collections exactly as they were published, with textual notes indicating revisions or first thoughts, he has attempted the impossible task of arranging the poems according to the order of composition. Fortunately (though inconsistently) he has left the twelve poems that give the volume its title in their calendar order (which was not the order of composition); but the remaining poems

[3] *The Prose of John Clare,* ed. J. W. and Anne Tibble (London, 1951), p. 107 n.

[4] As it happens, the limitations of Professor Tibble's edition are even more evident with some of Clare's other volumes. Of the seventy-three poems in *Poems Descriptive of Rural Life and Scenery,* for example, he omits sixteen. The prefaces and glossaries in the various volumes are also silently omitted. His text, which is based on the manuscripts, is highly unsatisfactory.

It is also worth noticing that Clare's letters contain numerous references to *The Literary Souvenir, The Anniversary,* and other annuals of the time. In December, 1825, we find him telling Hessey that he has "some other things scattered about in different periodicals" that he will mention to Taylor, since he considers them among the best poems that he has written (*Letters,* p. 179). Although I have made only a partial are rearranged in the following way (my page references are to the first volume of Professor Tibble's edition):

The Sorrows of Love; or, The Broken
Heart 462
Jockey and Jenny; or, The Progress
of Love . . . . omitted
The Rivals; A Pastoral 471
The Memory of Love; A Tale 483
Wanderings in June 341
To * * * * . . . . omitted
The Approach of Spring 348
To the Cowslip 352
The Dream 399
Life, Death, and Eternity 411
The Last of Autumn 353
Antiquity 412
Poesy 446

It will be noticed that Professor Tibble omits one of the group of "Village Stories" (which he renames "Village Tales"): that the second of the next four poems is

investigation of this, I find that seventeen poems by Clare occur in the twenty volumes of these annuals that are by me as I write. Two of these do not appear to be included in Professor Tibble's edition at all: a "Song" ("Love, practice not those wily ways") printed on the last page of *The Literary Souvenir,* ed. Alaric A. Watts, 1826; and a sonnet entitled "A Spring Morning" ("Spring cometh in, with all her hues and smells"), printed on page 416 of *Friendship's Offering,* 1829. With most of the others, the date given by Professor Tibble as that of first publication is later than that of the annual: as an extreme example, I may cite the sonnet "Autumn" ("Me it delights, in mellow Autumn tide"), which was printed in *The Amulet* for 1828, although Professor Tibble gives 1908 as the date of its first publication.

omitted: and that the remaining five poems are rearranged. It will be evident why I have gone back to the original editions in the following attempt to trace the first part of Clare's poetic career.

In the Introduction to *Poems Descriptive of Rural Life and Scenery*, published in 1820, John Taylor is quite explicit about the nature of the appeal he is making on Clare's behalf. "The following Poems," he writes, "will probably attract some notice by their intrinsic merit; but they are also entitled to attention from the circumstances under which they were written." It is often wiser to appeal to the heart of the English public than to its head, and there is little doubt that the success of the volume (which reached a fourth edition by 1821) owed more to the fact that it was the production of "a day-labourer in husbandry, who has had no advantages of education" than to the value of the poetry that it contained. The merit of the individual poems differs (indeed) greatly. The opening piece, "Helpstone," is precisely what Clare's readers must have been expecting:

> Hail, humble Helpstone! where thy vallies spread,
> And thy mean village lifts its lowly head;
> Unknown to grandeur, and unknown to fame;
> No minstrel boasting to advance thy name.

In "Helpstone" Clare is obviously indebted to Goldsmith. The second poem in the volume, "Address to a Lark, Singing in Winter," is as clearly the work of an admirer of

Burns. "The Fate of Amy" is a ballad of simple life of a kind that reminds us of the sort of inferior magazine verse that in some ways anticipated Wordsworth:

> Nor did she for the joys of youth
>   Forsake her mother's side,
> Who then by age and pain infirm'd,
>   On her for help relied.

In "Evening" we notice a striking and significant contrast between the tired "poetic diction" of the descriptive poetry of the later eighteenth century and Clare's instinct for the right word, however humdrum:

> Now grey-ey'd hazy Eve's begun
>   To shed her balmy dew,
> Insects no longer fear the sun,
>   But come in open view.
>
> Now buzzing, with unwelcome din,
>   The heedless beetle bangs
> Against the cow-boy's dinner tin,
>   That o'er his shoulder hangs.

As we read such a poem as "To an Insignificant Flower, Obscurely Blooming in a Lonely Wild," it is of Clare's patrons that we think, rather than of the poet himself. We know that certain passages had to be revised after the first edition because Lord Radstock complained that they contained "radical and ungrateful sentiments,"[5] and even in the poems as they first appeared we occasionally catch Clare glancing anxiously over his shoulder at the gentlemen in the next room. The fourth stanza of the "Elegy on the Ruins of Pickworth," for example, reads rather like a parody of *In Memoriam*, although the stanza used is different;

> Mysterious cause! still more mysterious plann'd,
>   (Although undoubtedly the will of Heaven:)
> To think what careless and unequal hand
>   Metes out each portion that to man is given.

Up to this point one reads through the volume with interest and a slightly condescending respect, as if wandering round an exhibition of week-end painters. And then one reaches "Noon," and there is no longer any question of making allowances:

> All how silent and how still,
> Nothing heard but yonder mill;
> While the dazzled eye surveys
> All around a liquid blaze;
> And amid the scorching gleams,
> If we earnest look, it seems
> As if crooked bits of glass
> Seem'd repeatedly to pass.

> .   .   .   .

[5] John and Anne Tibble, *John Clare: His Life and Poetry* (London, 1956), p. 72.

Not a twig is seen to shake,
Nor the smallest bent to quake;

. . . .

Bees are faint, and cease to hum,
Birds are overpower'd and dumb.
Rural voices all are mute,
Tuneless lie the pipe and flute:
Shepherds with their panting sheep,
In the swaliest corner creep,
And from the tormenting heat
All are wishing to retreat.
Huddled up in grass and flowers,
Mowers wait for cooler hours;
And the cow-boy seeks the sedge,
Ramping in the woodland hedge,
While his cattle o'er the vales
Scamper with uplifted tails.

Such a passage makes it evident that Taylor was fully justified in quoting in the Introduction, with reference to Clare, Wordsworth's complaint of the dearth of new images of external nature in English poetry between Milton and Thomson. It is the sort of verse that looks easy to write until one reflects how rare it is. In a general sense, no doubt, Clare is writing in the tradition of "L'Allegro" and "Il Penseroso," as developed in "Grongar Hill"; yet in poems of this sort he owes relatively little to any directly literary tradition, and much to direct observation—"if we earnest look." Whereas Milton looked at nature through the spectacles of books, Clare brought to his reading of books his own loving and minute knowledge of nature. The result, in each case, is fine descriptive poetry; but it is something different that is being described.

Since modern critics are apt to explain everything in terms of a poet's development, it is fortunate that we know enough about the dates of composition of the poems in the volume to see that Clare had neither steadily progressed nor steadily deteriorated. The contrast between good and bad is not that between early and late, or late and early. Taylor tells us that "Noon" was written before Clare was seventeen (although no doubt it was revised later); whereas "Summer Evening," another fine example of what Leigh Hunt would have called a "Now," was written not long before the publication of the volume. Some of the bad poems are early, some late. It was not a question of development, but of what Clare could and could not do.

There was also the question of what his readers wanted him to do. Since this was the Age of Genius, it is not surprising that the title poem of his next collection should have dealt with his own life. His readers were so interested in the phenomenon of the Peasant Poet that the least he could do was to provide them with a full self-portrait. Not that there is any reason to suppose that in this matter the taste of his readers conflicted with his own: it was the period of autobiography in verse, and Clare shared the sensibility of his age. The stream of autobiographical poems may be traced back (to go no further) to the publication of Book I of Beattie's *The Minstrel* in

1771, the year that also saw the appearance of Macken-
zie's *Man of Feeling*. Beattie was the first of many poets
to be obliged to admit, more or less unwillingly, that in
his hero he had "given only a picture of myself, as I
was in my younger days."[6] The concern of the poet was
to describe (usually in Spenserian stanzas or blank verse)
"The Growth of a Poetic Mind," the unusual pleasure
that he had taken as a boy in external nature and in
books, and his determination to devote himself to a life
of poetry or contemplation. Although he denied any obli-
gation to Beattie, it seems certain the Clare knew *The
Minstrel* before he wrote his own poem; but the resem-
blances between *The Village Minstrel* and "The Romance
of Youth," by John Hamilton Reynolds, the friend of
Keats, are hardly less remarkable. When Taylor drew
his attention to this poem, Clare wrote: "Its romantic
enough but there is good things in it how much the
outline is like mine one could hardly have concievd such
a similarity coud exist in different minds."[7] He particularly praises "that sombre sadness of memory" in the
poetry of Reynolds, adding that "that preaching to trees
to waterfalls & flowers is just what delights me." In fact,
"The Romance of Youth" is greatly superior to *The Village Minstrel,* but at the moment my point is that there is
a remarkable similarity between both poems and *The
Minstrel:*

[6] *The Poetical Works of James Beattie,* ed. Alexander Dyce (London,
1894), p. xxxvii.

[7] *The Letters of John Clare,* ed. J. W. and Anne Tibble, (London,
1951), p. 92.

Some say that from the cradle he was prone
To strange delights, unlike his simple kind;
That he did love to lie and be alone,
To creep from out his bed, when night was blind,
And listen at the window to the wind,
Singing in lofty elms;—to feed his eyes,
Which then were dark, and deep, and full of mind,
With sight of the wan moon in desert skies,
Till tears to those two orbs, like night stars would arise.

And oft he traced the uplands, to survey,
When o'er the sky advanced the kindling dawn,
The crimson cloud, blue main, and mountain grey,
And lake, dim-gleaming on the smoky lawn:
Far to the west the long long vale withdrawn,
Where twilight loves to linger for a while;
And now he faintly kens the bounding fawn,
And villager abroad at early toil.
But, lo! the Sun appears! and heaven, earth, ocean, smile.

O who can speak his joys when spring's young morn
From wood and pasture open'd on his view,
When tender green buds blush upon the thorn,
And the first primrose dips its leaves in dew:
Each varied charm how joy'd would he pursue,
Tempted to trace their beauties through the day;
Grey-girdled eve, and morn of rosy hue
Have both beheld him on his lonely way,
Far, far remote from boys, and their unpleasing play.

Although most readers will have guessed that one of these
stanzas comes from each of the three poems, not every-

one will be certain which comes from which, or even which was written half a century before the others.

The Village Minstrel is not a successful poem. The more directly Clare refers to himself, the more conventional he becomes:

> A more uncouthly lout was hardly seen
> Beneath the shroud of ignorance than he;
> The sport of all the village he has been,
> Who with his simple looks oft jested free;
> And gossips, gabbling o'er their cake and tea,
> Time after time did prophecies repeat,
> How half a ninny he was like to be,
> To go so soodling up and down the street,
> And shun the playing boys whene'er they chanc'd to meet.
>
> (XXXII)

As one would expect, the descriptive passages are much more interesting:

> And he would mark in July's rosy prime,
> Crossing the meadows, how a nameless fly
> Of scarlet plumage, punctual to its time,
> Perch'd on a flower would always meet his eye;
> And plain-drest butterfly of russet dye,
> As if awaken'd by the scythe's shrill sound,
> Soon as the bent with ripeness 'gan to dye,
> Was constant with him in each meadow-ground,
> Flirting the withering swath and unmown blossom round.
>
> (XXXVI)

Yet even in the better passages the Spenserian stanza does not give the impression of being the right meter: it is too elevated for Clare's immediate purposes, as if the Peasant Poet had dressed up in fine clothes to present himself to company.

It is a relief to turn to such a poem as "Holywell," in which the unpretentious economy of the description reminds us of "Noon" in the previous volume:

> While oft unhous'd from beds of ling
> The fluskering pheasant took to wing;
> And bobbing rabbits, wild and shy,
> Their white tails glancing on the eye,
> Just prick'd their long ears list'ning round,
> And sought their coverts under-ground.
> The heath was left, and then at will
> A road swept gently round the hill,
> From whose high crown, as soodling by,
> A distant prospect cheer'd my eye,
> Of closes green and fallows brown;
> And distant glimpse of cot and town;
> And steeple beck'ning on the sight,
> By morning sun-beams painted white;
> And darksome woods with shadings sweet,
> To make the landscape round complete;
> And distant waters glist'ning by,
> As if the ground were patch'd with sky.

As well as reminding us of Clare's debt to poetic tradition, such a passage makes it clear how appropriate it was that he counted the painters Rippingille, William Hilton, and Peter de Wint among his friends. Hilton was the painter of the finest of the portraits of Clare (first used as an engraving in *The Village Minstrel*), while De Wint—of whom we are told that he "was never so happy as when looking at nature"—painted the original of the engraving in *The Shepherd's Calendar*, a harvest scene that harmonizes perfectly with the poem it was designed to illustrate. In "Autumn" Clare is particularly successful in expressing the delight he feels as he contemplates the procession of the months:

> The summer-flower has run to seed,
>   And yellow is the woodland bough;
> And every leaf of bush and weed
>   Is tipt with autumn's pencil now.

One notices that he distinguishes the different sounds of the season with the particularity of a countryman: he mentions "The stubbles crackling with the heat,"

> And grunting noise of rambling hogs,
>   Where pattering acorns oddly drop;
> And noisy bark of shepherd's dogs,
>   The restless routs of sheep to stop;
>
> While distant thresher's swingle drops
>   With sharp and hollow-twanking raps;
> And, nigh at hand, the echoing chops
>   Of hardy hedger stopping gaps;

And sportsmen's trembling whistle-calls
　　That stay the swift retreating pack;
And cowboy's whoops, and squawking brawls,
　　To urge the straggling heifer back.

After such a passage, it is curious to see Clare swinging
back to the tired idiom of the Descriptive Muse, as he
does in the next stanza:

Autumn-time, thy scenes and shades
　　Are pleasing to the tasteful eye;
Though winter, when the thought pervades,
　　Creates an ague-shivering sigh.

There are other satisfactory poems in the collection:
"Rural Evening" is well managed, while "Cowper Green"
and "Solitude" are at least partly successful. The "Description of a Thunder-Storm" shows Clare's powers exercised on a theme closer to The Sublime than usual. Such
lines as these,

The very cattle gaze upon the gloom,
And seemly dread the threat'ned fate to come.
The little birds sit mute within the bush,
And nature's very breath is stopt and hush

read like a preliminary sketch for "The Dream," one of
the most remarkable poems in *The Shepherd's Calendar*.
"The Cross Roads" is an admirable example of the type

of tale also to be exemplified in Clare's next collection. But unfortunately a great many of the poems in *The Village Minstrel* are of little merit. "The Woodman," for example, a poem written in the manner of "The Cottar's Saturday Night" at the suggestion of the Rev. J. Knowles Holland, merely confirms the fact that Burns was a bad model for Clare. It contains one or two of the outstandingly inept lines that he was apt to write when he felt obliged to subscribe to the equity of the social system:

> The bed's warm comforts he must now forego;
> His family that oft till eight hath lain,
> Without his labour's wage could not do so,
> And glad to make them blest he shuffles through the snow.

The "Song of Praise," an avowed imitation of the 148th Psalm, is a conventional exercise in pious versifying, while the poem "To the Rural Muse" is equally devoid of interest. The collection of sonnets with which the second volume ends merely confirms the reader's impression that the poet is having difficulty in finding enough poems to fill his two volumes. He would have been well advised to wait a year or two until he had a larger body of poetry to choose from—or at least to have pruned the collection drastically, so that the good poems should not have been lost among the mediocre.

The Shepherd's Calendar was a very different matter. Since this volume contains by far the best of the poems that Clare published during his lifetime, a tentative account of its genesis may be of interest. As early as July, 1823, we find him writing to Taylor "respecting . . . the visionary Vol. which I wish to publish next winter," and informing him that he has obtained the consent of the Marquis of Exeter to receiving the dedication. His idea is that the volume should consist of "the pieces in the London with some new ones."[8] On the last day of the same month he wrote to Taylor again, mentioning that he had "talked to Hessey about the Poems publishing next winter," since he was dissatisfied with Taylor's opinion.[9] Taylor probably wanted Clare to take his time and produce a volume that would not be a mere collection of unconnected pieces. In his typescript dissertation on Clare, Mr. Robert Protherough has quoted from an unpublished letter written as early as January 21, 1820, in which Taylor "approved much" of an earlier project of Clare's for a poem "entitled a Week in a Village" and advised him to "divide the Week's Employments into the 7 Days, selecting such for each as might more particularly apply to that Day. . . . The Sports, & Amusements [he continued] should in like manner be apportioned out into the 7 Days;—and . . . one little appropriate Story should be involved in each Day's Description.—A different Metre might sometimes be introduced."[10] Another largely unpublished letter makes it clear that the title of *The*

[8] *Letters*, p. 149.
[9] *Ibid.*, pp. 150-51.
[10] British Museum MSS: Egerton 2245, d 1, 25v.

Shepherd's Calendar was Taylor's suggestion. "Talking
the other Day with Hessey," he wrote on August 1, 1823,
"it occurred to me that a good Title for another Work
would be—'The Shepherd's Calendar'—a Name which
Spenser took for a poem or rather Collection of Poems
of his.—It might be like his divided into Months, &
under each might be given a descriptive Poem & a Narrative Poem."[11] Later in the month Clare replied: "I am
very pleasd with the title of the new book but will the
subjects support it as it ought to be I fear T indulges too
great expectations on my new M.S.S. which he has not
yet seen . . . I shall be the worst off for a tale that most
assuredly ought to accompany every month I could soon
daub pictures anew [enough] for the Descriptions . . . I
will set seriously to work to make the thing as good as I
can."[12] A letter written on January 5, 1824, shows Clare
hard at work on the volume. "Any other things that you
may think woud make tales or any pictures you may
have noticd in the months of rural scenery woud be very
acceptable . . . Hessey proposd 'Harvest home' as a
'capital subject' but in my mind it is too barren of incident
unless it be connected with a story & I am looking over my
mind for one to suit it."[13]

The Monthly Magazine for the following month announced somewhat prematurely that "The New Shepherd's Calendar, by J. CLARE, may soon be expected,"

[11] British Museum MSS: Egerton 2246, d 2, 228r.
[12] *Letters*, p. 154.
[13] *Ibid.*, p. 156.

modifying this in March to the statement that Clare was "preparing a New Shepherd's Calendar."[14] During the succeeding year there seems to have been a good deal of discussion about the plan of the volume. A further stage of this is revealed by the following letter, which Taylor appears to have written early in June, 1825:

I have been reckoning the number of Lines and Pages which the present Plan of our new Volume gives us, and I find that we shall have about twice as much matter as we require—20 pages to each Month will make a Vol. of 240 pages, which alone is a large quantity—now the Cottage Evening alone extends to 19 entire pages,—and the Sorrows of Love make 16: to join both in one month will therefore swell the work out too much. What shall we do? —Shall we put only one piece of Poetry under each month? I don't know how we do otherwise.—In that Case we will keep the Cottage Evening for January, and instead of the verses descriptive of Febry we will insert the Valentine's Day alone, bringing The Sorrows of Love into March, and omitting the Descriptive Lines here again. What think you of this?—There is a Feeling of propriety in it I think, from the Character of the Stories,—but perhaps a very few Lines might be prefixed to each Story from the Descriptions—yet that would plunder them of their Sweets, and make a Sad Waste of your Labour.—Shall we insert the Descriptions only and leave the Tales for another Volume? "Clare's Cottage Stories" would not make a bad Title.—The most unlucky thing in such an arrangement would be the diminished Interest of the Descriptive Volume if the Stories were separated,—and the comparative sameness of the Pieces with some you have already published.

[14] Vol. LVII, pp. 74 and 162–63.

I am as you see at a Loss what to do, but let me have
your opinion, & in the meantime I will consider further of
the matter: perhaps between us we may hit on the best
plan.[15]

Clare replied on the nineteenth of June that in his view
neither the descriptive poems alone nor the narrative
poems alone would make a satisfactory book:

I think the best woud be to select the best parts of the
descriptive pieces as Introductions to the Months & then
let the story follow that was judged to be most suitable &
in some cases w[h]ere a Story was not to be had the
whole of the Descriptive Poem if good might be inserted
only such for instance as "Spring" for April which I consider one of my best Poems when it has undergone your
pruning ... W[h]ere the descriptive pieces contain nothing worth extracting then the Story may fill up the month
of itself but I woud always get a character of the month
w[h]ere I could—the insertion of the "Cottage Evening"
for January by itself & the "Valentine day" for February
without the descriptions are very good improvements as I
think for there is nothing in the Description for Feb[y] that
is worth preserving but I think the one for March is better
as there are images in it not noticd before by me or anyone else ... one of these is the description of the Droves
of Wild Geese that are very charact[er]istic companions
of this Month ... the "Sorrows of Love" will come in for
March very well.[16]

For various reasons, *The Shepherd's Calendar* did not
make its appearance until 1827. No full and accurate ac-

[15] British Museum MSS: Edgerton 2250, d 6, 329r and v.
[16] *Letters,* pp. 172–73.

count of the planning of the volume, or of the delays to which it was subject, will be possible until a good deal of further research has been done among Clare's manuscripts. Meanwhile, however, we may notice that when the book appeared the "Calendar" itself consisted of twelve descriptive poems alone, and was followed by four narrative poems (all dealing with love) under the general title of "Village Stories." Taylor's suggestion of using "The Cottage Evening" for January was adopted: "The Sorrows of Love" is printed among the "Village Stories": "Valentine's Day" appears to have been omitted: the descriptive poem with the fine passage about "the Droves of Wild Geese" is in fact the poem for March: the poem that Clare calls "Spring" may be the one used for April but is more probably "The Approach of Spring," which is printed among the nine miscellaneous poems at the end of the volume: while two of the other miscellaneous poems—"The Last of Autumn" and "Wanderings in June"—may at some time have formed part of the plan for the Calendar itself. It is clear that the volume as it finally appeared was the result of a great deal of anxious discussion. We must also notice that Clare was by now much more in the habit of revision than he had been earlier—schooled, no doubt, by Taylor's criticisms, which were often extremely shrewd. "I do assure you," Clare wrote to Taylor on March 18, 1826, "all that I write now undergoes severe discipline for if a first copy consists of a 100 lines its second corrections generally dwindle down to half the number & I heartily wish I had done so at first." "My judgment some years back," he wrote in another letter on September 3, 1827, "was as green as a child's in matters of taste & now I think it is ripened and good."[17]

The difference between *The Shepherd's Calendar* and Clare's earlier collections is apparent as soon as one opens the book. It contains no glossary and only a very brief Preface, written by the poet himself and expressing the hope that his "low station in life will not be set off as a foil against [his] verses." Whereas *The Village Minstrel* had contained a long poem and no fewer than sixty sonnets, as well as a great many miscellaneous poems apparently intended to demonstrate the sheer bulk of Clare's output, the emphasis is now on the types of poetry at which he excelled. There are no long poems (apart from the series of descriptive pieces forming the Calendar itself), and no sonnets.

The poems for the months are written in a variety of meters. "January," "May," "July," and "September" are in tetrameter couplets: "March," "June," "August," and "October" are in pentameter couplets: "November" is in Spenserian stanzas: while "February" and "December" are in eight-line stanzas of tetrameters rhyming *abab, cdcd*. "April" is in a purely lyrical meter in which alternate tetrameters and trimeters similarly cross-rhyme. This variety of rhythm helps to avoid the monotony that always threatens purely descriptive poetry, and distinguishes *The Shepherd's Calendar* sharply from *The Seasons* and Bloomfield's *Shepherd's Boy*. At times the contrasting meters have something of the dramatic effect

---

[17] *Ibid.*, pp. 187, 202.

of different movements in a musical composition. After the active movement of late harvesting in "September," for example—

> Harvest awakes the morning still,
> And toil's rude groups the valleys fill

—we find the slow-moving opening of "October"—

> Nature now spreads around, in dreary hue,
> A pall to cover all that summer knew

—followed by the somnolent Spenserian stanzas of "November." "February" (by way of contrast) begins *allegro vivace:*

> The snow has left the cottage-top;
>   The thatch-moss grows in brighter green;
> And eaves in quick succession drop,
>   Where grinning icicles have been.

The poems vary in length, as in meter. None has a narrative thread: the poet's method is rather to paint a series of pictures from a typical day in the season, so giving what he calls a "character" of the month. In two of the poems, "December" and "January," the scene is set indoors. "December" contains a description of a rural Christmas, with its morris dancers, its mistletoe, its was-

sail singer, and its distribution of toys. "January" is almost completely an evening poem—and we notice that
Clare has a laboring man's love of the evening:

> The shutter closed, the lamp alight,
> The faggot chopt and blazing bright—
> The shepherd now, from labour free,
> Dances his children on his knee;
> While, underneath his master's seat,
> The tired dog lies in slumbers sweet,
> Starting and whimpering in his sleep,
> Chasing still the straying sheep.

The description of bedtime stories by the fire could
hardly be bettered:

> The children steal away to-bed,
> And up the ladder softly tread;
> Scarce daring—from their fearful joys—
> To look behind or make a noise;
> Nor speak a word! but still as sleep
> They secret to their pillows creep,
> And whisper o'er, in terror's way,
> The prayers they dare no louder say.

In "February," where the scene moves out-of-doors,
Clare's method is particularly clear. We hear of the melt-
ing of the snow, of children hunting for pooty-shells and
prematurely building "their spring-time huts of sticks and
straw," and then, in succession, of a number of the key

figures in Clare's village—the milkmaid, the shepherd, sheep-dogs pursuing the sheep—

> While, following fast, a misty smoke
> Reeks from the moist grass as they run

—hedgehogs, pigs and horses, insects and birds. In "March" the list of *dramatis personae* grows longer: we hear of the woodman, the hedger, the ditcher, the sower, and the driving boy. The poem ends with a number of little pictures reminiscent of Bewick's woodcuts: girls stealing out to assignations: insects mistaking March for spring: a boy returning home at night terrified by superstitious stories: and an old woman leaving her spinning to pick a few flowers,

> In flower-pots on the window-board to stand,
> Where the old hour-glass spins its thread of sand.

To see how truly *The Shepherd's Calendar* is a countryman's poem one has only to glance at the references it contains to flowers, birds, and insects. In "March" (for example), we hear of primroses, hazel tassels, woodbine, sweetbriar, lad's-love and winter-aconite; while "May" and "June" are full of flowers—bluebells, lilies of the valley, corn-poppies,

Call'd "Head-achs", from their sickly smell;
And charlocks, yellow as the sun,
That o'er the May-fields quickly run,

"iron-weed", pimpernel ("the shepherd's weather-glass")
John-go-to-bed-at-noon, fumitory, and forget-me-nots.
From "January" onward, with its clouds of starnels,
rooks, crows, and jackdaws, the poem is equally full of
birds. In "March" no fewer than ten species of birds
are named, and we notice that they are brought in with
a naturalness and inevitability which show that for Clare
any account of village life without the birds that visit it
in the different seasons would be quite unthinkable. The
same is true of his treatment of insects. In the work of
most poets insects occur rarely, as images of disgust: to
Clare they are simply part of the life that he is describing. A stanza of "February" is devoted to gnats and to
the bemused flies

Along the sun-warm'd window-pane,
Like dreaming things that walk in sleep.

The last section of "March" is also devoted to "the insect-
world" and contains a description of how

Bees stroke their little legs across their wings.

In "May," we hear of crickets and bees, while "June" opens with a picture of insects dancing and "reeling in the sun," while

> The mottled spider, at eve's leisure, weaves
> His webs of silken lace on twigs and leaves.

Above all Clare emphasizes the contribution of the birds and insects to the chorus of country sounds. In September (we are reminded) the chirping of sparrows and the cooing of doves contribute to "morning's early sounds," while in October "the whirr of starling crowds" and the "quawking" of crows blend with the "feeble wail" of puddocks and the drone of beetles to compose the characteristic music of the time. No poet has ever captured the sound appropriate to each month more faithfully. In July,

> Scythes tinkle in each grassy dell,
> Where solitude was wont to dwell;
> And meadows, they are mad with noise
> Of laughing maids and shouting boys.

Early on a September morning, we hear

> [The] creaking noise of opening gate,
> And clanking pumps, where boys await
> With idle motion, to supply
> The thirst of cattle crowding nigh.

Throughout the poem this world of sounds helps to create the sense of purposeful busyness characteristic of Clare's description of the months. All the more impressive is the strange silence described in "July," the silence of noon on a midsummer day:

> Till noon burns with its blistering breath
> Around, and day dies still as death.
> The busy noise of man and brute
> Is on a sudden lost and mute;
> Even the brook that leaps along
> Seems weary of its bubbling song,
> And, so soft its waters creep,
> Tired silence sinks in sounder sleep.
> The cricket on its banks is dumb,
> The very flies forget to hum;
> And, save the waggon rocking round,
> The landscape sleeps without a sound.
> The breeze is stopt, the lazy bough
> Hath not a leaf that dances now;
> The tottergrass upon the hill,
> And spiders' threads, are standing still.

This passage may be compared with the lines in "August" that describe the village, deserted when its inhabitants have gone to help with the harvest:

> Silent the village grows,—wood-wandering dreams
> Seem not so lonely as its quiet seems;
> Doors are shut up as on a winter's day,

And not a child about them lies at play;
The dust that winnows 'neath the breeze's feet
Is all that stirs about the silent street.

In an appreciative notice of *The Shepherd's Calendar* in *The Monthly Review* for June, 1827, the writer objected to Clare's "use of vulgar epithets, or expressions."

> Such phrases as "dethering joys," "the tootling robin," "plopping gun," "quawking crows," "chimbled grass," and such words as "crimpling," "croodling," "crizzling," "pudgy," "poddle," "progg'd," are hardly allowable in familiar prose, and not at all in poetry, even though there may be such in common use. We are not disposed to be fastidious, especially in local descriptions; but we must protest against the introduction of these obnoxious sounds in metrical compositions. They do not occur so constantly in this, as in the former works of the author; but they are the progeny of a vicious taste, that cannot be too sparingly indulged in, nor too soon abandoned altogether.[18]

Since several reviewers had objected to such diction from the first, it is evident that Clare retained it deliberately; and there can be no doubt that his reason for doing so was his belief that it enabled him to gain a precision and fidelity of description otherwise unattainable. The note on "wood seers" in the Glossary to *The Village Minstrel* illustrates this:

> Insects that lie in little white knots of spittle on the backs of leaves and flowers. How they come I don't know, but

[18] Vol. V ("New and Improved Series"), p. 277.

they are always seen plentiful in moist weather, and are one of the shepherd's weather-glasses. When the head of the insect is seen turned upward, it is said to betoken fine weather; when downward, on the contrary, wet may be expected. I think they turn to grasshoppers, and am almost certain, for I have watched them minutely.

It is the same desire for accuracy that leads him to employ unusual words at the end of "February":

> The foddering-boy forgets his song,
> And silent goes with folded arms;
> And croodling shepherds bend along,
> Crouching to the whizzing storms.

We notice that he is particularly fond of unusual or provincial verbs:

> While, far above, the solitary crane
> Swings lonely to unfrozen dykes again,
> Cranking a jarring melancholy cry
> Through the wild journey of the cheerless sky.

This is the same power of observation that we see in these lines from "February":

> The flocks, as from a prison broke,
> Shake their wet fleeces in the sun,
> While, following fast, a misty smoke
> Reeks from the moist grass as they run,

or in the nostalgic recollection of children's games in May:

> The joys, the sports that come with Spring,—
> The twirling top, the marble ring,
> The jingling halfpence hustled up
> At pitch and toss, the eager stoop
> To pick up *heads*, the smuggled plays
> 'Neath hovels upon sabbath-days,—
> The sitting down, when school was o'er,
> Upon the threshold of the door,
> Picking from mallows, sport to please,
> Each crumpled seed he call'd a cheese
>
> .   .   .   .
>
> He sees, while rocking down the street
> With weary hands and crimpling feet,
> Young children at the self-same games,
> And hears the self-same boyish names.

At first sight, *The Seasons* and *The Farmer's Boy* might seem similar in their plan to *The Shepherd's Calendar*; but the briefest comparison will bring out differences more important than any similarities. *The Seasons* is the work of an eighteenth-century philosopher. Since he is interested in the universal causes of things, Thomson takes the whole world for his subject:

> . . . The shining Alps,
> And wavy Appenine, and Pyrenees,

are as much a part of his theme as the milder scenes of nature; and for the same reason he ranges freely backward and forward in time. Whereas Thomson has an intellectual belief in the ordering of things, one is tempted to say that Clare is himself a part of the natural order rendered articulate. His poem is as narrowly confined in time as it is in space, and while it is instinct with the happiness of living, he does not apostrophize Nature (as Thomson does) or cry

> How mighty, how majestic, are thy works!
> With what a pleasing dread they swell the soul!

One might apply to Clare what Nathan Drake wrote of Bloomfield, in comparison with Thomson: "The *Farmer's Boy* . . . [is] peculiarly and exclusively, throughout, *a pastoral Composition*; not like the Poem of *Thomson*, taking a wide excursion through all the phaenomena of the *Seasons*, but nearly limited to the rural *occupation* and business of the fields, the dairy, and the farm yard."[19] And certainly in one sense a comparison with Bloomfield is more apt than a comparison with Thomson; for Bloomfield had explicitly disowned Thomson's greater theme:

> No deeds of arms my humble lines rehearse,
> No *Alpine* wonders thunder through my verse,
> The roaring cataract, the snow-topt hill,
> Inspiring awe, till breath itself stands still:
> Nature's sublimer scenes ne'er charm'd mine eyes,
> Nor Science led me through the boundless skies.
>
> ("Spring," 7-12.)

[19] Robert Bloomfield, *The Farmer's Boy; A Rural Poem,* 3rd ed. (1800), pp. 113–14.

Bloomfield's example meant a good deal to Clare, and he thought so highly of him that at one time he was planning to write an account of his life and writings; yet what renders any comparison of *The Shepherd's Calendar* and *The Farmer's Boy* of little value is the immense inferiority of Bloomfield. He is much more given to moralizing than Clare, while his diction is often pestered by Latinisms reminiscent of the third-rate descriptive verse of the later eighteenth century, as when he writes of "The approv'd economy of crowded folds," or addresses Autumn in these words:

> O THOU, who bidst the vernal juices rise!
> Thou, on whose blasts autumnal foliage flies!

While there are tolerable passages in Bloomfield, there are others as inept as the farmer's question to Giles, the rather absurd hero of his poem:

> Left ye your bleating charge, when daylight fled,
> Near where the haystack lifts its snowy head?

Bloomfield and Clare exemplify the different effect that a common tradition may have on the work of a poet of talent and a poet of genius.

In the "Village Stories" Clare owes a greater debt to Crabbe than he owes to any previous poet in the *Calendar* itself. "I like the 'all ten' measure best of any now & shall keep on wi't," he had written in a letter that the

Tibbles date as having been written in 1820: "doubtless
they will next say in so doing I imitate Crabb." He went
on to acknowledge rather grudgingly that he liked touches
"here & there" in his *Tales*, but to complain of "a d---d
many affectations among them which seems to be the
favourite play of the parson poet ... I mean to have a good
race with him"—he continued—"& have consciet enough
to have little fears in breaking his wind."[20] Whereas critics
habitually contrast Crabbe's realism with the romanti-
cized Village of Goldsmith, Clare felt that Crabbe himself
knew little of the harsher realities of a laborer's life. In
his narrative poems, as in his descriptive, he wished to
give a more faithful account of country life than had
been given by any earlier poet. In "The Cross Roads; or,
The Haymaker's Story," the poem in *The Village Minstrel*
that anticipates the later narratives, Clare had as his
source a true story that he had often heard (as he told
Taylor) "from the simple old grannys of the village";[21]
and he added that he had tried to preserve "all their simplicity" by putting the story into the mouth of an old
woman. He uses the device of the storyteller admirably,
and the conclusion of this warning tale told to haymakers
during a storm is dexterously turned:

> . . . She pinch'd her box again,
> And ceas'd her tale, and listen'd to the rain,
> Which still as usual patter'd fast around,

[20] *Letters*, p. 75.
[21] *Ibid.*, p. 112.

And bow'd the bent-head loaded to the ground;
While larks, their naked nest by force forsook,
Prun'd their wet wings in bushes by the brook.

In "Jockey and Jenny; or, The Progress of Love," which Professor Tibble omits from his edition, the setting of the story is skilfully sketched in:

Where over many a stile, 'neath willows grey,
The winding footpath leaves the public way,
Free from the dusty din, and ceaseless chime
Of bustling waggons in the summer time,
Beyond a brook, where braving storms in vain
Two willows fell and still for brigs remain,
A humble cot, a sheltering hedge beside,
Lifts on the eye its solitary pride.
Its thatch, with houseleek flowers is yellow o'er,
Where flock the bees from hives against the door;
Trees, towering round it, hide returning rooks,
And twittering swallows seek its chimney nooks;
In peace, the sparrow chirps its joyous calls,
And takes the feather to its creviced walls;
Nor fail the harmless robin and the wren
To seek those sweet, secluded haunts again.

"The Rivals" and "The Memory of Love" both contain some excellent passages, but it is "The Sorrows of Love; or, The Broken Heart" that is Clare's finest achievement in this informal type of narrative. The old woman who tells the story begins by checking her facts in the family Bible,

> That lay with penny stories rustling near,
> And almanacks preserved for many a year.

Clare reminds us of the identity of his narrator by inserting passages in a simple, colloquial style into the body of the tale:

> I mark'd these things, for I was often by,
> And even thought the wedding-day was nigh:
> For, as a neighbour, oft by night and day
> I took my work in, to pass time away.

The conclusion is beautifully managed:

> She ceased her tale, and snuff'd the candle wick,
> Lifting it up from burning in the stick,
> Then laid her knitting down, and shook her head,
> And stoop'd to stir the fire, and talk of bed.

Of the remaining poems in the volume, "The Dream" is by far the most remarkable. In a letter written about the time of its publication in *The London Magazine*, Clare informed Taylor that it had been composed in a mood of depression due to his fear that *The Village Minstrel* had not been a success: "I feel somthing that tells me they don't go off like the others & I prevent that feeling as much as ever I can from damping my further exertions but I cannot help it doing so at some times—still I'm determind in the teeth of vexation to surmount dissapointment by unwearied struggles—under these feelings the dream was written & that is the reason of their explanation." [22] It also owed a good deal to the work of one of his fellow contributors to *The London Magazine:* in a note to a poem called "The Nightmare," first printed by the Tibbles (I, 404–8), Clare wrote: "I wish to acknowledge that whatsoever merit this and *The Dream* may be thought to possess they owe it in part to the *English Opium Eater*, as they were written after (though actual dreams) the perusal of that singular and interesting production." Clare must have read the *Confessions* as they originally appeared in *The London Magazine* for September and October 1821. In a later letter we find him asking whether Taylor and Hessey will give him a copy of the *Confessions* in book form, and mentioning that the Opium Eater "is a great favourite of mine."[23] Although several passages in "The Dream" are crudely written, the poem also contains some masterly passages. Elsewhere in this essay I have usually been able to find quotations which do not occur in the much briefer discussion of Clare in my book *English Literature 1815–1832*, but here I hope I may be allowed to quote the same passages. In his nightmare—in *The London Magazine* it was entitled

[22] *Ibid.,* pp. 131–32.
[23] *Ibid.,* p. 145.

IAN JACK

"Superstitions's Dream"—Clare has a vision of the end of the universe:

> When years, in drowsy thousands counted by,
> Are hung on minutes with their destiny:
> When Time in terror drops his draining glass,
> And all things mortal, like to shadows, pass,
> As 'neath approaching tempests sinks the sun—
> When Time shall leave Eternity begun.

In no other poem is Clare's imaginative power so clearly revealed:

> Winds urged them onward, like to restless ships;
> And Light dim faded in its last eclipse;
> And Agitation turn'd a straining eye;
> And Hope stood watching like a bird to fly.

Clare's vision of the end of the world is that of a countryman:

> The colour'd flower, the green of field and tree,
> What they had been, for ever ceas'd to be:
> Clouds, raining fire, scorch'd up the hissing dews;
> Grass shrivell'd brown in miserable hues;
> Leaves fell to ashes in the air's hot breath,
> And all awaited universal Death.

It is characteristic of him to remember the fate of the brute creation, the agonized death of the cattle, of dogs

and birds; and he gives us an extraordinary description
of the greatest horror of all, the death of light:

> The pallid moon hung fluttering on the sight,
> As startled bird whose wings are stretch'd for flight;
> And o'er the east a fearful light begun
> To show the sun rise—not the morning sun,
> But one in wild confusion, doom'd to rise
> And drop again in horror from the skies—
> To heaven's midway it reel'd, and changed to blood,
> Then dropp'd, and Light rush'd after like a flood.

The conclusion is perfect in its simplicity. As Clare awoke
from his dream in terror, he tells us,

> I heard the cock crow, and I blest the sound.

Clare considered "The Dream" "the best I've done yet"
and made a point of its being included in *The Shepherd's
Calendar*; yet he resolved not to attempt any more poems
of this sort for a while—and for a very revealing reason:
"I mustn't do no more terrible things yet they stir me up
to such a pitch that leaves a disrelish for my old accus-
tomd wanderings after nature."[24] The poem and the
comment form a somber epigraph to the lyrics that Clare
was to write during the later years of his life.

[24] *Ibid.*, pp. 131–32, 194.

A volume containing such poems as these should have established Clare more firmly than ever as one of the poets of his time; but although the writer in *The Monthly Review* considered that *The Shepherd's Calendar* was "likely to increase his fame," most of the other reviewers were unenthusiastic, and no second edition was ever called for. It is not really surprising. By 1827 the public was beginning to lose interest in the Peasant Poet—and it was beginning to lose interest in poetry. As early as 1820, Peacock had written, in a letter to Shelley:

> The truth, I am convinced, is, that there is no longer a poetical audience among the higher class of minds; that moral, political, and physical science have entirely withdrawn from poetry the attention of all whose attention is worth having; and that the poetical reading public [is] composed of the mere dregs of the intellectual community.

> (6 December, 1820)

If that had been an exaggeration when it was written, by 1827 it was beginning to be something like the truth. Within a few weeks of Byron's death we find a writer in *Blackwood's* remarking that nowadays "few write poetry ... and nobody at all reads it." [25] In 1826 Clare complained to Taylor that "the book trade is at a low ebb now," and on the twentieth of August the following year he wrote: "I feel very dissapointed at the bad sale of the new Poems but I cannot help it if the public will not read ryhmes

25 Vol. XV (June, 1824), p. 675*b*.

they must still read Colbourns Novels until they are weary ... —to tell them what they ought to think of Poetry would be as vain I fear as telling the blind to see[;] the age of Taste is in dotage & grown old in its youth."[26] This is not simply the grumbling of an unsuccessful poet. In 1830 we find John Taylor, perhaps the most enlightened publisher of verse in our history, describing himself as "no publisher of poetry now."[27] As Bulwer-Lytton was to write in his brilliantly perceptive *England and the English* in 1833, "Every time has its genius ... The genius of *this* time is wholly anti-poetic."[28] It was Clare's misfortune to publish his finest volume at a point when his countrymen were too deeply concerned with political and social reform to have any time to spare for poetry.[29]

[26] *Letters,* pp. 189, 200.

[27] Edmund Blunden, *Keats's Publisher* (London, 1936), p. 180.

[28] Book IV, chap. ii.

[29] Publication of this essay has been delayed, with the rest of the book. It was written in 1961, and at that time lent to Mr. Eric Robinson and Mr. Geoffrey Summerfield. They decided to publish a separate edition of *The Shepherd's Calendar,* and this appeared in 1964. It should be emphasized that their volume differs in two ways from that published in 1827: it contains only the title poem, without the "Village Stories, and Other Poems," which originally accompanied it; and it depends for its text on Clare's manuscripts. The account of Taylor in their Introduction seems to me unfair and misleading.

WAVERLEY AND
THE FAIR MAID OF PERTH

John Henry Raleigh

It is a commonplace of Scott criticism that his Scottish novels are his best, and that his early novels tend to be better than his later ones, such exceptions as *Quentin Durward* (1823) and *Redgauntlet* (1824), both rather late in his career, duly noted. Certainly the initial popular response to Scott would bear out this general judgment. *Waverley*, published in 1814, and the novels that followed so rapidly, enjoyed the first great mass market in publishing history. But after *Ivanhoe* (1819), itself a great success, Scott's sales began to fall off, and most of the rest of his novels were received with much less applause, and often with regret. However Scott tried to vary his formula or change his historical period, it was the combination of history and comedy, romance and tragedy, sentiment and realism, all shot through with Scottish archeology, anthropology, and sociology, that he had put together in varying ways in *Waverley, Guy Mannering, Rob Roy,* and the rest of the early Waverley series that remained the real Scott for his readers. The remainder of the novels were regarded, generally speaking, as a rather prolonged anticlimax. It has even been asserted that his very last attempts, in the late 1820's and early 30's, were the work of a man in his dotage, as *Count Robert of Paris* (1832) would seem to indicate. Added to these nineteenth-century gravamina is our own contemporary opinion that all of Scott's work, early and late, is hardly to be taken seriously, except for a kind of lip service in literary histories and college class rooms, for whose purposes, first, *The Heart of Midlothian* and, more recently, other Waverley novels have been accorded the tribute of paperback reprint. But the tribute is a dubious one at this date, and may only represent a response to the immense voracity of paperback publishers, insatiable for new titles. Whatever the reasons for the reprints, the work of Scott is not generally valued, and his later novels are double-deep down in obscurity—in common opinion, the senescence of a writer who was once thought to be major but is now labeled, perhaps definitively, as of the second rank.[1]

As a result, his last Scottish novel, *The Fair Maid of Perth* (1828), which is simultaneously his only Scottish novel with a medieval setting, his most unhackneyed and unconventional conception in the entire Waverley series, and one of the most interesting and original works he ever wrote, has been almost completely lost sight of; and, if one may be allowed an Irish bull, is even more unread than the earlier, more well-known, and more respected works. Furthermore,—leaving aside for a moment Scott

---

[1] I originally wrote this essay in the summer of 1961 for the present volume. Since that time, the rediscovery of Scott has gone on apace, as does the rediscovery of *The Fair Maid of Perth*. There is a discussion of it in Alexander Welch's excellent book, *The Hero of the Waverley Novels* (New Haven, Conn., 1963). More specifically, there is Francis R. Hart's *"The Fair Maid,* Manzoni's *Betrothed,* and the Grounds of Waverley Criticism," *Nineteenth-Century Fiction,* XVIII (September 1963), 103–18. This is a fine article, both perceptive and subtle. In contrast with mine, it is more analytical and less historical. I suggest the two be read as companion pieces. Both Mr. Welch and Mr. Hart have modified and extended my own views of *The Fair Maid.* But, understandably, I let my 1961 opinions stand as originally written.

the novelist—if Scott's work is still esteemed as a valid picture of Scottish history, the overall historical picture is again incomplete, and is certainly oversimplified, if *The Fair Maid of Perth* is left out of the total purview. Beyond that, *The Fair Maid* is both a companion piece and a pendant to *Waverley* itself, to which it bears a peculiarly intimate, intricate, and dialectical relationship. Both have the same setting, Perthshire, and share a distinct autobiographical element, but after that they diverge radically; in fact, the very character types, social and political conventions, and attitudes toward history that Scott first evolved in *Waverley* and upon which, with variations, he constructed novel after novel in the Waverley series, are, in *The Fair Maid of Perth*, his valedictory, either drastically modified or actually reversed. In a real sense, then, it can be said that *The Fair Maid of Perth* was his own "answer" to *Waverley*, and a kind of "retraction" of much of the subject matter of all the previous Scottish novels. Finally, *The Fair Maid* is his only historical novel that explores a historical "might-have-been." All the previous Scottish novels described what had actually happened in Scottish history. *The Fair Maid* likewise describes what had happened—none more grimly—but on one of its levels of meaning it is a pious and quite beautiful wish, a never-to-be-answered prayer, all expressed allegorically, for what Scott would have liked to have had happen in the long, intricate, glorious, and sad history of his native land.

I

Waverley and *The Fair Maid of Perth* share the kinship of a similar setting, a similar historical theme, and a large infusion of autobiographical material. Both take place in Perthshire, which for Scott was the most beautiful and varied county of Scotland. He had first visited the Perthshire highlands at the age of fifteen, and many years later, in the introduction to *The Fair Maid of Perth*, he described the experience:

> I recollect pulling up the reins without meaning to do so, and gazing on the scene before me as if I had been afraid it would shift like those in a theatre before I could distinctly observe its different parts, or convince myself that what I saw was real. Since that hour, and the period is now more than fifty years past, the recollection of that inimitable landscape has possessed the strongest influence over my mind, and retained its place as a memorable thing, when much that was influential on my own fortunes has fled from my recollection.

The archetypal movement in a Waverley novel is a journey, a retreat, an invasion, or an excursion, from the Lowlands to the Highlands, and in the first and last of the Scottish novels, this movement is into the Perthshire highlands.

To the geographical link between the two novels can be added a historical connection. Both novels are concerned with the Stuarts, *The Fair Maid* taking place in the reign of Robert III (1390–1406), when the long hereditary tragedy of the Stuarts began;[2] and *Waverley* dealing with the last, faint, pathetic exertion of Jacobitism, the abortive rebellion of 1745. Thus *Waverley* concludes a train of events that had its inception historically in *The Fair Maid of Perth*, and between them the two novels span what might be called the romance of Scotland; i.e., the story of the Stuarts. Again both novels deal with Catholicism: *The Fair Maid of Perth* with its death pangs as a national institution; and *Waverley* with its final extinction as a lingering national sentiment in eighteenth-century Scotland by the final and irrevocable crushing of the Jacobite power and the subsequent breakup of the clan system of the Highlands.

Finally, both novels are deeply autobiographical, although in quite different ways. On that first trip to Perthshire in 1786 or 1787, Scott had met a vigorous old man, Alexander Stewart, of Invernhyle, who was a genuine Highlander and Jacobite and had participated in the uprisings of 1715 and 1745. He was full of tales of alarms and battle, including a broadsword duel with Rob Roy. On the same trip, Scott got his first glimpse into the Highland way of life. Thus it might be said that this first excursion into the Perth highlands and the meeting with Alexander Stewart were the material cause, in Aristotle's sense, of the Waverley novels themselves. All this lore, as is obvious, was transferred almost directly to *Waverley* and to subsequent novels. Waverley himself is given one part of Scott's character—the sensitive, romantic, desul-

[2] For a sketch of the historical events relating to *The Fair Maid of Perth* and what Scott did with them, see Appendix, p. 263.

torily but widely read young man who, upon entering the Highlands, thinks he has walked into the past. This is Waverley on his introduction to the Highlands:

> Here he sat on the banks of an unknown lake, under the guidance of a wild native, whose language was unknown to him, on a visit to the den of some renowned outlaw, a second Robin Hood. . . .

The autobiographical element then in *Waverley* is evocative of youth, promise, beauty, and romance. The novel itself was written in a lighthearted and offhand fashion. *Waverley*, so the story goes, was begun in 1805, put aside, taken up again in 1813, finished in six weeks, and published in 1814. As it was an immediate success, and since Scott had just previously weathered a financial crisis, he took off happily on a vacation. He was very deprecatory about the book—"a small anonymous sort of novel"—and its feckless hero. He was off with a light heart on a new career that he did not take very seriously.

But the autobiographical element in *The Fair Maid of Perth* is at one and the same time more obscure and more complex, at once sad and defiant. He wrote it in 1827 and 1828: he was ruined financially; his wife was dead; old friends were dead, or dying, or ill; his own health was gone; he was laboring—vainly as it turned out, although he never knew this—to pay off completely a mountainous debt; and he had fears that his own mind was threatened as well. Thus his *Journal* for February 17, 1828:

A day of hard work. . . . yesterday, at dinner time, I was strangely haunted by what I would call a sense of preëxistence—videlicet a confused idea that nothing that passed was said for the first time—that the same topics had been discussed, and the same persons had stated the same opinions on the same subjects.

But most of the time his mood was either sad and regretful, or defiant and courageous. On November 7, 1827, just beginning *The Fair Maid*, he wrote in the *Journal*:

This is sad work. The very grave gives up its dead, and time rolls back thirty years to add to my perplexities. I don't care, I begin to grow overhardened, and, like a stag turning at bay, my naturally good temper grows fierce and dangerous.

This combination of sadness and defiance got into the novel in several ways.

The sadness is embodied in the character of Conachar, a young Highland chieftain who was Scott's most ambitious attempt at a complex character. In fact, in Scott's fictional world Conachar was a walking contradiction, a cowardly Highlander. And as Balzac (who declared no one but Scott would have risked such an attempt) saw, no simple coward either. Scott's conception was of a man who was constitutionally timid but whose emotions and feelings, such as jealousy, honor, and sense of duty, held him up until his moment of crisis. The crisis for Conachar comes at the climax of the novel in a battle between two Highland clans. Only Conachar, on one side, and Henry

Smith, the hero of the novel and a mighty warrior, on the other side, are left standing. They are old enemies and rivals for the hand of Catherine, the Fair Maid herself. (Smith is not a Highlander but a citizen of Perth, who joined the battle of the clans when one side proved short a man.) At this point, Conachar breaks and runs. In his *Journal* for December 3, 1827, Scott characterized him as "my brave coward or cowardly brave man." Behind this conception was an act of sorrowful expiation: the character of Conachar, who is treated very sympathetically and understandingly, is based upon Scott's brother Daniel. Daniel Scott was the black sheep of the Scott family. Dissipated, he got into a scrape with a woman in Edinburgh and was shipped off to Jamaica. There he played the coward in a Negro uprising. Shipped back to Scotland, he sank into his old ways and died. Scott refused to see him, declined to go to his funeral, and would not wear mourning for him. But the years shamed him for this adamantine behavior, and the character of Conachar, as he told Lockhart, was his attempted expiation.

At the same time, Scott's personal sadness tended to pass over into a historical sadness for Scotland itself. On December 28, 1827, well into *The Fair Maid* and very much aware of its gloomy subject matter, he complained in his *Journal:*

> . . . Surely we ought to close one volume at least of Scottish history at a point which leaves the kingdom triumphant and happy; and alas! where do our annals

present us with such an era excepting after Bannockburn?
[Strictly speaking, even this was not true, for what followed after Bruce's victory in 1314 was a period of terrible economic distress.]

All historians agree that the time of Robert III was one
of the most dreary and hopeless in all Scottish history.
Thus while, like *Waverley, The Fair Maid of Perth* has
a conventional happy ending as far as the plot is concerned, its historical import is unrelievedly somber. The
historical movement in *Waverley* is upward and consum-
matory, ending in the triumph of the orderly modern
world and the final extinction of the attractive but impossible Jacobites. In *The Fair Maid of Perth*, there is
no historical movement—only an anarchic and tragic
stasis.

The other personal feeling, the "stag at bay" attitude
that Scott professed at this time, is expressed in the novel
by an obsession with the ironies and complexities of courage and cowardice. In fact, one might say that this is
what the novel is really about. In *Waverley*, it is taken
for granted that English soldiers and Highland warriors
will possess, simply, courage, which they do. But *The
Fair Maid* is an anatomy of the ranges and the complexities of both bravery and cowardice, and characters
do not always act out their prescribed roles. Always characters are faced with danger or death, and they do not
always behave in expected ways. In the anatomy of cowardice, there is not only the extended and complex portrait of Conachar, but there are also three other and

briefer pictures, one comic and two serious. The comic aspect is embodied in a minor character, a bonnet-maker named Oliver Proudfute, who is the stock braggadocio of English drama and fiction. Serious but briefer variations on Conachar, with the outcome of the fatal ambiguity being resolved on the side of courage, are embodied in the characters of Albany, the king's brother, and Sir John Ramorny, one of the many villains in the novel. Albany is an old man who has the same moral constitution as Conachar: "But if he had not courage, he had wisdom to conceal and cloak over his want of that quality . . . ":

> He also had pride enough to supply, in extremity, the want of real valour, and command enough over his nerves to conceal their agitation.

Ramorny is still another variation on this same type. At the point of death, "endeavoring in vain to conceal his fear," his "spirit of pride" sustains him.

The gallery of courage is larger and even more varied. The epitome of courage is the dauntless armorer Henry Smith—"insouciance" is the word Scott uses to describe his bravery. It is almost irresistible not to think that Scott was associating himself with this character: the man who will do battle, no matter what the odds. Scott liked to think, anyway, that had he lived in another age, he would have been hanged; and his last sad years were, in fact, solaced by the universal admiration expressed at his own courage for carrying on. Courage is likewise described in other manners and guises in the novel.

There is the wild, instinctive, ferocious bravery of the Highlanders; the cool, efficient, haughty command of Douglas; and the dedicated idealism of Father Clement, a Carmelite, who denounces the corruptions of the church and is declared a heretic accordingly.

But the two most interesting and complex examples are embodied in Henbane Dwining, an apothecary, who illustrates the courage of evil, and Simon Glover, the father of the Fair Maid, who illustrates the courage of normality. Dwining, with Ramorny and others, is implicated in the murder of Rothsay, the king's oldest son. Douglas captures them all and pronounces drumhead justice upon them. Douglas' lieutenant, who is carrying out the sentence of hanging, is mystified by Dwining, the "poor dwindled dwarf," "who never wielded sword or bore armour," yet who had an air of "undaunted resolution." He laughs in the face of Douglas' lieutenant and calmly takes some poison he has secreted on himself, dying with "the contemptous sneer still on his countenance." But the longest extended discussion in the novel on the nature of courage is put into the mouth of Simon Glover. What Glover represents—at the opposite pole from Henry Smith—is normal, average courage: the courage of a responsible citizen who would never do battle of his own volition but who would never shirk it in the line of duty. He explains his psychology in an extended monologue to Conachar. Glover had once, as a citizen, to defend Perth against invading Englishmen. The gist of his explanation of his feeling on that day is that while he was at times afraid, he was sustained by patriotism and by the fellowship of comrades in battle. In the actual heat of the battle itself, he lost his fear:

> Other dangers I have had, which I have endeavored to avoid like a wise man, or, when they were irresistible, I have faced them like a true one. Upon other terms a man cannot live or hold up his head in Scotland.

Thus, whereas in *Waverley* courage is a simple matter, in *The Fair Maid of Perth* it is complex. Given the minimum of psychological analysis in a Scott novel, it is extraordinarily complex. For Scott had finally come to realize that neither cowardice nor bravery were simple matters, and *The Fair Maid* is his testimony to the discovery.

II

The autobiographical differences between *Waverley* and *The Fair Maid of Perth* point to other and more fundamental differences. In fact, the two novels are almost schematic in their antitheses: the one modern, the other medieval; the conflict of England and Scotland in the one, the internal conflicts of Scotland in the other; the one based on living memory, the other on medieval history; the one based on straight historical fact, the other on the juggling of historical facts and legends.

Even more important, however, are certain radical departures in *The Fair Maid of Perth* that set it off not only from *Waverley* but from all the other Scottish novels. The first and most obvious departure is a new and different attitude on Scott's part toward his own materials and conventions. That *The Fair Maid of Perth* was something new and different in subject matter and attitude was recognized by nineteenth-century Scotto-lators. For example, Albert Canning, who wrote two books about Scott and celebrated the genial, warm, good-natured aspect of the Waverley novels, and who admitted, gladly, that throughout his career as a historical novelist Scott had a tendency to make all his historical characters appear in the best light, did not quite know what to make of *The Fair Maid of Perth*. In his concluding remarks on it in his *Philosophy of the Waverley Novels* (1879), Canning said that although the novel had a nominally happy ending, it was so concerned with human crime and suffering and so unrelieved by wit and cheerfulness that its final and total effect was depressing, if powerful. The novel would hardly, I suppose, be called "powerful" today; but in the context of the Waverley novels, it is striking for the grimness of its subject matter and tone, and for the manner in which it reverses some of the basic conventions of the Waverley novels as a whole.

As for subject matter and tone, the first thing that strikes one is that, despite the fact that *The Fair Maid of Perth* is a medieval novel, there is little in it to glorify the Middle Ages or to exalt the feudal system; and the picture of the Catholic Church is unrelievedly black. There are touches of the romanticization of medievalism in the opening pages, as if, out of sheer habit, Scott fell into his accustomed ways before his "stag at bay" attitude prevailed. Thus when Catherine, the Fair Maid, is introduced, the reader is told that in that age of chivalry female beauty was much more admired and valued than it is now. There is, too, at this point, some of the familiar *ubi sunt* feeling with which Scott often enveloped the past, as when it is observed that a bottle of liquor then was equal to at least three quarts in "these degenerate days." But these are only opening touches, and we are soon out of the realm of fancy and into a reality composed of treachery, blood, violence, mutilation, murder, and corruption. King Robert says that the first words stammered by a Scotch infant are, "combat-blood-revenge." At the close of Shrovetide evening, in the first part of the novel, Scott reports, ironically, that all was rather quiet. The common people had toiled and struggled at football; the aristocracy had watched cock fights and listened to wanton music; and the citizens had gorged themselves on pan cakes fried in lard. There had been only a "few" casualties: three deaths and some broken limbs; but since these mishaps had happened to persons of little consequence, no one cared. So it goes, throughout the novel in which we either witness, or are told about, the "corruptions of the church," "the mismanagement of the nobles," and "the wild ignorance of the poor."

Scott's plot reflects this sense of evil and anarchy at the fictional level. At the beginning, Sir John Ramorny, Rothsay's evil accomplice, has had his right hand cut off by Henry Smith when Ramorny and others are attempting to abduct the fair Catherine for the pleasure of Rothsay. After the fray, the hand is discovered in the street and picked up by Oliver Proudfute. This bloody hand becomes a sort of emblem for the novel in its entirety. The whole story of Ramorny is grisly, cruel, and appalling. His physical sufferings, consequent to the amputation, are described in detail, as he is alternately cured physically and goaded emotionally by his diabolical physician, the evil apothecary Henbane Dwining. Ramorny is cruelly tormented, verbally, by Rothsay on the loss of his right hand—in those days and in his station, an incalculable loss. But neither is Rothsay spared, and at the end he is lingeringly starved to death by Ramorny and his accomplices. To maintain the grisly atmosphere that had first been generated by the bloody hand, Scott makes Rothsay's end appropriately ghastly. As he lies starving in a dungeon, Rothsay is confronted at night by Bonthron, one of Ramorny's menials.

> —"But look up—you were wont to love delicate fare— behold how I have catered to you." The wretch, with fiendish glee, unfolded a piece of raw-hide covering the bundle which he bore under his arm, and, passing the light to and fro before it, showed the unhappy prince a bull's head recently hewn from the trunk, and known in Scotland as the certain signal of death. He placed it at the feet of the bed, or rather lair, on which the Prince lay. "Be moderate in your food," he said; "it is like to be long ere thou get'st another meal."

The ending for all is appropriate: the prince dies; the grim Black Douglas arrives at the castle and pronounces doom on Ramorny, Bonthron, and Dwining, sentencing them all to be hung. Ramorny pleads that, as a knight, he should be decapitated rather than suffer the ignominy of hanging. By a dark logic he is granted his wish:

"The Douglas never alters his doom," said Balveny [Douglas' lieutenant]. "But thou shalt have all thy rights—Send the cook hither with a cleaver." The menial whom he called appeared at his summons. "What shakest thou for, fellow?" said Balveny; "here, strike me this man's gilt spurs from his heels with thy cleaver—And now, John Ramorny, thou art no longer a knight, but a knave—To the halter with him, provost-marshal! hang him betwixt his companions, and higher than them if it may be."

In this account of total evil happening to totally evil men, Scott managed to suggest a darker range of human experience than in any of his previous novels, albeit with the usual melodramatic overtones and phraseology.

If *The Fair Maid of Perth* is unusual for its picture of human cruelty, it is even more unusual for the freedom with which Scott broke out of most of the conventions that he had first formulated in *Waverley* some thirteen years before. Significantly, too, he stayed within the bounds of the one convention that over the years he had tried to break through. Right from the start of his career Scott had attempted to get away from the conventional heroine—sweet, demure, blameless, helpless—by creating heroines who were unconventional, independent, intelligent, voluble, satirical—in short, feminists before their time. Flora McIvor of *Waverley* was the first of this type and Diana Vernon of *Rob Roy* was the most famous. Julia Mannering of *Guy Mannering* is another example: romantic, satirical, vivacious, intelligent, a little haughty, a little bashful, shrewd, and with a vein of impudence.

When she meets Dominie Sampson, the ugly, slow-moving, goodhearted, comic eccentric of the novel, she exclaims: "I shall never forget the extraordinary countenance he has been pleased to show us." At this sally, her father—humorless, orderly, conventional—frowns. But Scott's heroines in this vein are never quite convincing (although they had their admirers in the nineteenth century) because the very anti-conventionality never quite becomes absorbed into genuine character sketches. And their fates are conventional enough: they marry the usually innocuous hero. In *The Fair Maid of Perth*, Scott gave up, as he had at times before, on the pre-Meredithian heroine and created Catherine Glover, dazzlingly beautiful, spotlessly pure, endlessly beloved, inveterately pursued by a variety of men, and, for all that, reasonably convincing for the very reason that she is a conventional heroine in a historical romance. She is given some substance by being lent a point of view, for in this bloody novel she is the voice of peace. And poignancy is added to her position because the man she loves and who loves her is the greatest warrior, and thus the greatest killer, of them all, Henry Smith.

But in most other aspects of the novel, Scott followed his own instincts rather than the dictates of publisher's wishes or public taste; especially was he independent in the handling of his braggadocio and coward, Oliver Proudfute. Proudfute is brisk, forward, corpulent, voluble, and likeable, one of the few comic figures in the novel, and the kind that in an earlier work would have been kept around to the end. But he is killed off fairly early in the proceedings. (He has borrowed Smith's dress to walk home at night, and is assassinated in the street by a professional murderer who has been hired to kill Smith.) Ballantyne, Scott's publisher, objected strongly to Scott's taking from the scene so early in the novel such a laughable, and saleable, character. But Scott was adamant, both on the grounds of expediency (he would have to cancel much subsequent writing if he revived Proudfute), and of artistic propriety (he remembered, painfully, what a mistake it was to bring back Athelstane from the dead at the end of *Ivanhoe*.) Thus he wrote to Ballantyne in 1828 (this quotation is from notes quoted by John Lockhart, who conjectures that they were written during the Christmas holidays of 1828):

> I cannot afford to be merciful to Master Oliver Proudfute, although I am heartily glad that there is any one of the personages involved sufficiently interesting to make you care whether he lives or dies. But it would cost my cancelling half a volume, and rather than do so, I would . . . kill the whole characters, the author, and the printer. Besides, *entre nous,* the resurrection of Athelstane was a botch. It struck me when I was reading *Ivanhoe* over the other day.

To his *Journal* on February 22, Scott confided:

> J. B. is outrageous about the death of Oliver Proudfute, one of the characters. But I have a humour to be cruel.
> "His business 'tis to die."

Where Scott genuinely transcended his own conventions was in the creation of his two chief male characters, Conachar and Henry Smith. If Conachar was, psychologically, Scott's expiation for his inhuman treatment of his brother Daniel, he was also a complete inversion of Scott's general picture of the Highlanders. For more than a decade, Scott had been pouring out armies of Highlanders whose prime characteristics were massive physiques and indomitable courage, the Falstaffian Rob Roy, and a few others, excepted. Generally speaking, all of Scott's Highlanders can be subsumed under a spectrum that at one end is occupied by the noble savage and at the other, by the rogue. But it was the image of the noble savage that loomed the largest in the world of Waverley, and in the mind of the reading public.

That some, though by no means all, of the Highlanders in Bonnie Prince Charlie's last vain attempt of 1745 proved cowardly or mercenary (at least one thought he was on a cattle-raid into England), and that those who were captured proved to be of poor physique and to average five feet four inches in height, did not matter. The whole English-reading world was now convinced by the power of Scott's myth, that the Highlanders were, or had been, populated by a race of superhumanly brave giants, simply comic or simply austere. Some of Scott's early descriptions of this imaginary breed had been awe-inspiring, and had even been elaborated into a kind of mystique. In *A Legend of Montrose*, there occurs the inevitable expedition into the Highlands by the Lowlanders. They come into the smoky hall and meet the legendary giants. Allan McAulay strides in: of "lofty stature," in "complete equipment," with "dark eyes and wild and enthusiastic features." He is half-mad, with a deep and stern voice, full of superstitions, gloomy, noble, severe, and unpredictable. He suddenly seizes upon an English officer, a big, strong man who is helpless in the grip of "the gigantic mountaineer." Suddenly, Allan flings him off and the officer crashes to the ground. Peace is made, and they enter the banquet hall:

> Behind every seat stood a gigantic Highlander, completely dressed and armed after the fashion of his country, holding in his right hand his drawn sword with the point turned downwards, and in the left a blazing torch made of the bogpine. This wood, found in the morasses, is so full of turpentine, that, when split and dried, it is frequently used in the Highlands instead of candles. The unexpected and somewhat startling apparition was seen by the red glare of torches, which displayed the wild features, unusual dress, and glittering arms of those who bore them, while the smoke, eddying up to the roof of the hall, over-canopied them with a volume of vapour.

Except for that prosaic (and inevitable) historical explanation about the bogpine, this is all standard Scott myth.

But his Highland chieftain of *The Fair Maid* is altered both in form and character. It is true that he is surrounded by the usual courageous giants, but Conachar himself is something new in Scott's Highland world. He is complex, cowardly, and rather conventionally handsome, like Scott's early Lowland heroes, such as Waverley himself. On being introduced, Conachar is described as "tall," "handsome," with "fine limbs," and "curled tresses"—in short, a certain femininity is suggested. He is hotheaded and precipitate, but his impulses arise from irritability rather than genuine valor. His last act, after his disgrace in the battle of the clans, is to fling himself over a precipice into a raging cataract; the body is never found. Two legends then evolved about him: one, that he swam safely to shore and remained in the wilderness as a hermit; the other, that he was snatched from death by fairies, to wander in the forest, wild and armed, but always fleeing when his courage was called on. These legends, said Scott, were founded on two "peculiar" points in his story:

> —his evincing timidity, and his committing suicide, both of them circumstances almost unexampled in the history of a mountain chief.

The conception of the character of the hero, Henry Smith, is as novel and original in its way as that of Conachar. In a letter of June 26, 1828, to a certain Mrs. Hughes, Scott wrote:

> I am glad you like Gow-Chron [Smith]. He is rather a favorite of my own. But Henry Wynd's *insouciance* always delighted me in the story. A man who plunged into such a mortal combat without knowing which side he was fighting on [the historical Smith did not know which side was which] must have been a queer fellow anyhow.

As Conachar is a physical and moral reversal of the Highland chieftain, Henry Smith is a physical and moral metamorphosis of the conventional Scott hero. Since the Waverley physiognomy and stature had been dealt out to

Conachar, Scott invented a new one for the smith. He is below the middle stature but remarkable for the breadth of his shoulders and the length and brawniness of his arms. He is bandy-legged and possessed of one of "the deepest voices that ever answered question." His forehead is "high and noble, but the lower part of the face was less happily formed." He has a large mouth, furnished with a set of "firm and beautiful teeth." Everything about him indicates personal health and muscular strength. He has a short thick beard, mustaches, thick curly black hair, and a resolute eye that in the presence of Catherine only turns bashful. In short, here is a picture of masculinity and potency. He is also favored by class. Not of the gentry —and he is careful not to overstep the line by dress or manner—he is a burgher of wealth and consideration. Furthermore, he is a member of the only constructive social group in the entire novel, for in this dark world the only ray of light emanates from the "burgher craft of the better class," to which Henry Smith, Simon Glover, and Catherine, all belong. This assertion of Lowland bourgeois superiority may seem to be merely the traditional Scott answer to all of Scotland's problems, namely, that in the last analysis, after one has expatiated on the bravery of the Highlanders, the color and romance of the past, the poetic appeal of the Stuarts, the power and attractiveness of the "auld ways," it was with Lowland Scotland and middle-class Scotland, with its bourgeois virtues of regular work and systematic saving, that the future of Scotland lay. This Scott truism certainly does apply, partially anyway, to *The Fair Maid*; but as with everything else in the novel, there are complications. In the first place, although a Lowland burgher and a crafts-man, Smith is in all ways a lone wolf, committed to nothing except his own notions of justice. He has fought —and every time he fights a man dies—with literally everyone: " 'To my shame and sin be it spoken, I have feuded with Highland and Lowland, English and Scot, Perth and Angus.' " Beyond that, he differs from the archetypal Scott hero in three important respects. First, he has nothing but contempt for the Highlanders who for him are objects of ridicule. Their inordinate pride, so admirable in earlier novels, is presented as being silly in his eyes. Further, he can beat them at their own game, for he is a stronger and greater warrior than they. Second, as a lone wolf, Smith is not subject to the con-flict of divided loyalties that plagued the earlier Scott heroes. The king, the nobility, the Highlanders, the burghers, the gentry, the poor—all are the same to him. His last action in the novel is to refuse the service of the haughty Douglas, and gain thereby his disapproval. "I fought for my own hand," he says to Douglas. Third, and most important, he is a killer on a vast scale. In all of the other Scottish novels, the hero, while often nominally involved in war, never actually kills anybody. Again *Waverley* is the *locus classicus*. In the village of Cairnvrecken in the Highlands, Waverley stops to have his horse shod by the local blacksmith. Waverley's ap-pearance arouses suspicion, and he is soon in trouble. Confronted by a mob, he draws a pistol. The blacksmith rushes at him, and in "self-defense" he discharges the pistol. The blacksmith falls, and Waverley feels a "thrill of horror." But after tantalizing the reader with the thought that Waverley may actually have killed somebody, Scott reports in the next chapter that the blacksmith was only grazed. Now, of course, the medieval setting of *The Fair Maid* had much to do with Henry Smith's freedom to kill. Waverley and the other earlier heroes, like Osbaldistane in *Rob Roy*, Latimer and Fairford in *Redgauntlet*, Morton in *Old Mortality*, and others, are conceived of as modern gentlemen, no matter what the historical date of the novel in which they appear. They come right out of the drawing rooms of nineteenth-century, middle-class England and Scotland. It is inconceivable that they should actually kill anybody. But Smith is a medieval man, and not a "gentleman," and is therefore free to commit carnage on a vast scale and yet be the "hero."

Still the irony remains that the gentle and peace-loving Fair Maid of Perth finally marries the sole survivor of, and the most active participant in, the bloody battle of Perth. This is not to mention his previous record and career. After the marriage of Catherine and Smith, however, it is promised that Smith will never again draw his sword, except in defense of Scotland. It is as if Rosa Bradwardine, "the sweet young thing" of *Waverley*, had finally not been married off, as she was, to the gentle and studious Waverley, but to the Richard the Lion Hearted of *The Betrothed*, *The Talisman*, and *Ivanhoe*.

What Scott did, then, with his last Scottish hero was to remove him from modern society and from all sense of divided loyalties and inner conflicts, with the accompanying sense of fatality that plagued all his earlier heroes. Though a Lowland burgher, he has the strength, courage, and fighting ability of a Highlander. Cheerful, industrious, humorous, he is one of the most likeable, besides being the least priggish, of Scott's heroes. He is, so to speak, released from the intricacies and toils of Scottish history and enjoys a freedom, including the freedom to kill in a wholesale fashion, that is given to no other hero in the whole Waverley series.

III

The second major way in which *The Fair Maid of Perth* diverges from *Waverley* and the other Scottish novels is in its allegorical evocation of a Scottish historical "might-have-been." Practically all the characters in the Waverley novels have a double dimension: they exist both as fictional individuals and as embodiments of some class or force or aspect of Scottish history. Their fictional destiny is thus a correlative of Scottish historical destiny, as, for example, the execution of MacIvor at the end of *Waverley* signifies the end of Jacobitism and the impending breakup of the clans—that is, what had actually happened in history after 1745. The collective fate of all the Waverley characters thus constitutes an allegory about Scottish history. Where *The Fair Maid of Perth* differs is that in this novel alone Scott has managed, without expressly violating any historical facts, to group and interrelate his characters in such a manner as to suggest, at the level of the historical allegory, a kind of national idyll or pastoral, a dream of what might have happened in Scottish history.

At the beginning of the novel, after the beauties of Perth have been described, the first character introduced is the Fair Maid herself. Of this most beautiful region in Scotland, she is the most beautiful inhabitant. She is, then, the spirit of the place, the living embodiment of its natural beauty and its natural peace; and is thus the soul, or the anima, or the spirit, of Scotland herself. She in turn is being wooed or pursued by a dissolute prince (Rothsay), a Highland chieftain (Conachar), a Lowland burgher-artisan-warrior (Smith), and the Catholic church (Father Clement, a friend and confidant, has urged her to take the veil). Since the novel takes place before Knox and the Reformation, these were, in fact, the very forces that were struggling against one another and fighting for the soul of Scotland in the late fourteenth century, and throughout succeeding centuries as well, with the addition of Presbyterianism later on. It is instructive to contrast the varying successes and failures of the respective suitors. Least successful are Rothsay and Father Clement, and in Scottish history these are precisely the two medieval forces that were first to disappear as genuine national powers: the monarchy and the Catholic church. Rothsay's dissolute character seems to signify the weakness of the Scottish throne, which only became strong when it became English. And Father Clement's hold on Catherine is as a man, not as a priest; and in the novel, he is declared a heretic by the church for denouncing its corruption. It is Catherine who secures his escape to the Highlands and who says of him:

> If you judge Father Clement by what you see him do and hear him say, you will think of him as the best and kindest man in the world, with a comfort for every man's grief, a counsel for every man's difficulty, the rich man's surest guide, and the poor man's best friend. But if you listen to what the Dominicans say of him, he is . . . a foul heretic, who ought by means of earthly flames be sent to those which burn eternally.

Again this indictment is historically accurate. The Catholic church never had any great power in Scotland, and at the time of which Scott writes it was notoriously dissolute and corrupt. One of the many reasons for Knox's incredibly complete success lay in the fact that he came into a vacuum.

Conachar, the Highlander, never has a real chance either, but at least what he stands for—Highland nobility—is taken with some degree of seriousness. Significantly, Catherine's chief endeavor with him is to woo him from his rude Highland ways. But the whole picture of the Highlands in *The Fair Maid* is practically devoid of serious meaning. Two bands of barbarians slaughter one another, and a chief flees in disgrace. Clearly, the future does not lie here. And the one other great power, the nobility, is spurned by Catherine's intended, the smith, when he refuses to serve Douglas.

For it is the Lowlander who conquers both in love and war. What Scott has done is to take Highland physical strength and bravery and join it to Lowland common sense, industry, and middle-class orientation. In turn, this paragon is joined by holy matrimony to the "soul" of Scotland, and settles down in the beauty of Perth to produce the Scotland of the future. As Scott had given way to his medieval romanticism at the beginning of the novel, he gave way at the end to his Scottish romanticism, besides providing the conventional happy ending. For we are told at the conclusion that ten months after the wedding a "gallant infant" was being rocked in the cradle to the tune of:

> Bold and True
> In bonnet blue

The names of the boy's sponsors are recorded, as "Ane Hie and Michty Lord, Archibald, Erl of Douglas, one Honorabil and gude Knicht, Schir Patrick Charteris of Kinfaums, and ane Gracious Princess, Marjory Dowaire of his Serene Highness David, umquhile Duke of Rothsay." Under such patronage a family rises fast; and several of the most respected houses in Scotland, but especially in Perthshire, and many individuals, distinguished both in art and arms, record with pride their descent from the *Gow-Chron* and the *Fair Maid of Perth*.

This, it seems, is what Scott's dream of Scotland would have been were it not for one thing—England. England is thus kept off the scene in *The Fair Maid*, although its hovering presence is mentioned near the end. But England or no, the tangled complexities and inner conflicts of Scottish history itself would probably never have allowed such a happy conclusion as that implied by the marriage of Scotland's beauty and peace as exemplified in the Fair Maid, and Scotland's bravery and strength, as personified in Smith, who would be henceforth warlike only in the face of a common enemy—having disposed of the monarchy, the church, the Highlanders, and the nobles, all in the name of the sanity, normality, and strength of the middle-class Lowlands. And thus there is the paradox that onto his grimmest Scottish novel, with its authentic history, Scott managed to graft, without any contradictions, a national idyl or pastoral. Taken in this sense, the idyllic part of *The Fair Maid of Perth* is Scott's *The Tempest*, the final act, the conclusion, the place where art and history part—where the wizard brings everything together, resolves all conflicts, and takes his leave.

APPENDIX

Since few modern readers are acquainted with *The Fair Maid of Perth*, much less the actual history of the period, and since a knowledge of this is necessary to my argument here (and to the contrast to *Waverley*), I append a sketch of the events and a brief summary of what Scott did with those events.

Robert III was old, lame (he had been kicked by a horse), kindly, sad, and ineffectual. The epitaph he composed for himself was: "Here lies the worst of kings and the saddest of men." Robert was actually controlled by his wily brother Albany. Robert's eldest son, Rothsay, was the first "bonnie Prince Charlie," imperious, capricious, dissolute, and engaged in a tug of war for power with his uncle Albany. Rothsay was betrothed to marry the daughter of the Earl of March but married instead, for a larger dowry, the daughter of the Earl of Douglas. Since marriage did not improve his ways, he succeeded in alienating not only the offended March, who went over to the English King, Henry IV, but his father-in-law, Douglas, as well.

The weak monarch and his scheming court could exercise no real control over the kingdom. The Highlands were in a continuous uproar, not the least of their troubles being the ravages of the King's half-brother the Earl of Bucham, or "The Wolf of Badenoch," who was sent there supposedly to control matters.

In 1396, a long-standing feud between two Highland clans threatened to convulse the mountain country north of Perth. It was finally decided that the two clans should battle it out, in the presence of the king, on the North Inch of Perth, a piece of level ground by the River Tay. This kind of barbarity seems out of keeping with the known character of Robert; presumably it was the nobles, principally Albany, who persuaded him that the best way to deal with the clans was to let them kill one another off. Accordingly, thirty champions were chosen from each side, and they met on the Inch of Perth in pitched battle (one tradition has it that the battle took place in the fall; another [Scott's], that it occurred in the spring, on Palm Sunday). Proven historical facts about this conflict are scanty, although legends are many. It does seem that one side was short one man. Tradition has it that one Henry of the Wynd, or Henry Smith, a Perth armorer, agreed to take the man's place, merely for joy of battle (and for a slight fee). Traditions vary as to how many were left after the slaughter. Eight or twelve were left alive on Smith's side, and only one (Scott's Conachar) on the other. There was peace in the Highlands for years.

In the Lowlands at this time, the chronicles are full of complaints from the poor who suffered unmercifully from marauding groups of disbanded soldiery. The ostensible shepherd of the flock, the Catholic church, was notoriously corrupt and universally hated. Foreign relations generally were peaceful, but in 1400 Henry IV of England conducted an invasion up to the gates of Edinburg. He did no pillaging or burning, and finally retired.

Douglas and Albany agreed on only one thing: the necessity for removing Rothsay from power. They persuaded the king that his son needed to be put under restraint. Accordingly, the prince was captured by one Sir John Ramorny and committed to prison in the Castle of Falkland in Fifeshire. The queen, who was the last powerful supporter of Rothsay, had died in 1401. Rothsay died, under mysterious circumstances, in early 1402. Rumor had it that he was starved to death, and his body was found in a horribly emaciated condition (perhaps dysentery). There was a public outcry against Albany and Douglas. In May, 1402, they were examined by Parliament and were acquitted, but the rumors never ceased.

The remainder of Robert's life was equally oppressive. On September 14, 1402, the English defeated the Scotch at Hamildon Hill, the Earl of Douglas being taken prisoner. The final blow for Robert came in 1406. His only surviving son, James—later James I of Scotland—who was being sent to France for his education, was captured and taken to London. Robert died shortly thereafter or at about the same time.

Such then were the facts and legends at Scott's disposal.

What Scott did was to increase the impact of all these dire events by telescoping them. Historically, the battle of the clans had taken place in 1396; Rothsay died in 1402; and James I was abducted in 1406. Scott made Rothsay's death immediately precede the battle of the clans and implies, anyway, that James's abduction occurred shortly thereafter. Thus the poor king suffers a rapid succession of blows. At the same time, the invasion of Henry IV is left out—although one is hinted at near the end of the novel—in order to make all the troubles internal. Scott also invented a whole set of imaginary characters and with considerable skill fitted them into the authentic history.

TRENDS IN MINOR ROMANTIC NARRATIVE POETRY

Karl Kroeber

Many romantic poems are stories, and most Romantic lyrics, dramas, and didactic works are influenced by narrative conceptions and techniques. The Romantics' ideal poet is no mere storyteller, but his function and character cannot be disassociated from the function and character of the popular teller of tales. The sophisticated complexity of Romantic poetry is often rooted in the simplicity of story; the Romantic style is to some degree a narrative style.

Romantic narrative developed from the ballad. Wordsworth, Scott, and Coleridge were interested in ballads in their youth. The interest was a heritage of mid-eighteenth-century traditions of literary antiquarianism and primitivism. Each of the poets turned to more complex narrative, but not before their diverse talents had lifted the literary ballad from the sloughs of archaism and established it as a respectable form in the repertoire of the sophisticated lyricist.

Coleridge and Wordsworth absorbed the ballad into a more complex and lyrical kind of verse story.[1] The process of absorption is revealed by Coleridge's successive emendations to *The Rime of the Ancient Mariner*. In the original poem, an ostentatiously balladic story serves to present "literal" magic, supernatural events, interesting

[1] Blake, too, moved from conventional ballad imitations, *Fair Elenor* and *Gwin, King of Norway* through the ballad-related *Songs of Innocence* and *Songs of Experience* to, finally, complexly symbolic stories which nevertheless retain significant balladic characteristics—for example, *The Mental Traveller, The Crystal Cabinet*. These poems also illustrate the Romantic fondness for a "circular" narrative form (adumbrated in some popular ballads) suited to a secular and experiential mythopoeism.

because they are sensational. Revisions, culminating in the addition of the prose gloss, de-emphasize the balladic story *per se*. In the final version, narrative symbolically orders the complex interpenetration of the natural with the more-than-natural, and makes possible a meaningful interplay between past and present, prose and verse, ordinary and suprasensory reality.

A parallel development may be traced through Wordsworth's reworkings of *Peter Bell:* belligerently "unpoetic" language and deliberately crude dramatization are tempered to an increasingly symbolic purpose. As illuminating is the sequence of *The Idiot Boy* (1798), *Michael* (1800), and *The White Doe* (1807), which illustrates the same movement away from naturalistic diction and stress upon simple story in itself toward elaborate language and the treatment of story as the organizing system of vision.

Balladic narrative perhaps attracted Coleridge and Wordsworth at first by its literalness. In one kind of ballad, supernaturalism was appropriate and therefore "credible." In another kind of ballad, the flattest naturalism was appropriate and therefore "justified." But Coleridge's and Wordsworth's interest in literal magic and literal realism soon changed to concern with the organic unity of the natural and the more-than-natural. As they lost interest in the literal, they lost interest in the ballad as ballad.

Scott's art evolved along another route, toward social realism. From translations of Bürger and balladic wonder-mongering appropriate to M. G. Lewis' collections, he advanced to the longer historical narratives of *The Lay of the Last Minstrel* and *Marmion*. In *The Lady of the Lake,*

Gothic sensationalism is supplanted by the wonder of actual history and actual scenery. Cultural history provides the medium through which Scott's version of Romantic organicism finds expression. Wordsworth and Coleridge in their later narratives elaborate and intensify the significance of progressively fewer details; their subjects become stylized. Scott's art becomes progressively less stylized and more crowded with naturalistic detail. His stories become the embodiments of historical forces in action. His protagonists serve to make visible suprapersonal powers operating within or between cultures. *The Lady of the Lake* is more than melodrama because the conflict between James and Roderick dramatizes how a primitive civilization was not simply destroyed, but was assimilated into a more progressive one.[2] *The Lady of the Lake* adumbrates the theme of the best Waverley novels and suggests that Scott's mature art can best be understood not as a "reconstruction of the past," but as a portrayal of the temporal dimension of sociocultural events, whether contemporary or ancient.

Artistic necessity as much as the challenge of Byron's popularity drove Scott from narrative poetry to the novel. He needed a larger, looser form to portray the growth

---

[2] Precisely because James and Roderick represent different cultural values, their simple, unitary personalities can evoke ambiguous responses in the reader: one recognizes, for example, that Roderick, though impeccably "honorable," "deserves" to be defeated. This ethical complexity depends upon a historical vision which undermines the sociocultural stylization inherent in traditional tragedy. Much of the Romantic leaning toward melodrama (as well as toward narrative) seems to me traceable to an intensified awareness of historical and cultural processes —an awareness most apparent in Scott. The best study of Scott's handling of history is Georg Lukacs' *The Historical Novel,* translated by Hannah and Stanley Mitchell (London, 1962).

of societies. He tended to define heroism as the ability to assimilate into social advances toward new economic, juridical, and spiritual complexities the simple virtues of more primitive ways of life. Many of the Scottish novels are stories of moderates caught between opposing fanatics: on one side, those defying inevitable progress toward new forms of civilization, on the other, those who would totally extirpate older, simpler fashions of life. Thus the evolution of Scott's art parallels that of Coleridge and Wordsworth, although Scott moved into naturalism and prose while they moved toward the mythopoetic. But all three strove to encompass within ever more comprehensive unities their intense value for the individual, the local, the experiential.[3] This striving explains why none of the three abandoned narrative form however much they modified it; for of all poetic forms, story, perhaps, best combines broad scope with emphatic dramatization of particularized detail.

Among the second generation of "great" Romantics, only Byron pursued Scott's direction. Byron added, of course, a flamboyant individualism that challenged the worth of any and all cultural progress. For Byron, social rules must be judged against personal experience. Hence his protagonists tend to be exiles and extremists, not moderates trapped among fanatics. For him, narrative

---

[3] *The Excursion* interestingly illuminates this development when it is contrasted with the first (1805) version of *The Prelude*. The basic story of *The Excursion* is simpler, yet it encompasses a more intricate multiplicity of subnarratives; and, though literally and figuratively more pedestrian, the later poem is more dramatic, since its basic structure is dialectical, while its more systematized and formalized symbolism is embodied in more consistently localized, and even more particularized, realities.

serves to unify two passions almost unknown to Scott—the passion that seeks lyrical self-expression and the passion that finds outlet in satire. Yet Byron, like Scott, moved toward social realism.

In his first stories, *The Giaour, The Bride of Abydos, The Corsair,* and *Lara,* narrative objectifies self-expression. The need thus to objectify differentiates Byron from Coleridge and Wordsworth. Like them, he finds only in the integrity of his own experience a secure foundation for his art and a valid basis for judging his society, but he is perhaps more conscious of the conditioned nature of personal experience. So almost from the beginning of his career, Byron concentrates on the shifting relationships between the individual and his social environment and strives for a more than lyrical and more than satirical form of utterance. This he found first in melodramatic narrative or semi-narrative *(Childe Harold)*. As he matured, his narrative form became more complicated until, in *Beppo* and *Don Juan,* story and Byron's comments about the story are intermingled in a kind of super-narrative that forces us to recognize the difficulty of identifying the true motives of sophisticated, self-conscious people, the true meaning of "grand" social undertakings such as war, and the true emotions expressed through the necessary but falsifying artifice of civilized intercourse. Through Byron, as well as Scott, Romantic narrative contributed significantly to the progress of the novel[4]—

4 As is always true in the evolution of literary styles, there was feedback in the influence of poetry on prose. For example, Scott moved from ballad to long narrative poem to novel, but the novelistic qualities of *Don Juan* (particularly in the last cantos) owe something to Byron's reading of Scott's novels.

but Byron's contribution was to enrich the ironic modes of novelistic art.

Shelley and Keats continued along lines laid out by Coleridge and Wordsworth that led toward mythopoetic narrative. The younger poets early turned to myths and stories from older literature, not because these stories were antique, but because they provided a ready-made escape from the confines of literal realism (the result of seeing *with* and not *through* the eye, in Blake's terms) and served as compositional systems for the representation of that creative experience wherein "spirit" and "sense" operate as one—the most intensely *human* experience to these antiorthodox poets. But the younger men, unlike their predecessors, who had enjoyed the democratic idealism liberated by the French Revolution, could not identify personal ecstasy with social fact. Hence *The Prelude*, Wordsworth's "epic" of the French Revolution, is less visionary than Shelley's *The Revolt of Islam* or Keats's "Hyperion." Keats's and Shelley's stories tend toward private fantasy, since for them narrative is less a matter of ostensible subject than a matter of inherent form, less the substance of their poetry than its structural system. Yet their "self-indulgence" is meant to illuminate more than private truths. Narrative serves them as a means of personal re-entry into traditional mythology. Inheritors of the first generation of the Romantics' revolt against conventionalized literary mythologizing, Keats and Shelley return to the creative experience beneath the overlay of formalized classical imitations.

In broad outline, then, Romantic narrative evolves along two paths. On the one hand, it moves in the direction of social realism. To this development, Scott contributed, above all, an understanding of societies and cultures as organisms whose flowering or decay could be embodied in stories of individuals who participate in more than one phase of a civilization's progress. Byron contributed above all a complexly ironic and colloquial technique for criticizing both the passionate life of the individual and the organization of his society. These are two aspects of the same evolution. Waverley and Don Juan are both young men introduced into strange societies, but Waverley represents the intrusion of sophistication into a "primitive" group, while Don Juan represents the eruption of "primitive" desires within ultra-refined circles. Waverley's sophistication is tempered and educated into imaginative sympathy for older virtues; Don Juan's naturalness is sophisticated to the point of corruption, but in a fashion that illuminates the psychologically ambiguous and morally ambivalent systems of civilized relationships.

The other course of early nineteenth-century narrative leads toward what one may call mythological romances, poems that escape from story as substance, story as credible report, into story as the organizing system of more-than-rational experiences of preternatural significance. The characteristic form of these romances is myth-like in its simplicity. The plot can be summarized in a sentence or two. But within this simplicity the poet elaborates the processes by which, at its highest intensity, the imagination experiences the synthesis of the supra-sensory with the sensory from which it emerges.

Within this general pattern, the principal trends of minor Romantic narrative verse are to be distinguished. I shall try to define these trends by commenting on a few poets who seem to exemplify them most clearly. Crabbe, for instance, illustrates how narrative form accompanied the growth of social realism during the Romantic era, but the development of his art is paralleled in other poets, such as Ebenezer Elliott.

The Village (1783), Crabbe's first major poem, is static, descriptive, satiric. *The Parish Register* (1806) is a mechanically organized collection of summarized biographies. *The Borough* (1810) includes developed life histories, such as that of Peter Grimes. *Tales in Verse* (1812) is purely narrative, comprising twenty-one stories, each of which is something more than simple biography, and *Tales of the Hall* (1819) encloses even more complicated narratives in a framework hinting at the recessed perspectives of *Wuthering Heights*. As Crabbe's art becomes more an art of storytelling, his subject matter becomes less abstract and mechanical, more problematical and sociological. His first protagonists are examples of the deterioration induced by specific vices; every one is the victim of moral flaws in his character. Crabbe's first stories are, in fact, versions of Hogarth's "Progress" series, and his realism is the descriptive, intellectual, analytical realism typical of that form. His conventional, conservative morality is equally typical of that "Progress." In his later stories, however, the protagonist is one of a group of interacting characters, not the isolated personification of a special failing. Nor in the later tales is the protagonist always sole architect of his doom; society may bear some blame for the individual's disaster. A complication in Crabbe's view of the relation of individual personality to social pressure leads him to question neoclassic concepts and precepts. Narrative gives order and focus to Crabbe's new questioning. Story for him—as for his contemporaries —provides a means to explore the nature of unique men, not typical men, under the pressure of a society understood to be mobile and evolving, not hieratic and fixed.

But Crabbe was born too early (1754) and was by temperament too conservative to participate fully in the central movement of Romantic art. His verse is valuable as a revelation of how eighteenth-century attitudes and techniques yielded to new pressures. To understand the nature of those pressures in their own right, we must turn to Robert Southey and Walter Savage Landor, the first of the minor Romantics. In their own day, the former was more important, but today it appears to be the latter who accomplished more of permanent value. The reversal of opinion implies a change in critical sympathy for narrative verse (Southey is primarily a narrative poet, Landor, only secondarily), and unless we recognize the profundity of that change, we are likely to misunderstand the necessary part played by story in the emergence of the Romantic style.

Southey never liberated himself from the Ossianic heritage common to the Lake poets. Unlike Coleridge

and Wordsworth, he could only transform the sensationalism of his youthful works into a sober historicity that
is, in fact, a respectable disguise for superficiality of inspiration. *Madoc* is more coherent than *Thalaba* but it
possesses no more poetic truth or beauty.

It is becoming customary once again to speak kindly
of Southey. I confess, however, that I find his poetry
tedious. His importance seems to me to rest upon his
poetic deficiencies. Southey might not even have attempted verse (as a prose writer, he is far from despic-
able) had his age not favored narrative poetry. He is
incapable of lyric passion or of dramatic excitement. He
has few ideas, his sensibility is often coarse, and his moral
imagination is frequently convention-bound. But he con-
ducts a narrative competently and, in his early works
(especially *Joan of Arc* and *Kehama*), he embellishes his
stories with happily flamboyant imagery.

Southey's mistake lay in his effort to write epics.[5] His
greater contemporaries avoided the conventional epic
form. Although they believed in the transcendent importance of poetry, desired to write works possessed of
all-encompassing unity, and often employed the narrative
mode, they turned away from the traditional epic. If
The Prelude is an epic, it is a subjective one. The strength
of Scott's narrative poems lies in their modesty, in their
refusal to claim a too great seriousness. Scott and Byron

[5] In fairness, one should note that Southey distinguished, as most
critics have not, between his "romances," *Thalaba* and *Kehama*, which
are written in free stanzaic forms, and his epics, *Joan, Madoc,* and
Roderick, written in blank verse. I find the "romances" more vigorous
and interesting, though parts of *Joan of Arc* are animated—probably by
a genuine republican fervor.

believed in the aesthetic value of a good story well told. Their narratives never pretend to epic grandeur, except where, as in *Don Juan* and, in a different fashion, in *The Bridal of Triermain* and *Harold the Dauntless*, the epic pretension is treated ironically.

Southey's solemnity about his epic-like narratives betrays his attachment to the spirit of Macpherson, Percy, and Chatterton. Like Macpherson (and unlike Coleridge), Southey describes marvellous events without participating imaginatively in their strangeness. Perhaps he should have taken opium. At any rate, his approach is archaistic. *Thalaba, Madoc,* and *Roderick* are learned histories of wonderful occurrences. His greater contemporaries delighted in the marvelous and were fascinated by history. Story for them was a means of uniting these interests, a means of fusing their capacity for wonder with their realistic comprehension of the systems of social and psychological process, a means of celebrating the romance of reality and the reality of romance. *The Ancient Mariner, The Prelude,* and *The Lady of the Lake* have little in common, but in each it is narrative that blends "wonder" and "history" into a poetic substance that is neither purely fabulous nor purely historical. This fusion Southey never achieves.

Neither does Landor. Yet Landor's best verse possesses imaginative fieriness and verbal toughness, and *Gebir*, his best known narrative, repays study.[6] It seems full of typically Romantic imagery and certainly points to some

[6] "Crysaor" is perhaps a better work of art and may more significantly anticipate some of Keats's and Shelley's (and even Tennyson's) narratives.

Romantic predelictions; for example, the tendency to represent ancient civilization as admirable not for its Roman, toga-wrapped dignity, but for its youthful, uninhibited vigor, "half-naked, loving, natural, and Greek." In *Gebir*, we find passages such as this:

> Arabian gold enchased the crystal roof,
> With fluttering boys adorn'd and girls unrobed;
> These, when you touch the quiet water, start
> From their aerial sunny arch, and pant
> Entangled 'mid each other's flowery wreaths,
> And each pursuing is in turn pursued.

And *Gebir* contains some Romantic themes. Gebir is destroyed not alone by personal failure but also by a heritage of guilt. Like Byron's heroes, Gebir is a noble soul predestined to damnation. Even more significantly, like the younger Wordsworth of *The Prelude*, Gebir struggles with social problems that cannot be solved merely by the exercise of conventional rectitude, that, in fact, call for a drastic moral revaluation, a redefinition of the relationship between personal responsibility and social duty.[7]

Why, then, does *Gebir* fail? Because its images, techniques, and themes are static, not dynamic. These images,

---

[7] Gebir's fate is meant to be a warning against British interference with French democracy. The true "hero" of the poem is Gebir's pacifist brother Tamar. *Joan of Arc,* also written in the 1790's, is likewise an "inverted" epic: not only is the protagonist a woman, but the national cause celebrated is that of France, not Britain.

techniques, and themes in the hands of other poets appear in a continuous process of transformation. Both the intensity and instability of the Romantic manner lies in a restlessness that strives to image the budding rose above the rose full blown. The sculpturesque quality of Landor's verse (often justly praised) lacks the dynamism of the full Romantic style, for which story, a developing structure, frequently supplies an appropriate organization.

Whereas Southey fails to unite narratively romance with reality, Landor does not control the techniques upon which such fusion depends for its effectiveness. One thinks of Keats's poetry, I suppose, as descriptive and static. Yet contrast the passage from *Gebir* quoted above with its obvious parallel in the "Ode on a Grecian Urn." The figures on the urn strike us as vital beings arrested at the climax of action. The "struggles" on the urn, one might say, are the efforts of an intensely imagined vitality to break free from an imprisoning, if immortalizing, medium. Landor's figures are visualized as inanimate beings endowed with a spurious activity. And, though the philosophy of *Gebir* may suggest *The Prelude*, Landor's presentation is abstract and stylized; he has none of Wordsworth's understanding of the fluid complexity of social and psychological development.

All this is said not to derogate Landor and Southey but to suggest that there is an organic connection during the Romantic era between narrative form, dynamic imagery, and themes of growth and transformation. It is not, therefore, special pleading to emphasize the importance of story in early nineteenth-century literature. Indeed, between 1810 and 1820 more significant narrative verse was published than in any other decade of English literary history. To this decade, in one sense the high point of Romantic art, belong Leigh Hunt's *Story of Rimini* and Thomas Love Peacock's *Rhododaphne,* and if these poems are of the second rank, for that reason they define the forces other than personal genius that shaped a climactic epoch. I shall treat them as exemplars of the chief trends in narrative verse of the decade.

Both *Rhododaphne* and *Rimini* loosen metrical forms traditional in narrative verse: Hunt softens the taut strength of the heroic couplet with the relaxed grammar of long but unperiodic sentences in which emphasis falls on modifiers, particularly adverbs; and Peacock modulates the jolting regularity of the octosyllabic couplet with clusters of trochaic lines and variations in rhyme pattern. Both poems are extended non-satiric narratives, more than ballads but less than epics. Their inspiration is doubly literary, Peacock drawing not only on the history of ancient life but also on Hellenistic and Renaissance embroideries of that history; and Hunt, of course, reworking Dante's treatment of what was already in the thirteenth century a literary motif. But neither of the poems is formalistic or imitative. They are animated by a sense of rediscovery. Hunt's revived medievalism possesses the bright naïveté of a fairy tale, and Peacock's romance of Thessalian magic escapes the pomposity of neoclassic, as well as the pedantry of pre-Romantic, reconstructions.

In both poems, description dominates over characterization. In both, also, story per se is less important than as a compositional principle. Weak characterization and de-emphasis of story as story are features of the Romantic mythological romance. These characteristics perhaps result from the poets' desire to celebrate a universal spirit for which the particular and personal is but the transient embodiment. They may also result from the probing, exploratory inclination of poets less interested in restating traditional solutions to eternal problems than in suggesting new possibilities of imaginative and moral questing. At any rate, feeble characterization and disregard of story as story produce weaknesses; both Hunt and Peacock tend to escape into self-indulgent fantasy—with consequent errors in taste: there is, for example, too much water in *Rimini* and too much refulgence in *Rhododaphne.*

Two other elements in the latter poem (not so well known as *Rimini,* but of equal value as a work of art)[8] are illuminating of the purposes and techniques of the mythological romances. Peacock, like Shelley and Keats, is above all concerned with the intermingling and differentiation of sensual love and spiritual love, both of which spring from "primogenial or Creative Love," according to Peacock's Preface. Anthemian (Peacock's hero) wanders through landscapes appropriate to *Alastor* and undergoes an enchantment like that cast by Lamia upon Lycius, to attain, finally, a climactic sensual-spiritual bliss akin to that portrayed in *Endymion* and *Epipsychidion.* The

---

[8] Hunt's other narratives impress me as being more trivial and belletristic than *Rimini,* although *Bacchus and Ariadne* probably influenced Tennyson.

common ideal of these romances is clear: the highest and only enduring love is that in which Uranian love is embodied in Pandemanian love, for only by the identification of the spiritual with the sensory can man experience the eternal power of Primogenial Love, the abiding spirit and wisdom of the universe. These poems, then, are not merely erotic fantasies, nor do they evade the reality of life's hazards. In *Rhododaphne*, typically, the promise of ecstasy evokes the presentiment of despair.

> The sun upon the surface bright
> Poured his last line of crimson light,
> Half-sunk behind the hill:
> But through the solemn plane-trees past
> The pinions of a mightier blast,
> And in its many-sounding sweep,
> Among the foliage broad and deep,
> Aerial voices seemed to sigh,
> As if the spirits of the grove
> Mourned, in prophetic sympathy
> With some disastrous love.

Intense joy is achieved only at the risk of catastrophe. In fact, the title of Peacock's poem might stand as a symbol for the ambiguities that for the Romantic circumscribe his search for life's high meed.

Rhododaphne also illustrates the function of magic for poets who are anything but superstitious—indeed, who incline toward the scientific. Magic liberates those powers that reason confines. Any human capacity may explode

to destructiveness: Rhododaphne, like La Belle Dame
and Lamia, brings sorrow and death with her strange
power. But fear of destructive forces within us should
not constrain us to pure rationality. With reason alone
we can never reach that truth of beauty that the Witch
of Atlas reveals, or of which Rhododaphne sings:

> The Nereid's home is calm and bright,
> The ocean-depths below,
> Where liquid streams of emerald light
> Through caves of coral flow.
> She has a lyre of silver strings
> Framed on a pearly shell,
> And sweetly to that lyre she sings
> The shipwrecked seaman's knell.

One should not minimize the eroticism of Romantic
mythological romances. But in these poems love is associated with magic because the love celebrated is beyond
all else "primogenial," creative—an activation of the
entire personality. It would be only a slight exaggeration
to say that when the later Romantics write of magical
love, they write of what Wordsworth and Coleridge had
called imagination. The distinctions between and unity
among Primary imagination, Secondary imagination, and
Fancy, elaborated by Coleridge, might be used to eluci-
date Peacock's system of primogenial, spiritual, and
sensual love. The terminological difference is important;
it suggests, for example, a retreat from confidence in the
public and practical relevance of poetry toward yearning

for private and aesthetic satisfaction. That the change is in part only verbal, however, helps to explain why the second generation of Romantics continued the practice of narrative verse. They, like Coleridge and Wordsworth, found the flowing, developing design of story helpful in expressing the nature of imaginative life, to them the only authentically vital life.

In the "Neo-Jacobean" narratives of the 1820's, however, eroticism takes on a more sinister coloring. In these poems, too, there is a return to the dark magic of early Romantic Gothicism, observable, for instance, in the first version of *The Ancient Mariner*, "Monk" Lewis' ballads, and Scott's first narratives.[9] But the macabre joking and grotesquerie of the later Romantics is not to be explained, in my opinion, solely as literary imitation, either of Jacobean drama or of early Romantic balladry. Thomas Hood, W. M. Praed, T. L. Beddoes, and George Darley, at least, are poets of talent, each in his own way dedicated to his art. But each gropes vainly and with conscious uneasiness for a form of expression appropriate to his genius.

Beddoes' *Death's Jest Book* is, on the one hand, evidence of how dominance of narrative hindered development of dramatic forms. Yet the play's haunting, distorted power derives in part from the way Beddoes assimilates into the drama much of the manner and inspiration of the mythological romances. The unfinished

[9] Apparent here, I believe, is a pattern of development common to many artistic styles. After the peak of a style is reached, the beginning of a decline is marked by younger artists' return to elements important in the origin of the style but subordinate during its culmination.

Nepenthe of Darley reminds one of Beddoes, both in its erratic structure and its passages of brilliant imagery— and in its vivid expression of pathological mental conditions. Beddoes and Darley, remarkably gifted men, best exemplify the chief failing of all late Romantic poets: lack of confidence. The great Romantics were great, in part at least, because they were confident of the truth of their vision. The failure of poetic nerve in Beddoes and Darley signals the transformation of Romantic assurance into Victorian doubt.

Yet it is a mistake, I believe, to read these late Romantics merely as forerunners of a Victorian dead end. They pave the way for the "Spasmodic" poetry of the 1830's and 40's, and, while no one could claim that school as one of the glories of English literature, its influence upon some major poets, Tennyson, for example, should not be underestimated. One might argue, further, that the mixing of narrative and dramatic forms, so characteristic of the late Romantics, may have contributed to the development of the dramatic monologue. A more concealed line of influence is suggested by George Macdonald's *Phantastes*, which owes much to the late Romantic narrative tradition, and which, on the testimony of C. S. Lewis, is not without relevance to developments in twentieth-century literature and criticism.

Thomas Hood and W. M. Praed seem less anguished and unsure than Darley and Beddoes, and it is significant that Hood and Praed, in different senses of the term, were "popular" poets. Praed has affinities to a conservative narrative tradition of the Romantic era, one which preserves some eighteenth-century tastes and sensibilities. To this tradition belong Campbell's *Gertrude of Wyoming* and *Theodoric*, Rogers' *Columbus*, and Moore's *Lalla Rookh* (part prose and part verse). Praed's immediate master, however, is Byron,[10] and in clever sophistication the Etonian boy-wonder is no unworthy pupil of the author of *Mazeppa* and *Beppo*. In *The Legend of Drachenfels*, Praed retells a folk story with tact and rapidity; in *The Red Fisherman*, he skillfully counterpoises excitement with humor; and in *Gog*, he proves himself a master of something like the Pulcian manner. What Praed lacks is the emerging Byronic personality. Praed is scarcely impersonal, but his narratives are not means of discovering and fostering unknown or unexploited aspects of his personality. In both *Childe Harold* and *Don Juan*, the relation between the poet and his protagonist changes as the poems progress. The relation could shift, of course, because the composition of the poems occupied years and Byron matured. But Byron valued change for its own sake; much of his art (not just his long poems) served as a means of self-revelation as well as a means of self-expression. The same is true of Shelley and Keats; their egocentricity is exploratory. Romantic emphasis on self cannot be separated from the Romantic conception of self as free, developing, and latent with potentiality. The Romantics liked the narrative form because it could be

---

[10] Byron was associated with Moore and Rogers, but a more intriguing because less noticed "conservative" influence on Byron may have been that of Sir John Henry Moore. Some passages in his "Duke of Benevento," first published in 1778, sound as if they were cribbed from *Don Juan*.

adapted to progressive self-revelation. Praed retains the form, but without stress upon self-discovery. As a result his quick-moving, neatly turned lines are often belletristic, and his shifts between straightforward narration and witty digression strike one as empty contrivances.

Thomas Hood, not an ornament of polite society, but a poor, punning radical sweating for his bread, followed Keats and Shelley, rather than Byron; yet Hood also missed the essential qualities of his masters, even though poems such as *Lycus* and *The Two Swans* are patently derivative. But Hood was no mere imitator, as is proved, paradoxically, by his *Hero and Leander*, which, unlike Hunt's version, possesses an original point of view and moments of poignancy. Hood's chief contributions to narrative art, however, were his macabre melodramas, especially *The Last Man, The Dream of Eugene Aram*, and *Miss Kilmansegg.*

In these poems, Hood mingles psychological horror with social criticism in a fashion that foreshadows the art of his friend and fellow radical Charles Dickens. Hood, in fact, is one of the writers responsible for the transposition of Romantic themes, techniques, and ideals into the mainstream of the early Victorian novel. His weird settings, grotesque *personae*, and semi-colloquial language are manifestations of his transitional role. That the novel gained most from Hood's work suggests the aesthetic limitations of his verse, but his accomplishments deserve more attention than they have yet received.

One hint as to their importance must suffice here. It has been argued that caricature originated in Renaissance paintings and drawings as the counterpart of an idealistic art. The first caricatures were inverted idealizations that developed eccentric particularities into "the perfection of ugliness." Trivial though they may have been, these experiments in caricature led the way toward more realistic styles in painting.[11] Hood's narrative poems serve an analogous function in nineteenth-century English literature. In them, social radicalism and criminal psychology are unified by stories that are melodramatic because they are nearly mythical.[12] Hood's imagination, as one would expect of a disciple of Coleridge, Shelley, and Keats, tends toward the mythopoetic. His protagonists are impressive because they are like the characters of legend, supranatural. At the same time, they are part of the sordid, vulgar, urban life of industrial England. No wonder they are grotesque. But their distortions and the distortions of Hood's language (those hideous puns!) are signs of the awkward emergence of new literary techniques and purposes.

I have tried to suggest some ways in which minor Romantic narrative poems are worthy of attention.[13]

[11] Werner Hofman, *Caricature from Leonardo to Picasso* (New York, 1957).

[12] William Godwin in *Caleb Williams* was perhaps the first writer effectively to combine criminal pathology and social protest, but Godwin did not have a mythological imagination.

[13] I have, of course, omitted many writers. Some who would surely be mentioned in an exhaustive survey include: James Hogg, whose narratives in *The Queen's Wake* are not only interesting in themselves but also as imitations of contemporary poets; "Monk" Lewis who helped to popularize (simultaneously) Gothic ballads and parodies of Gothic ballads; Mrs. Hemans, whose verses were quite popular, and about whom the perfect comment was made in a prefatory note to an American edition of her works: "There is in her writings much which both appeals, and

Taken altogether, they are interesting, to my mind, in confirming a Romantic tendency toward *subjective narrative*, wherein the "objective" sequence of events becomes separated from (and sometimes subordinate to) the "story" of the psychological development of the protagonist or narrator. This tendency leads, on one side, toward the dramatic monologue, on the other side, toward the allegorical romance.

But study of minor Romantic narrative poems also confirms a different tendency, perhaps best dramatized by Walter Scott, the one Romantic poet who became a successful novelist. Probably all modern estimations of Romanticism are inadequate because today we cannot take Scott seriously. We should like to deny what he admitted cheerfully: a story is almost by definition an entertainment. Hence we underestimate how eagerly story poems were sought as entertainment by readers of the early nineteenth century.[14] Alone among the principal British writers of his time, Scott was willing fully to accept the limitations and responsibilities (as well as the rewards) of satisfying this popular taste. In the 1830 Introduction to *Rokeby* he observed: "I conceived myself

deserves to appeal, to many gentle, sweet, pious, and refined souls . . . ";
Richard Harris Barham, whose *Ingoldsby Legends* throw light on the
audience for which Hood wrote; Bryan Waller Procter ("Barry Cornwall"), Thomas Wade, and R. H. Horne, all of whom illustrate later
developments of the Romantic mythological romance. I think it might
be useful to confront John Clare's pastoralism with Blake's to define
different fashions of introducing narrative elements into lyrical forms.

[14] I have found no fully satisfactory explanation for the popularity
of narrative poetry during the first years of the nineteenth century. My
best guess is conventional: the industrial revolution raised to positions
of relative affluence and leisure a considerable number of people who
lacked literary sophistication but who desired "culture."

to understand, more perfectly than many of my contemporaries, the manner most likely to interest the great mass of mankind."[15] His understanding led him from narrative verse into a new form of novel. In making this transition, Scott did not merely reveal his inherent Philistinism. He also carried forward some of the impulses that gave rise to Romanticism: democratic idealism, historical awareness, desire for new forms of literary expression. Knowledge of minor Romantic narratives, I believe, may help us to judge Scott's achievement more precisely and sympathetically, and thus enable us to appreciate both the subjective and the popular aspects of Romanticism. "The poet," said Wordsworth, "is *a* man speaking to *men.*"

---

[15] In a letter, Scott express the same point more pungently: "I thank God I can write ill enough for the present taste." The solemnity of modern criticism is too outraged by such happy self-deprecation to consider the positive as well as negative implications of such an attitude.

PERIODICAL LITERATURE

William S. Ward

"Worlds of fine thinking lie buried in that vast abyss, never to be disentombed or restored to human admiration. Like the sea it has swallowed treasures without end, that no diving bell will bring up again; but nowhere, throughout its shoreless magazines of wealth, does there lie such a bed of pearls, confounded with the rubbish and purgamenta of ages." Though Thomas De Quincey was thinking primarily of his friend Coleridge and of the *Morning Post* when he wrote these lines, his statement (in "Samuel Taylor Coleridge") applies also to scores of other writers and to the many periodicals for which they wrote. Indeed, it can be applied in the broadest sense to the whole content of periodical publications, for within them lie not only the unidentified writings of many important literary figures, but also a mass of other materials in which may be found a remarkably complete record of the culture of the day and of the full range of opinion on every major question that troubled the age. In order to understand the place of this "vast abyss" in literary history, however, and gain the perspective essential to an evaluation of its contribution to the Romantic period, it is necessary first to take a fresh look at some of the periodicals themselves, and even to repeat a few well-known facts.

During the years that brought the eighteenth century to a close, there was no single periodical that constituted an important part of the country's reading. Interesting things were going on in the development of the newspaper press, but periodicals were rocking along in the old, accustomed ruts. Criticism was still in the hands of the *Monthly Review* and the *Critical Review*, but both, despite the fact that they had their dutiful readers and still carried considerable weight, had fallen off since the days of Goldsmith and Smollett. The *British Critic* purveyed its particular line of religious and critical orthodoxy, and the *Gentleman's Magazine*, the oldest of them all, contained (in addition to its miscellaneous matter) notices of books and maintained something of the tone of scholarliness. But despite their good, gray respectability and the diligence with which they must have been read, not one of them could possibly have had much to say to a younger generation—or even an older one—that was increasingly aware of the revolutionary ideas with which Europe was astir. Nor could anyone have really felt that either literature or literary criticism was taken very seriously by those who wrote about it. But mediocre though these periodicals were, the age had nothing better to offer.

If one looks carefully, however, he will find signs of something better to come. Thus gradually through the eighteenth century, reviews had come to replace the abstracts and summaries of earlier years, and the review, as a distinct periodical type, to hold a place beside the more common magazine. Also, by 1788 the *Analytical Review* was proposing to look at books more "analytically" than was generally the case with its more perfunctory contemporaries; and not long afterwards, the liberal, forward-looking *Monthly Magazine* (founded in

1796) came into being, while Griffiths, editor of the conventional *Monthly Review*, at least took a step in the right direction by engaging experts to review books in their various fields. Unfortunately, however, Griffiths (as well as his son, who succeeded him) had editorial policies which required that the style of each of his authors, as well as their opinions, theories, and attitudes, be consistent one with another and that collectively they write as one person. It is no great wonder, therefore, that in the end the *Monthly* never really moved forward into the nineteenth century even though it survived until 1845.

But while the magazines and reviews were running along in their old accustomed grooves, the French Revolution had stirred men's imaginations as they had not been stirred for many years. Old beliefs were being shaken to the very bottom; the air was full of questions and doubts; restlessness and uncertainty were everywhere. But despite all the ferment there was no forum of discussion, no means by which active and original minds could come into communication, no organ that showed evidence that it was alive to the vital topics of the day.

It was three young men in Edinburgh—Sydney Smith, Francis Jeffrey, and Francis Horner—who seized upon this opportune moment and founded the review that was to work a revolution in journalism and to lift book reviewing for the first time to the level of criticism. The story of the *Edinburgh Review* has been told too often to require retelling again. Suffice it to say that almost from the moment the first number appeared, in October, 1802, it was clear that the *Edinburgh* belonged to the new age.

A literary or social historian writing long after the event has taken place must note, of course, that Jeffrey and his fellow contributors were far from embracing the Romantic point of view and the more liberal social and political philosophy of the age. At the time, however, the important thing was that they had moved far away from their forebears, and that they seemed able and willing to come to grips with the important issues and problems of the day.

Perhaps one would have had to be living at the time in order to gain a full understanding of the electric effect that issue after issue of the *Edinburgh* had. "No genteel family," Scott wrote to George Ellis in 1808, "*can* pretend to be without it, because, independent of its politics, it gives the only valuable literary criticism that can be met with." A little later, Carlyle spoke of it as "a kind of Delphic oracle and voice of the inspired for the great majority of what is called 'the intelligent public.'" And according to Hazlitt, once a writer had an article printed in its pages, he kept it ever afterwards as a "kind of diploma and unquestionable testimonial of merit." By 1813, it is estimated, the *Edinburgh* had a circulation of more than twelve thousand, and Jeffrey himself in a letter to Thomas Moore in 1814 estimated that each issue, within a month of publication, was read by at least fifty thousand people.

There were, of course, many reasons for this popularity and influence. For one thing, the *Edinburgh* treated all subjects with forthrightness; it was bright, lively, and talented in a way that none of its contemporaries were;

and above all, it took the business of book reviewing seriously and maintained a general tone more elevated that that of any of its predecessors. For another thing, in declaring itself to be fiercely opposed to the domination of booksellers and publishers, it paved the way for honest, independent criticism based on merit. Before long, chiefly through Brougham's influence, it was to bend too much to partisan politics; but for the moment, it was significant that an important reviewing journal was not dominated by a publisher with books to sell, and that threats of the withdrawal of advertising could not elicit a favorable verdict from a reviewer.

More important, however, was the selectivity that it exercised in determining the books to be reviewed. Whereas the older reviews—usually monthlies—undertook to run reviews and notices of a high percentage of the books that were printed, the *Edinburgh Review* selected only the ones that "have attained or deserve a certain portion of celebrity," and that could serve as the starting point for the discussion of matters of lively concern at the time. Thus Carlyle's "Essay on Burns" was originally written as a "review" of Lockhart's *Life of Burns*, and Macaulay's famous essay on Milton as a "review" of *De Doctrina Christiana*. And since the *Edinburgh* reviewed books dealing with almost every imaginable subject, it was able through its gifted contributors to provide its readers with the opinions of some of the best-trained minds of the day on a remarkably wide variety of topics.

Still another reason for the success of the *Edinburgh Review* was that it set up a scale of remuneration that induced the brightest young men of the day to become contributors. For fifty years, if an occasional exception may be allowed, two guineas a sheet (i.e., a "sheet" of sixteen printed pages) had been the going rate. When, therefore, Sydney Smith suggested to Archibald Constable, publisher of the new review, that "if you will give £200 per anum to your editor, and ten guineas a sheet [to your contributors], you will soon have the best review in Europe," it is not surprising that Thomas Longman, who shared the risk with Constable, should have characterized the terms and the publisher's acquiescence as "without precedent."

In the beginning, of course, Jeffrey and his friends had an idea that no one should receive any remuneration at all, for when the eighteenth century drew to a close, reviewers, with few exceptions, were £2-a-sheet hacks who were completely dependent on editors, and these in turn were dependent on the booksellers who financed the reviews that advertised ("puffed") the books they printed and sold. At first, therefore, the young *Edinburgh* reviewers felt, as Lord Cockburn put it, that their role should be "all gentlemen and no pay"; otherwise, their critical independence would be in danger of being jeopardized. After the excitement of producing the first few numbers had worn off, of course, it became apparent to all concerned that the venture took up far more of the contributors' time than they could afford to give. Despite this realization, however, Jeffrey at first hesitated to accept the editorship because of "the risk of general degradation"; but in the end, he found the "dividend to the editor" (as John Murray put it a little later) such "a monstrous bribe" that he accepted Constable's offer and therewith began a twenty-six year "reign" that was to produce results heretofore undreamed of in the history of periodical literature. Before Jeffrey ended his editorship, his salary had been increased to £800 and the minimum to contributors from £10 to £16 per sheet, though according to Jeffrey himself, two-thirds of the articles were paid for at a much higher rate, £20 to £25 being the average. With the precedent established, not only the *Quarterly*, from the time of its inception, but also the other better magazines and reviews had to follow suit in order to compete for the services of talented writers. Not everybody could hope for the £100 per article that Southey came to draw from the *Quarterly*, but the pay was still good, and it was small wonder that the better part of the profession should be drawn into the ranks of the reviewers.

To write at such length of the *Edinburgh Review* and much more briefly of other reviews and magazines is in no way to detract from the importance of the excellent periodicals that came after it. It is simply that Jeffrey and his fellows created a new era in periodical literature and marked out a course that was to remain essentially unchanged for many years to come. Even the *Quarterly Review*, coequal though it was of the *Edinburgh,* really contributed nothing new; and neither did the other reviews that were contemporary with it. Some of them, in fact (and notably the *British Critic*, the *Eclectic Review*, the *Monthly Review*, and the *Critical Review*) continued on their way little changed from what they had been in the eighteenth century.

It would be somewhat surprising if the important advances made by the reviews during the early nineteenth century were not accompanied by comparable advances by the magazines, for those which moved forward into the new century were no better geared to the new age than were the reviews of the same period. Almost without exception, they were little changed from the *Gentleman's Magazine* when it was first founded by Edward Cave in 1731. That is to say, the term "magazine" implied a storehouse of information, a repository of all sorts of facts, fancies, and entertainment. Poems, essays, and other forms of belles-lettres were not uncommon in a given issue, but a magazine made up of a miscellany of original works of the imagination or one marked by the spirit of a new age was still several years away.

The break-through came quickly for the reviews, of course, but for the magazines it did not come till the founding of *Blackwood's Magazine*, in 1817, though some bright spots can be seen as one looks back in perspective. The liberal *Monthly Magazine* (founded in 1796), for example, was generally better in quality and more forward looking in viewpoint than its contemporaries. The *Monthly Repository* (1806–37) anticipated a later day by combining serial narratives with its regular news-with-comment feature. By and large, however, the force of tradition was greater than any desire for change, so that poetry, essays, bankruptcies, foreign affairs, meteorological reports, obituaries, stock prices, book reviews, and agricultural notes continued to rub elbows indiscriminately.

As already indicated, it was with the founding of *Blackwood's Magazine* that important changes in magazine-making were wrought. Founded by Tories of a younger and nimbler sort than those associated with the *Quarterly*, *Blackwood's* (after a poor start under two uninspired editors) quickly created a sensation without equal in magazine history. Just as the *Edinburgh* and the *Quarterly* provided an intelligent reading public with serious discussions of matters of political and cultural interest, so *Blackwood's* satisfied the need for a lighter, more varied miscellany of general reading matter. It did not enjoy the authoritative status of the *Quarterly*—and made no pretense of doing so—but with its liveliness and wit, its mischievous, rollicking fun and audacity, it quickly captured an audience comparable to that of the great reviews. That the *Chaldee Manuscript* and the *Noctes Ambrosianae* were sometimes in bad taste, and the assaults on Coleridge, Hunt, Hazlitt, and Keats irresponsible and inexcusably vicious, is not to be denied; but the fact remains that the articles were written by gifted, clever young men whose devastating hilarity caused others than Crabb Robinson to conclude, not without some misgivings, that "the fun makes one overlook the knavery."

Even *Blackwood's* daring and abundance of talent did not take the full step to a completely new type of magazine at once. As late as 1825, for example, it still dutifully carried the usual chronicle of deaths, births, marriages, storms at sea, market prices, and all the rest, like the other magazines of the day. By 1827 (perhaps under the influence of the *New Monthly Magazine*), the "Chronicle" heading was dropped and the material normally appearing under it began to appear irregularly, and finally, in 1831, disappeared altogether. In the meantime, more original criticism and more poetry and fiction were being included in each issue. With the final elimination of the Chronicle, therefore, and the replacement of it with original matter, the modern literary magazine, made up entirely of original articles, was finally born.

Three years after the first number of *Blackwood's*, the *London Magazine*, under the editorship of John Scott, began its short but brilliant career. Not only did it devote a greater portion of its contents to literary matters than any magazine had ever done before, but its quality was unexcelled. De Quincey's *Confessions of an English Opium-Eater*, Lamb's *Essays of Elia*, and Hazlitt's *Table Talk* may be better known than the other contributions, but excellence was not limited to them; and John Scott's appraisals of his contemporaries prove him to have been one of the wisest judges of literature in his day. After Scott's untimely death, of course, the quality of the *London* fell off, but not before its recognition of the "Cockneys" and its stand against *Blackwood's* had given new breadth to the taste of the day.

In the same year that the *London* was founded, the *New Monthly Magazine* (founded in 1814) came under the editorship of Thomas Campbell and became one of the best magazines of the day, both because of its original articles and poetry, and because of the excellent criticisms of Wordsworth by Thomas Noon Talfourd and the appreciative judgments of Keats and others of the "new school" of writers. Its stress on original literature is important in the development of literary periodicals, for, as already noted, this emphasis may have had its influence on *Blackwood's* and other magazines of the day.

Side by side with these magazines, of course, were scores of others, but perhaps only *The Liberal* of Lord Byron and Leigh Hunt deserves particular mention because of its quality, and not one of them because it made a notable contribution to the development of periodical literature. *Fraser's Magazine* and *Tait's Edinburgh Magazine* (both founded in 1831) achieved their own particular distinction, but their story belongs primarily with the age to follow.

Significant also during the first three decades of the nineteenth century is the development of the weekly journal of belles-lettres. The evolution of the review and the magazine stems from the preceding century, but the weekly journal is more distinctively the product of the early nineteenth century. It is this development that leads ultimately to periodical criticism as a profession.

Though at least two other weeklies devoted to literature (*The Literary Journal* and *The Director*) preceded the *Examiner*, it was Leigh Hunt's celebrated publication (founded in 1808) that really established the form and set the standard for the weekly journal of belles-lettres for a good many years to come. In the beginning, of course, the *Examiner* had given short shrift to literature; but the vilification of Shelley and Keats, especially between 1816 and 1822, at the hands of the *Quarterly* and *Blackwood's*, was provocation enough for Hunt to make his paper the principal champion of the younger generation of Romantic poets and the first weekly literary journal worthy of the name.

With the *Examiner* establishing the lead, the weekly journal of belles-lettres became pretty well standardized as a sixteen-page folio, usually published on Saturday, and containing, as a rule, reviews, original literature, letters, anecdotes, and other lesser forms of intelligence about literature. There were some notable imitations during the years ahead, of course, among them William Jerdan's *Literary Gazette* (founded in 1817) and the *Literary Journal* (1818–19), but none of them really contributed anything new. The *Athenaeum* (1828–1921) did get beyond mere imitation, but its period of greatest development and influence lies well beyond the years of this survey.

By the end of the Romantic period, in short, the three main types of English literary periodical—the review, the magazine, and the weekly journal—had taken the shape they would retain throughout the century, and even, if minor modifications be allowed, down to the present day. And to this evidence of maturity it can be added that the number of periodicals being published was increasing with astonishing rapidity. Thus during the first decade of the century, the average year saw the birth of approximately forty new periodicals (including newspapers). During the decade to follow, the annual average moved up to fifty-five, but it was during the 1820's that the rate of increase really began to gather momentum. During these ten years, the annual average doubled to 110, rose sharply to 175 in 1831, and far more than doubled the average of the preceding decade by rising to 250 in 1832, the year commonly assigned as the terminal date for the Romantic period. The time had come when there was a magazine for every interest and every taste.

But an account such as this—a sort of success story concerned primarily with those periodicals and those contributors that have survived through the years and that contributed most to the shape of things to come—by no means constitutes a complete record. So far as mere numbers are concerned, for example, all but a few periodicals that came into being during the period were strictly mediocre, and a very high percentage of the total did not survive beyond a few issues. Most of them, the new and the old alike, continued to employ undistinguished writers who, like the periodicals that employed them, continued on their way as if the *Edinburgh* and the *Quarterly* and their distinguished contributors had never been. Nor had all problems been solved so far as doing justice to an author or his work is concerned.

The quarterlies, for example, making far too little pretense of impartiality, continued on their pontifical way wherever politics and literature crossed paths. And not even the "puffing" that the *Edinburgh* came into the world to oppose had been routed, as an 1830 *Edinburgh Review* article (51:193–210) on "Mr. Montgomery and Puffing" makes quite clear.

Despite growing pains and shortcomings, however, it is evident that the burgeoning years are ahead, and that the Age of Periodicals, as Wilkie Collins was to call it a few years later, was just coming into its majority.

As for a judgment on the merits of the stout-spoken men who wrote for the great reviews and magazines, it is doubtful whether even yet their work has been finally appraised. That they said many wise things and rendered important service to periodical literature and to practical criticism is readily granted by all; but the mistakes they made, their dogmatic manner, and the personal abusiveness they were constantly capable of and frequently indulged in, has made it difficult for them, even a century and a half later, to be judged without prejudice. Perhaps, therefore, it is well to look more closely into the sources of their critical behavior.

First of all, we need to remind ourselves that the critical tradition that Jeffrey, Gifford, Croker, Lockhart, and the rest fell heir to was that of the dogmatists—the tradition of Rymer, and Dennis, and Johnson. In this tradition, the critic operated from the point of view that his special knowledge and equipment made him the final authority in all matters involving literature. Thus when the great reviews and those who wrote for them spoke, they did so as infallible judges from whose decisions there was no appeal in either this world or the next.

Likewise, we need to remember that the code of the day seems to have accepted as normal a kind of literary violence and personal abuse that apparently was much less shocking to the high days of the Regency than it is to our own. The editor of the *London Magazine*, John Scott, did deplore the critical excesses of the times, but his intemperate charges against Lockhart led to a duel that ended with his death at the hands of Lockhart's second. Stout language was the order of the day, and a man hardly dared to enter the lists as an author unless he was willing to be proved a fool as well as a bad writer.

Finally, we need to remember that there were political considerations that on occasion called out "Jeffrey's gang"—or Gifford's "slash reviewers"—or *Blackwood's* "crew"—and caused critical principles to be cast to the winds. Throughout its history, journalism has been no stranger to politics; but at no time, perhaps, have the two been more closely in league with the reviews and the magazines than between the perilous days of 1789 and the Manchester Massacre of 1819—and beyond. "The Review has but two legs to stand on. Literature, no doubt, is one of them: but its Right leg is politics," wrote Francis Jeffrey to Walter Scott, and one can be sure that the truth of his observation was by no means applicable to the *Edinburgh Review* alone. Sometimes, of course, party loyalty led to eulogy of works with small literary value, but more spectacular and more relevant here were those occasions when a purpose could be served by finding a victim to gibbet. It is clear, for example, that the *Edinburgh* noticed *Hours of Idleness* mainly because of the opportunity it provided to chastise a presumptuous young aristocrat, and that *Blackwood's* abuse of the "Cockneys" had little to do with literary principle. And no doubt Leigh Hunt and William Hazlitt were far more right than wrong when they charged that it was necessary only for the *Examiner* to praise an author in order for the *Quarterly* to assassinate him. One can hardly claim, however, that the fault lay wholly on the side of those who represented the Establishment. Hunt and Hazlitt appear to have enjoyed the name-calling battles well enough, and the liberal periodicals—the *London*, the *New Monthly*, the *Literary Gazette*, and the *Westminster*, as well as the *Examiner*—to have been influenced by considerations that were non-literary.

And above and beyond any political advantage to be gained, of course, such doings stirred up interest among readers and attracted widespread attention. Neither the *Edinburgh* nor the *Quarterly* was blind to the advantages to be gained from finding a "dunce," and, as is well-known, *Blackwood's* "crew" set out deliberately, by fair means or foul, to gain attention: in the *Chaldee Manuscript*, the *Noctes Ambrosianae*, and, of course, the series on the Cockney Poets. Even as late as 1823, *Blackwood's* (13:321) declares, "We have been looking about for some person or other to immolate to our fury—some victim to break upon the wheel, and to whom we might give, with soft reluctant amorous delay, the coup-de-grace. . . . It is not a mere blockhead we are in search of; for in that case, we should only have to go into the Phrenological Society. . . . Neither is your absolute knave the man for our purpose, otherwise a Radical or Cockney would come quite pat." Mischief of this sort was good business, for it sold magazines.

To convict Jeffrey, Croker, Lockhart, and others of shameful critical conduct can but rub some of the gloss off men whom it would be pleasanter to think of as always motivated by invariably high principle. At the same time, it is well to remember that more is involved than just being right or wrong. Thus even when they were right in complaining about the puerilities in some of Wordsworth's ballads, of Shelley's strained metaphors, and Keats's shortcoming in *Endymion*, they seem more at fault than does Leigh Hunt when he uses strong language in calling the Prince Regent a fat Adonis of fifty who has not one single claim on the gratitude of his country; or Hazlitt, when he spoke of William Gifford as a low-bred, self-taught, servile pedant, admirably qualified by a combination of defects to be the editor of the *Quarterly Review*. Here, as elsewhere, prejudice and a point of view become inextricably involved.

For sometimes being wrong and for being abusive and unjust, at least as judged by the standards of our own age, time has dealt harshly with these judges, for today the mention of any one of them calls to mind not his best criticism but his worst. Thus with many students of

English literary history, Jeffrey is largely remembered
for his judgment of Wordsworth, Croker for his heresy
concerning Keats, and Lockhart for his attacks on "The
Cockney Poets." Somehow it is not so easy to remember
that Lockhart shares with John Wilson (Christopher
North) the honor of being one of the first to uphold
the name of Wordsworth; that Croker, despite the one
review for which posterity remembers him, was often a
discerning critic, as witness, for example, his excellent
criticism of Maria Edgeworth (*Quarterly Review*, June,
1812); and that Jeffrey, more than any other one person,
started reviewing on its way to becoming a high profession and left behind him a body of sound and judicious
criticism that deserves to be rememebered at least along-
side the passages and reviews that are regularly alluded
to in footnotes, or are included when "infamous" reviews
of the nineteenth century are reprinted.

This is not to say, of course, that a critic is not to be
held accountable when he is wrong, or that the critical
utterances of these practicing reviewers deserve to stand
beside the work of giants like Coleridge and Hazlitt. Still,
a matter of distortion is involved and some correction
needs to take place, and doubtless will, as more scholarly
investigation is done and the work of these writers is seen
in clearer perspective. Perhaps, too, we need to remember
that they had their blind spots of prejudice, and we
should make generous or amused allowance (just as we
do regularly with Dr. Johnson) when it is obvious that
their judgment has been led astray. Without claiming
for any one of them that his was a great seminal mind or
that his rank is among the great critics, it is necessary to

remember that they were practicing critics who placed their judgments on record day after day, and that actually these judgments have stood up remarkably well. A considerable portion of what they left behind not only reads well, but is worth reading even a century and a half later.

This is not the place to attempt to enumerate the contributions that they made or to measure the stature of individuals. It is to their everlasting credit, however, that they took the criticism of literature seriously, that they considered it their business to hold up exacting standards without compromise, and that despite the lapses that will long be remembered, they were nevertheless motivated by a spirit of justice that not only established a new form and set the tone for a new and honorable profession, but advanced it well on its way. Even before the third decade ended, men like Macaulay and Carlyle had developed this new type of review—or essay—to the point where it had earned the right to exist as an independent composition. In short, the period ends at a world's remove from the days of "all gentlemen and no pay." How great the distance was is very well suggested, in 1834, by an anonymous writer in *Blackwood's Magazine* when (pleased with the present status of his profession) he declares, "We recollect the time when our aristocratic exclusives sneered at the editor of, or contributor to, a Review, and would have thought it an insult to be asked to meet the editor of a newspaper" (36: 373–91).

Today—a century and a half later—these periodicals, the good and the poor alike, are an important source of knowledge about the past. One would not, as already stated, go to them in order to find the origins of the great ideas that altered the course of English thought, or to discover the poems or the criticism that changed the directions of English poetry. One could expect, on the other hand, to discover reactions to matters such as these and to find the means for gauging the interests of the time, for detecting trends, and for otherwise gaining insights that can be found in no other place. Thus through a study of the periodicals of the early nineteenth century, one can learn much about how Wordsworth, the "new poetry" (as it was commonly called), and the "new criticism" fared in a world long accustomed to another manner.

He can learn, for example, that the critical reaction to *Lyrical Ballads* and the second edition, containing the Preface, was not at all what he might have expected; that there was neither a rousing welcome nor reactionary disapproval but instead an apathetic acceptance that makes it clear that the reviewers were in no sense aware of Wordsworth's (or Coleridge's) genius or of the fact that a new school of poetry and criticism had just made its way into the world. He can learn, further, that it was the *Edinburgh Review*, in 1802 (I, 53–83), that first accused Wordsworth of leading a conspiracy to revolutionize and ruin English poetry and thus paved the way for the critical and personal abuse that was to characterize much of the criticism of Wordsworth during the next two decades.

By studying the periodicals, he can learn also that with a shift in perspective the Age of Wordsworth can be called the Twilight of English Classicism as appropriately as it can be called the Flowering of Romanticism, and that literary tastes change much less rapidly than is generally assumed by the literary historian who writes long after the change has taken place. That is to say, he can discover that Dryden and Pope and Johnson were still strong favorites; that it was their works, far oftener than not, that were held up as the only proper models for anyone who hoped to achieve lasting literary fame; and that despite current dissatisfaction with the level of poetic excellence, any efforts at reform "should stop short of revolution."

And still again, he can learn how the disturbed national state conspired to bring about a thoroughly uncritical outlook and to make the age a most unpropitious one for launching a new literary system; and how with the typical reviewer the social, political, and moral leanings of an author or his work were likely to distort critical judgment and to take precedence over literary merit. He can see, for example, how Wordsworth's "Jacobinical tendencies" in his earlier life and works got him into trouble; why Byron's "elegant outlaws" and their "high souled villainy" were condemned as subtle betrayers of public and private morality; why "that atheist" Shelley stirred up the furor that he did; and why one of the two most enlightened periodicals of the day (*Edinburgh Review*, 36:53) was well pleased when Thomas Bowdler "bowdlerized" Shakespeare and published the results as *The Family Shakespeare.*

These and many other matters vital to an understanding of the Romantic Movement he can find in the periodicals. Much investigation has already been carried on, of course, but in a very real sense only the surface has been scratched. Some work has been done on poetic theory and on the attitude toward the "new poetry," for example, and there has been some study of the novel and of the development of the essay as a literary form. Much more remains to be done on all three, however; and the drama and the stage have barely been touched at all. Interesting chapters remain to be written on such miscellaneous matters as the sonnet, historical criticism, the picturesque, the sublime, public taste, and so on. Some reputation studies have been completed, and some insights into the age that produced both authors and works have been achieved; but despite gains such as these and the others that have been cited, an expert use of periodicals and newspapers can do much more to reproduce the climate of opinion that was experienced by those who lived through the days of the French Revolution, the Napoleonic wars, and the years that led up to the Great Reform Bill.

The study of the periodicals of the English Romantic period—De Quincey's aforementioned "vast abyss"—falls into two fairly distinct stages. These two stages, however, are preceded by two periods of preparation: one of contemporary criticism and self-scrutiny, the other of memoirs and recollections.

An early instance of contemporary criticism may be found in Robert Southey's complaint to John Rickman in 1804: "I look upon the invention of reviews to be the worst injury which literature has received since its revival. People formerly took up a book to learn from it, and with a feeling of respectful thankfulness to the man who had spent years in acquiring that knowledge, which he communicates to them in a few hours; now they look only for faults. Every body is a critic, that is, every reader imagines himself superior to the author, and reads the book that he may censure it, not that he may improve by it." Edward Copleston's satiric *Advice to a Young Reviewer* (1807), written to poke fun at the method of criticism in the *Edinburgh Review,* is well known, of course, as also is Hazlitt's angry regard for Gifford and others of his breed a little later. More temperate, but in the same general vein, is John Keats's view as expressed to his brother George (February 24, 1819): "I have no doubt of success in a course of years if I persevere—but it must be with patience—for the Reviews have enervated and made indolent men's minds—few think for themselves." And even the periodicals themselves reveal a concern about the nature of contemporary criticism. Thus *Blackwood's* (October, 1818) observes that "the author is nothing—the Reviewer every thing. They rule the authors and readers of the freest country in Europe, with as arbitrary and merciless a sway as was ever exerted over the civil and political world by a sportive Nero."

The *Monthly Magazine* on several occasions (from October, 1819, to December, 1820) expresses concern about just criticism and party prejudice, and the *Edinburgh Review* (May, 1823) echoes the question commonly put or implied by writers of the day: "Whether Shakespeare could have written as he did, had he lived in the present day," subject to the kind of criticism that regularly appears in the periodicals.

The period of memoirs and recollections asserted itself, naturally enough, as the century lengthened and it became apparent both to participants and observers that certain men—and, of course, certain periodicals—had had a remarkable influence on their age, and that their accomplishments deserved to be recorded. Thus James Grant devoted the second volume of his *The Great Metropolis* (1837) to his recollections of newspapers and periodicals and to the men associated with them; J. W. Robberds' *Memoir* of William Taylor of Norwich (*Monthly Review*) in 1843; the *Memoirs and Correspondence* of Francis Horner (*Edinburgh Review*) in the same year; the *Life and Correspondence* of John Foster (*Eclectic Review*) in 1848, and his *Life and Thoughts* in 1849; Cockburn's *Life of Lord Jeffrey* (*Edinburgh Review*) in 1852; the *Autobiography* of William Jerdan (*Literary Gazette*) in 1852–53; *A Memorial* of Christopher North (*Blackwood's Magazine*) in 1854; the *Autobiography* of James Silk Buckingham (*The Athenaeum*) in 1855; and the memoirs of Sydney Smith (*Edinburgh Review*) in 1855, Robert Chambers (*Chambers's Edinburgh Journal*) in 1872,

Macvey Napier (*Edinburgh Review*) in 1879, and John Wilson Croker (*Quarterly Review*) in 1884. At the same time, selections from the major reviews and magazines and their contributors began to be reprinted: *Selections from the Edinburgh Review* in 1833; the *Critical and Miscellaneous Writings* of Henry Brougham (*Edinburgh Review*) in 1841, and those of Christopher North (*Blackwood's Magazine*) in 1842; John Foster's contributions to the *Eclectic Review* in 1844; the *Works* of Sydney Smith (*Edinburgh Review*) in 1844; *The Recreations of Christopher North (Blackwood's Magazine)* in 1848; *Essays Contributed to Blackwood's Magazine* in 1857; and *Essays Contributed to the Quarterly Review* in 1860.

Another important mid-century development in the study of periodical literature was the increased frequency of appearance of magazine articles dealing with periodicals and newspapers of former years. It would probably be too much to speculate that this development stemmed from the founding of *Notes and Queries*, in 1849; but it does seem apparent that the establishment of this publication provided an excellent vehicle for capitalizing on Victorian England's growing interest in the past, and for ferreting out and reporting information that might not be readily recovered in any other way. At any rate, *Notes and Queries*, particularly after the mid–1860's, does become a valuable source of knowledge about the periodicals and newspapers of earlier years, as well as a stimulus to an increased interest in them. Nor can one fail to note that it was in 1848 that the original edition of *Poole's*

Index (only 154 pages) made its appearance. In the years ahead, it also was to play a role in stimulating interest in the periodicals of earlier times.

By the 1880's, the above-mentioned accumulation of memoirs and recollections—coupled with the notes, queries, and longer articles and studies that were appearing with increasing frequency—had paved the way for the first stage in the serious study of periodicals, and had given them for the first time a place of respect in English literary history. Thus in 1882 (the year that also witnessed the much enlarged edition of *Poole's Index*), Mrs. Margaret Oliphant spent an entire chapter on early nineteenth-century periodicals in her *Literary History of England, in the End of the Eighteenth and Beginning of the Nineteenth Century*, and three years later, the editors of the *Encyclopedia Britannica*, in the ninth edition, first gave substantial space both to "Periodicals" and to "Newspapers." In the next decade, Mrs. Oliphant again gave ample attention to nineteenth-century periodicals in her *Victorian Age of English Literature*, and George Saintsbury (1896) devoted a chapter to "The Development of Periodicals" in his *A History of Nineteenth Century Literature* (1780–1900).

During these same years, the study of the periodicals gained attention in various other ways. For one thing, Cornelius Walford proposed to the Library Association (October, 1881) that a Catalogue of British Periodical Literature "from the earliest period" be set up; and a few months later, W. J. Thoms urged the establishment of a new library in London "to consist entirely of magazines and other records of contemporary matters" (*Bibliographer*, I [1882], 98). Despite the favorable response to both proposals, neither, of course, produced tangible results. The fact that the proposals were made does reflect the growing interest in the periodicals, however, while at the same time provoking the modern researcher to ponder what the difference might have been if such a bibliographical aid and central depository of periodicals and newspapers had come into existence almost a century ago.

And there were, of course, other new ways in which the periodicals and periodical writers of the early nineteenth century came to the fore as the old century ended and the new one began. In 1883, for example, Hall Caine in *Cobwebs of Criticism* devoted an entire volume to a discussion of the adverse criticism of the English Romantics that appeared in British periodicals between 1800 and 1825, and following his lead, E. Stevenson and J. L. Haney reprinted a number of reviews of the major Romantics in 1890 and 1904 respectively. And still other new kinds of studies were being undertaken: S. J. Reid, Samuel Smiles, and Andrew Lang published studies of Sydney Smith (1884), John Murray (1891), and John Gibson Lockhart (1896) respectively; W. A. Copinger published a monograph *On the Authorship of the First Hundred Numbers of the "Edinburgh Review"* in 1895; J. H. Pence prepared an index and "guide to the mass of literature the magazines have published concerning the acting drama and the men and women directly connected with it" (*The Magazine and the Drama*, 1896); Mrs.

Oliphant published her *Annals of a Publishing House: William Blackwood and His Sons* (1897); and Walter Bagehot (*Literary Studies*, 1898), Leslie Stephen (*Hours in a Library*, 1899), and Lewis E. Gates (*Three Studies in Literature*, 1899), all devoted chapter essays to what they called "The First Edinburgh Reviewers."

Up to this point, it will have been observed, almost all of the studies that have been cited were written by British authors and have dealt mainly with the *Edinburgh*, the *Quarterly*, *Blackwood's*, and the celebrated contributors who wrote for them. The second stage of the study of periodicals appears to have started when research in them began to invade American graduate schools and scholars began to make adequate tools for the study of them available. The first such study was apparently William B. Cairns' dissertation *On the Development of American Literature from 1815 to 1833, with Especial Reference to Periodicals* (University of Wisconsin, 1897). This was soon followed by other dissertations that dealt exclusively or in part with American periodicals: S. H. Goodnight's *German Literature in American Magazines Prior to 1896* (University of Wisconsin, 1905), William Ellery Leonard's *Byron and Byronism in America* (Columbia University, 1905), Elizabeth C. Cook's *Literary Influences in Colonial Newspapers, 1704–1750* (Columbia University, 1912).

Interest in the periodicals of the English Romantic period apparently followed hard upon the interest in American periodicals. At any rate, three Columbia University Masters' essays that made use of them—"English Reviews from 1830 to 1840," "The Review Article from 1800 to 1825," "Literary Criticism in the Leading Periodicals of the Early Nineteenth Century, 1802–1835"— were published in 1911, 1912,and 1915, respectively; and shortly thereafter, the late Walter Graham wrote the first dissertation dealing with British periodicals (*Tory Criticism in the "Quarterly Review*," Columbia University, 1919). To identify the real point of origin of these studies may not be possible at this late date, but it may well have been in the classes of Professor Ashley Thorndike. At any rate, writes Professor Emery Neff, "When I was a student in his nineteenth-century seminar in 1915–16," he was suggesting the periodicals as a fruitful source of research; and it was, of course, under his supervision that Walter Graham began the above-mentioned investigations, which started with the *Quarterly Review* and ended several years later with the highly influential and still standard *English Literary Periodicals* (1930).

While the periodicals were thus becoming a subject for research in graduate schools, the study of them was also becoming more firmly established in the literary histories that were being published. Thus Saintsbury gave space to "Periodical Criticism" in his monumental *History of Literary Criticism* (1904); Oliver Elton devoted a long chapter to "The Official Reviewers" in his *A Survey of English Literature, 1780–1830* (1912); and the *Cambridge History of English Literature* (1916) included a section (by Arthur R. D. Elliott) on the "Reviews and Magazines in the Early Years of the Nineteenth Century." By 1920, in short, the study of British periodicals had become a firmly established feature of literary scholarship.

A new stimulus to research—the development of helpful "tools"—comes during the 1920's. Already, however, some steps in this direction had been taken, and these deserve mention first, for they have been almost entirely neglected up to this point. First came the above-mentioned original edition of *Poole's Index* in 1848 (the fuller and better known edition and supplements in 1882 and following), and not long thereafter a series of volumes dealing with Irish periodicals: John Power's *Irish Literary Periodical Publications* (1866), Richard Robert Madden's *History of Irish Periodical Literature from the End of the Seventeenth Century to the Middle of the Nineteenth Century* (1867), and E. R. Mc Dix's series of articles and monographs beginning in 1904. After these came W. J. Couper's *The Edinburgh Periodical Press* (1908). And during approximately the same period, a number of libraries in both the United States and the British Isles were publishing checklists of their periodicals holdings. Important though these were for the great collections in the Bodleian Library, the British Museum, the New York Public Library, and elsewhere, however, the great need was for a "union" list. This came, in 1927, with the publication of the *Union List of Serials in the Libraries of the United States and Canada* (new edition in 1943), and with R. S. Crane and F. B. Kaye's *A Census of British Newspapers and Periodicals*, 1620–1800. The first British Union List (though limited to university libraries) appeared in 1937 as the *Union Catalogue of Periodical*

WILLIAM S. WARD

Publications in University Libraries of the British Isles,
and was replaced (1955–58) by the more comprehensive
British Union Catalog of Periodicals. William S. Ward's
*Index and Finding List of Serials Published in the British
Isles, 1789–1832* (1953), though covering only the Romantic period, represents the final step in the development
of an aid of this sort in that his listings are for both American and British libraries, and include newspapers as well
as the usual periodicals of the weekly, monthly, and
quarterly sort.

From these beginnings, and with these aids, interest
mounted rapidly during the 1920's, and reached a peak
during the 1930's that has shown no signs of dropping off.
The range of studies, too, has increased greatly. Strong
interest has continued in the famous reviews and magazines already mentioned, of course, and in those who
founded them, but its scope has broadened so as to include a great many other periodicals and the men who
wrote for them. Thus at least seven periodicals have been
the subject for full-length, comprehensive studies, and
half a dozen others have prompted book-length studies
of a more specialized sort. At the same time, the principal
editors and contributors—men like Jeffrey, Lockhart,
Gifford, Croker, Cobbett, Sydney Smith, Christopher
North, and others—have also called forth full-length
books, and sometimes two or three. And during the same
period, the periodicals have been searched for the light
they shed on critical theory and literary developments, on
authors, on the age they lived in, on the reception accorded them by their contemporaries, and so on. To try

to rehearse the subjects dealt with in books and in the many articles that have appeared during the past forty years would be tedious indeed. Suffice it to say, therefore, that historical and critical studies of every sort have drawn upon the periodicals in one way or another. Despite all that has been done, however, the surface has only been scratched; and once adequate aids (some of them requiring cooperative effort) have been made available, important studies can be undertaken that heretofore have been too formidable for one individual to attempt alone.

Undoubtedly, the research tool for which there is the greatest need is an index to authors and contents. Just as Ward's *Index and Finding List of Serials Published in the British Isles, 1789–1832,* solved the big problem of knowing the magazines of the day and where to find copies of them, so now there is the urgent need for an index that will enable each researcher to find his materials without having to turn thousands upon thousands of pages as he searches for the information that bears upon his own specialty. For more than a century, of course, there has been *Poole's Index,* and more recently (1957) Marion V. Bell and Jean C. Bacon's *Poole's Index: Date and Volume Key.* But despite their unquestioned value, these volumes have their limitations and need to be replaced by indexes that do the job more adequately.

One such index is under way, in fact, though by being concerned primarily with a later period, it will be helpful only to those who are interested in the latter years of the Romantic period. This is the Wellesley index to Victorian periodicals, 1824–1900, which is being edited at the Wellesley College Library under the direction of Walter E. Houghton. When completed, the Wellesley index (limited to monthlies and quarterlies) will provide three indexes: to subjects, to authors of books reviewed, and to writers (so far as they can be identified) of articles and reviews. The first volume is scheduled for publication in 1965, the second in 1967.

Perhaps it should be mentioned at this point also that Professors Powell Stewart and W. O. S. Sutherland, Jr., had at one time (the mid-1950's) developed plans, even to the point of initiating a pilot study, for preparing a subject index of eighteenth-century periodicals. Unfortunately, the great expense involved and the inability of an interested group to secure financial backing led ultimately to the abandonment of the project, and at present the prospects for reviving it are not bright.

A major job to be done, therefore, is an index comparable to the Wellesley index which covers the Romantic period up to 1824. Some of the work has been done so far as the identification of authors is concerned. Thus Hill and Helen C. Shine have published *The Quarterly Review under Gifford: Identification of Contributors, 1809–1824* (1949); Benjamin C. Nangle (in 1934 and 1955) has published *The Monthly Review: Indexes of Contributors and Articles* (two volumes); Alan Lang Strout (1959) has identified most of the contributors to *Blackwood's (A Bibliography of Articles in Blackwood's Magazine, 1817–25);* and Esther Houghton is working on identifications of contributors to the *Edinburgh Review, 1802–*

1824. Obviously, these studies are but a beginning on a limited aspect of a tremendously big project; but as is true with so many aspects of the periodicals research problem, long journeys, as well as short ones, must start with a single step.

Another bibliographical project—a much smaller one—that needs to be done is the preparation of a bibliography of printed books and articles dealing with the periodicals themselves; materials having to do with editors, publishers, contributors, and readers; special studies on printing, circulation, freedom of the press, and so on—a volume, in short, comparable to Weed and Bond's *Studies of British Newspapers and Periodicals from their Beginnings to 1800: A Bibliography*. Here, fortunately, progress can be reported, for William S. Ward has made a substantial beginning on both the titles and the annotations, and hopes to have a completed manuscript in 1966.

Another desirable development is a revival of *The Periodical Post Boy*. In the beginning, as explained by its first editor, Richmond P. Bond, "a group of scholars in 1947 conducted an informal poll to find an effective, cooperative method of promoting sound research in the field of the periodical. The result was a loose organization . . . guided by a small committee which would encourage the study of the American and British periodical press from the beginning to the present and would edit a bulletin of news and views thereon." The first number of this bulletin, *The Periodical Post Boy,* appeared in March, 1948, the last, in June, 1955. Once again, in 1965, as in 1948 and 1955, there is reason to hope that the *Post Boy* will again be published, not only because of the information it could carry, but because of the interest it could stimulate and the bond it could provide between those who work in the field.

Strictly speaking, attention to newspapers lies outside this essay. So similar are their contribution to a depth study of a period, however, and so similar are the problems associated with a study of them, that a brief consideration of them here seems appropriate. Books and articles about journalism, journalists, and particular newspapers began to appear as early as the 1790's and generally paralleled studies of the periodicals throughout the nineteenth century, both in time and number. The amount of work that has been done on matters of a literary nature, however, is relatively small in comparison with that done on the periodicals. One reason, no doubt, has been that traditionally the newspaper has been less concerned with purely literary matters than have the magazines and the reviews. And another, of course, has been that in so many instances complete files, or even good ones, are exceedingly hard to come by. Not only do they not reside in any one library, even if all known copies were brought together in one place the result would be that only scattered issues for some years would be known. What is needed first, therefore, is a major archeological project of unearthing all existing issues and, after that, of gathering them (or photographic copies of them) together in one place, either as a central depository or so that microfilm copies can be made for all libraries that desire them. The situation is bad for newspapers like the *Courier* and the *Morning Post*; it is even worse for many others, such as the *Oracle*, the *Telegraph*, and the *World*.

Despite this interest in the history of English journalism, and even of particular newspapers, however, *De Quincey's Editorship of the "Westmoreland Gazette"* (1890) by Charles Pollit, is one of the very few studies that were concerned with either the literature of the period or with authors. The increased interest in periodicals during the 1920's and 30's did lead to a vigorous interest in Leigh Hunt's *Examiner* and, to some extent, in John Scott's *Champion*; and at the same time, Coleridge's work as a journalist became more inviting. It is only in very recent years, however, that scholars have undertaken to complete the canon of certain ones of the major Romantics. Into this category falls the work of David Erdman on Coleridge's contribution (both prose and verse) to the *Courier* and the *Morning Post*; R. S. Woof's work on Wordsworth's poetic contributions to the same papers; Carol Landon's work on Wordsworth and the *Morning Post*; Lucyle Werkmeister's projected biography of the Stuart brothers and her studies, ranging from Burns to Wordsworth and Coleridge, and their contributions not only to the *Morning Post* and *Courier*, but to the original *Star*, the spurious *Star*, and the *Oracle*; Carl Woodring's book on Coleridge's political verse, much of the materials drawn from the Stuart newspapers; and Stuart Tave's work on the *Edinburgh Saturday Post* (later *Edinburgh Evening Post*) in order to identify the contributions of Thomas De Quincey to that newspaper.

But here, as with the periodicals, much, much more remains to be done, and the problem of finding complete— or even good—files is not only extremely difficult, but even, perhaps, impossible. A major undertaking for the future, therefore, is a concerted effort to provide microfilm copies of all known issues of important newspapers, much in the manner that University Microfilms has made available to libraries more than a score of the harder-to-get and more important periodicals that were published between 1789 and 1832. Unless copies do become available, in fact, De Quincey will indeed have been right about the worlds of fine thinking that "lie buried in that vast abyss, never to be disentombed or restored to human admiration."

The task of providing "texts" and of preparing guides and indexes to periodicals—reviews, magazines, journals, and newspapers—is a big one, of course, and calls for cooperative effort on a scale that may be without precedent. The former is minimal, however, and the latter essential, if senseless duplication is to be eliminated as scholars turn the pages of thousands upon thousands of volumes in their search for the "swallowed treasures" that lie confounded with what De Quincey so aptly characterized as the "rubbish and purgamenta of ages."*

* Since neither of the reviews of research in the earlier volumes of this series included the subject of periodicals, Professor Ward has added to his essay a useful section surveying bibliography and problems of research in this area.—Eds.

INDEX

INDEX